WITHDRAWN

Kirtley Library
Columbia College
8th and Rogers
Columbia, MO. 65201

Public relations and survey research

Business Series
STANLEY F. TEELE* and DAVID W. EWING, Editors

Dean S. Ammer, *Manufacturing Management and Control*

Gerald A. Fleischer, *Capital Allocation Theory: The Study of Investment Decisions*

Samuel Fox, *Management and the Law*

Thomas M. Garrett, *Business Ethics*

Thomas M. Garrett, Raymond C. Baumhart, Theodore V. Purcell, and Perry Roets, *Cases in Business Ethics*

David J. Luck and Arthur E. Prell, *Market Strategy*

William H. Reynolds, *Products and Markets*

Edward J. Robinson, *Public Relations and Survey Research*

Chester R. Wasson, *The Economics of Managerial Decision*

Chester R. Wasson, *Research Analysis for Marketing Decision*

Albert K. Wickesberg, *Management Organization*

Walter E. Willets, *Fundamentals of Purchasing*

* Deceased, May 29, 1967.

Public relations and survey research

ACHIEVING ORGANIZATIONAL GOALS IN A COMMUNICATION CONTEXT

Edward J. Robinson, Ph.D.
DIRECTOR, TRAINING DEVELOPMENT CENTER,
A DIVISION OF STERLING INSTITUTE

APPLETON-CENTURY-CROFTS
EDUCATIONAL DIVISION
MEREDITH CORPORATION
NEW YORK

Copyright © 1969 by
MEREDITH CORPORATION
All rights reserved

This book, or parts thereof, must not be used or reproduced in any manner without written permission. For information address the publisher, Appleton-Century-Crofts, Educational Division, Meredith Corporation, 440 Park Avenue South, New York, N.Y. 10016.

649–1

Library of Congress Card Number: 77-79167

PRINTED IN THE UNITED STATES OF AMERICA

390–74805–6

TO OUR CHILDREN,
Karen Lynn
Dodd Edward
John Olden

Acknowledgments

The writer wishes to convey his thanks to all those persons who cooperated with him in obtaining case materials for this volume. Those deserving particular mention are the ones associated with the seven cases in Part III of this volume all of whom cooperated with the author over a prolonged period of time and corresponded extensively to provide the writer with the necessary background and details so as to be able to write the cases.

Case 1: Lt. Col. Frank Doyal, USAF, Communication Studies Group SAFOI-XD, Bolling Air Force Base, Washington, D.C., and Mr. Donald Kent, Director of Information, State University College, Newpaltz, New York, and formerly a Major in the USAF, functioning as an Information Officer.

Case 2: Mr. Phelps H. Adams, Administrative Vice President—Public Relations, and Mr. William W. Cook, Director—Public Relations Research, United States Steel Corporation.

Case 3: Edwin E. Dowell, Director of Public Relations, Western Mining Divisions, Kennecott Copper Corporation, Salt Lake City, Utah; Nelson W. Aldrich, Former Director of Public Relations, Utah Copper Division; and K. E. Kefauver, incumbent Director of Public Relations, Utah Copper Division, Kennecott Copper Corporation.

Case 4: Frank R. Neu, Director, Public Relations Division, American Dairy Association.

Case 5: Because of their desire to remain anonymous we are unable to credit the persons and organizations associated with the Petroil Oil case.

Case 6: Robert B. Cunningham, Supervising Statistician, and Charles J. Sherrard, Community Relations Supervisor, both of the American Telephone and Telegraph Company, New York, New York.

Case 7: Arch McKinlay, Jr., Director of Public Information, National Safety Council, and John Naisbitt, former Director of Public Information, National Safety Council.

Preface

For a number of years it has been the contention of the writer that all applied fields, such as advertising, marketing, public relations—all the sub-specialties under the heading of business administration—will demand of their practitioners increasing rigor in their day-to-day work. Practitioners in all applied fields will be expected to support their decisions with evidence while solving day-to-day problems. They will be asked increasingly such questions as "How do you know?" "What are your data to support your decision?" "How do you know that you have solved your problem?" "What will it cost to achieve such a goal?"

What is true of applied fields in general is, of course, true of public relations in particular. Public relations practitioners will also have to face the questions asked above. The old "flying by the seat of the pants" approach to solving public relations problems is over. While there will always be a need for the intuitively based decision under some circumstances, decisions based on hunch, guessing, experience, and the rationale that "this is the way we have always done it" are a thing of the past. Hunches, guessing, previous experiences, and an awareness of prior practice are all appropriate under certain circumstances, but *none of these* is a substitute for decision making based on reliable research data. There is little question in the mind of the writer that the public relations practitioner of the future (regardless of what his title might be) will function as an applied social and behavioral scientist. He will draw upon the sciences that are logically related to public relations practice—psychology, sociology, economics, to name but a few—to help him solve his public relations problems with greater precision.

One aspect of the function of an applied social and behavioral scientist is the proper use of research to help in the problem solving process. If one defines research as a method by which we obtain reliable knowledge, it becomes clear that the most powerful tool available to the applied practitioner to help him achieve the rigor demanded of him is research. So it was that the writer began the task of developing this volume with the intent of generating a synthesis of how public relations practitioners made use of social and behavioral science research methods to help solve their public relations problems. This synthesis was to include a series of cases illustrating how the various research methodologies were helpful. Three simple yet logical criteria were set up to guide case selection. (1) The nature of the public relation problem faced by the practitioner, the information available to him, and his reasons for adopting a particular research methodology to help him solve his problem. (2) The accessibility to the writer of the complete research report containing all the usual details found in a research report. (3) How the research results were utilized in subsequent planning and execution of a public relations program.

What happened? As time passed it became quite clear that the "methods" in use by practitioners essentially boiled down to one method: survey research. In addition, the criteria listed above proved to be quite a filter. Again and again, a potential case had to be discarded because one or more of the three criteria were not met satisfactorily. Consequently, a decision was made to change the focus of the book and restrict the cases cited (with one exception) to the use of survey research as a tool to help solve public relations problems. To that end, the case selection was made with an eye toward portraying the extremely broad range of contexts within which public relations practitioners function and find survey research helpful to them.

One additional point should be made about the research methods used by public relations practitioners. Hundreds of people were contacted by the author, both in person and by mail; nevertheless, my efforts constitute one man's sample of what is going on in the field—and a biased sample at that. While I feel quite certain that the experiences recorded here are an accurate reflection of reality—that is, that the overwhelming preponderance of research done by public relations practitioners is survey research—they should not lead the reader to conclude that no other types of research are being utilized at the present time. Indeed, the writer himself has samples of other methodologies used. The generalizations made here about the uses of research are the result of one particular range of contacts and the strict application of one set of criteria to guide the selection of cases.

When the decision was made to limit the book to survey research, the evolution of a plan for the volume became comparatively simple. The first three chapters (Part I) would be devoted to spelling out a definition of public relations and to placing the function of the practitioner in a communication model context. Within that framework, the relationship of research to the quest of the practitioner for reliable knowledge followed logically. The next three chapters (Part II) present survey research in a "nutshell." These chapters contain the highlights of what a public relations practitioner should know about survey research to use the tool intelligently, but obviously, not in enough detail so as to be able to do survey research himself. The last seven chapters (Part III) consist of seven different cases illustrating how survey research was utilized by a public relations practitioner to help solve his public relations problem(s). Each case is long enough and presents enough details, including research findings, so that the

PREFACE

cases can be used as they should be used—as a "simulation" of real life which serves to stimulate, involve, provoke, and otherwise encourage a student to think and learn in a manner that will prove to be fruitful later "on the job."

One last point. If public relations practitioners of the future are going to take their place along with other applied practitioners as applied social and behavioral scientists, then the actions of the practitioners described in these cases will, before very long, appear to be quite primitive. Furthermore, the information about survey research contained in Part II will be considered too basic, and more advanced treatments of this topic will be quickly assimilated. Lastly, while the dominance of survey research may continue because of its particular appropriateness for so much of what a public relations practitioner does, books describing many other methodologies will become quite commonplace. In a word, if the field of public relations is to continue to grow and thrive and mature, this volume will become too elementary in a comparatively short time. If this book can make a modest contribution to this evolution, then one of its most important functions will have been served. If, on the other hand, the day-to-day sophistication of public relations practice does *not* render this volume obsolete in a reasonably short period of time, then the field itself is in real trouble. The demand for rigor referred to earlier is going to be inexorable, and public relations practitioners, along with all applied practitioners, must face up to this fact, and quickly.

I am particularly indebted to the Foundation for Public Relations Research and Education for their grant which helped to make this book a reality. Also, thanks are due to Milton Fairman, President of the Foundation at the time the grant was made to the writer, for his encouragement to complete this project, and to Foundation members, Dudley L. Parsons and G. Edward Pendray. Former graduate students of the writer were particularly helpful, especially Jack Van Hee, Adrianne Weir, and Frank Small. I am also grateful to those who read drafts of the manuscript and gave many helpful suggestions. Noteworthy are Dean Gerhart Wiebe and members of my own Divisional Faculty, Dr. F. Earle Barcus and Dr. George Gitter. Special thanks are again due my secretary, Mrs. John Clausen, who typed the manuscript and took care of a hundred and one details associated with the efforts to contact people for case materials. I wish to acknowledge the support and help of the co-editors of the series of which this volume is a part, David W. Ewing and Stanley Teele.

As before, I want to call particular attention to the ever-present help and inspiration of my wife, Priscilla, who joins with me in dedicating this book to our children.

E.J.R.

Foreword

"Public Relations and Survey Research" is the product of a grant made to Dr. Edward J. Robinson in November 1963 by the Foundation for Public Relations Research and Education, which I was serving at the time as president. The Foundation is an independent, nonprofit organization established by members of the Public Relations Society of America in 1956 to foster, sponsor and conduct basic research and study in the general field of public relations and to disseminate information developed through such efforts.

In furtherance of its objectives, the Foundation has organized a number of projects which it considers of significant value in promoting the understanding and development of public relations. Chronologically, Dr. Robinson's book is among the later projects, but in the sequence of an orderly study of the public relations complex it belongs near if not at the beginning.

Public relations is an amalgam of many disciplines. Through education, experience, and exposure, most of today's public relations practitioners have attained a good working knowledge of most of these disciplines. Of these, they are perhaps least proficient in the social and behavioral sciences. There seems to be an awesomeness about these sciences that dazzles the public relations practitioner and blinds him to their usefulness. In his defense, however, it can be said that few behavioral scientists have shown much willingness to shed their golden armor and get into working clothes.

Dr. Robinson is a behavioral scientist in overalls, offering the highly sentient practitioners of public relations the objectivity and detachment of the trained scientist. He views public relations as "an applied social and behavioral science," in that "nearly all public relations problems can be reduced to attitude and behavior change goals." This is a major premise of his book, and while some may quarrel with the narrowness, none can seriously challenge the validity.

"Public Relations and Survey Research" is an important contribution to the public relations literature for two reasons: it is the first time, to my knowledge, that the approaches to and the techniques, evaluation, and application of survey research to public relations practice have been put together between the covers of one book; and it is the first full-scale study of public relations survey research that dispenses sound scientific principles and precepts in layman's language.

Dr. Robinson's book is only secondarily a "do-it-yourself" guide. His purpose is to encourage the public relations practitioner to use survey research by exposing the extent to which its methods are rooted in everyday experience. In achieving this, Dr. Robinson has not subtracted a single cubit from his profession's stature; rather, he makes those of us in public relations consciously aware of how much the social and behavioral sciences add to our common body of knowledge.

For those who earn their livelihood from public relations, this is a useful book. For those concerned with the future of public relations, and particularly with its sources of development and authority, it is an important book, with a strong claim to a place in the basic literature.

Milton Fairman

Contents

Preface   ix
Foreword   xiii
Introduction   1

PART I.   *Public relations and research in a communication model context: some perspectives*

1   Public relations: a definition and some implications   5
2   Public relations: the need for research and the quest for reliable knowledge   9
3   Public relations: relationship to the process of communication   18

PART II.   *Survey research in a nutshell*

4   Survey research: relationship to other means of obtaining reliable information   35
5   The survey research process   50
6   Survey research checklist: step one   55
7   Survey research checklist: step two   58
8   Survey research checklist: step three   77
9   Survey research checklist: steps four through seven   96

PART III.   *Seven cases: the use of survey research*

10   Introduction to the cases   105
11   Case 1. Improving the attitudes of U.S. Air Force personnel toward their host country   111

12	Case 2. Assessing the effectiveness of a speech reprint program upon certain features of the United States Steel Corporation's corporate image	137
13	Case 3. Television and public relations: The Kennecott Copper Corporation	155
14	Case 4. The cholesterol scare and the diet-heart disease problem: what the American Dairy Association did about it	182
15	Case 5. Petroil Development and Research Corporation: how one company assessed its reputation as a research organization within the scientific community	205
16	Case 6. American Telephone and Telegraph Company: a research-based effort to decentralize community relations planning and programming	237
17	Case 7. Promotion of seat belt acceptance and usage by the National Safety Council	258

Index 279

Public relations and survey research

Introduction

THIS BOOK deals with the topic of public relations. However, it is concerned with public relations in a very special way in that we will be concentrating primarily on how the public relations practitioner attempts to solve the problems he faces daily in his work by utilizing survey research methods.

Briefly, the plan of this book is to provide first, in Part I, a context into which to place public relations; that is, to elaborate upon a schema which relates research in general to survey research in particular, and which does so within the framework of a communication theory model. Part II will present survey research in a nutshell, a synthesis for persons who will probably never *do* such research but who will undoubtedly have many occasions to *use* the results in the course of their work. Part III consists of a series of cases depicting seven widely differing problem situations in public relations. In spite of their diversity they all have one thing in common: in each instance the public relations practitioner utilized survey research to comprehend what he faced more intelligently and to shape a more accurate public relations program to solve his problems.

These cases serve a number of purposes:

1. They illustrate in concrete terms what a public relations practitioner *does*. It is one thing to define the term *public relations,* but it is another to convey, by means of the written word, what a public relations man does from day to day. Cases are very useful in this regard.

2. As is true of most case material, they should enable the reader to enlarge his own knowledge of the subject matter involved by making him think about what he might have done and why, had he been in the same situation.

3. They lend themselves to discussions which relate the cases to other subjects that bear on them.

4. They should enable the reader to broaden his grasp of survey research, because they contain a fair amount of actual survey research data, along with interpretations of these data. The reader will have an opportunity to relate the more academic and theoretical discussion of survey research in Part II to the cases in Part III.

5. They should help the reader see the relationship between survey research data and the *application* of these data to problems in public relations. Thus, in each case, deliberate efforts have been made to show as explicitly as possible how the practitioner *utilized* this information to shape his public relations program. By following along with the practitioner and looking over his shoulder, so to speak, the reader should sharpen his ability to relate research data to applied problem situations.

6. Finally, the questions asked in the critique portions of each case should enable the reader to go beyond the confines of the case and consider what might have been done differently. What other research approaches might have been utilized? With these data in mind, what other steps might have been taken that were not taken? These and many other questions designed to continue to link theory and practice should increase the reader's grasp of survey research and public relations, and should aid him in using the former to solve problems of the latter.

PART I

Public relations and research in a communication model context: some perspectives

1 | Public relations: a definition and some implications

AS A starting point in developing the several perspectives pertinent to an intelligent presentation of the relationship between survey research and public relations, let us first define the term *public relations*. To do so we will borrow a definition developed by the writer in another book:

Public relations as an applied social and behavioral science is that function which:

1. measures, evaluates, and interprets the attitudes of various relevant publics;[1]
2. assists management in defining objectives for increasing public understanding and acceptance of the organization's products, plans, policies, and personnel;
3. equates these objectives with the interests, needs, and goals of the various relevant publics; and
4. develops, executes, and evaluates a program to earn public understanding and acceptance.[2]

---

[1] The word *public* is used throughout this book to refer to any group of people who share a common interest. The employees of a company are an example of a public—good pay, the company's stability and future, and the opportunity for advancement are a few of the common interests. Some publics, such as employees, are part of an organization and are called *internal* publics. In contrast, customers are an example of an *external* public—as are suppliers, retail dealers and the community. Internal and external publics will differ from one organization to another.

[2] Edward J. Robinson, *Communication and Public Relations* (Columbus, Charles E. Merrill Books, Inc., 1966), pp. 51–52. Because of our particular objectives we will not devote space to a detailed examination of this definition; nor will we develop arguments as to why, for example, the public relations practitioner must think of himself as an applied social and behavioral scientist. This has already been done in the volume cited here, and the reader is encouraged to read the first three chapters as useful background to the content and point of view to be examined in the present book.

This definition suggests several implications that should be examined. We will dwell here on those portions of the definition that have greatest relevance for the research function of the public relations practitioner.

A FIRST IMPLICATION

The beginning of the definition stresses the fact that public relations is an applied social and behavioral science. The reason for this contention is that, in the opinion of the writer, the goal in nearly all public relations problem situations is to change attitudes and behavior. That is, whenever one examines the objectives in a public relations project one discovers that the practitioner is trying to modify the outlook and actions of some particular public or group of publics; this is exemplified in the cases in Part III.

For example, in Case 5 (pages 205–236), we see that the public relations practitioner wanted to change the attitudes of the scientific community (researchers in all sorts of settings, college professors, and so forth) about Petroil Development and Research Corporation's role in basic research as compared with applied research. He wanted to have these people believe that because significant research was being conducted there, Petroil was a desirable place for a scientist to work. In Case 7 (pages 258–278), the public relations practitioner for the National Safety Council is concerned with the public's attitudes toward highway safety and how to improve them, and particularly with how to induce more of the motoring public to accept and use seat belts.

We do not have the space to do so, but every one of the seven cases could be translated into a practitioner's list of desired attitude and behavior changes. In fact, as mentioned earlier, it is the author's contention that stimulating these changes represents the very heart of public relations work. All of the other activities of the practitioner—writing articles, publishing brochures, arranging for an open house or speakers' bureau, and so forth—are generated in the hope of bringing these shifts about. The reader should keep this point in mind so that he can either verify or reject it as he comes to the cases in Part III. Also, he is invited to adopt this point of view with any other case material or actual public relations problem situation he may be aware of to determine whether this generalization is substantiated.

If one grants the basic argument developed in the above paragraphs, it follows that the public relations practitioner in effect functions as an applied social and behavioral scientist. Therefore, he must know a great deal about these disciplines, for they are logically related to his work and help him achieve his goals—just as the physical sciences help the engineer solve his applied engineering problems.[3] Knowledge of research is one factor in

[3] The reader is reminded of the suggestion in footnote 2 concerning the material in *Communication and Public Relations,* for it makes a detailed attempt to associate the logically related social and behavioral sciences—such as psychology and sociology

the ability of the public relations practitioner to utilize the social and behavioral sciences. He must be able to read and interpret technical journals describing all sorts of psychological studies. Like the engineer, physician, chemist, or geologist, he must understand enough about research design, sampling, and so forth, to intelligently assess the studies and relate the findings to his own work.

A SECOND IMPLICATION

A second major implication lies in the first part of the definition which states that the attitudes of the various relevant publics must be measured, evaluated, and interpreted. This portion of the definition shows that survey research, among other techniques, is a prerequisite to the function of measuring, evaluating, and interpreting. As we shall see, each of the cases in Part III illustrates how survey research was structured to help solve a particular problem faced by a practitioner.

A THIRD IMPLICATION

The last implication we should like to highlight is based on the fourth part of the definition which states that another key aspect of public relations is the need to develop, execute, and evaluate a program that will earn public understanding and acceptance. To develop and execute a public relations program is one thing; but its evaluation usually requires some sort of research on the part of the practitioner.

There are many more implications of this definition that might be discussed—such as the need for careful planning or the obvious importance of communication. However, as our primary concern is the role of research in public relations practice, we shall focus on the research implications only. If the public relations practitioner examines his research needs, he finds again and again that he must know about the attitudes of a particular public toward his organization or toward some action his organization plans to take in the future. He may also need to find out the attitudes of the public *after* a particular public relations program has been in effect for a period of time in order to evaluate how effective his program has been.

Survey research generally becomes the answer to some of his research needs. Thus, it is hardly surprising that, as one tries to find examples of the utilization of research by a public relations practitioner, it almost al-

---

—to the practice of public relations. In this book, however, we can only touch upon this rather fundamental point stated in the author's definition of public relations above.

ways turns out to be some sort of survey research.[4] Before we can profit by a discussion of this, however, we need to examine additional perspectives which provide a framework for our cases and which demonstrate why the public relations practitioner must be research oriented. In addition, a simple communication theory model will enable us to understand better the relationship between communication as we know it in public relations practice and feedback of information. This is one approach to the relationship between research and communication.

ADDITIONAL PERSPECTIVES CONCERNING SURVEY RESEARCH AND PUBLIC RELATIONS PRACTICE

It is probably accurate to say that the most common use of survey research in public relations practice is to help ascertain the reaction of a given public to some feature of the organization's public relations program. To put it another way, we tend to go to the public to see how "they" react to what "we" choose to do. This is a perfectly valid utilization of survey research (or of any research, for that matter—and one which, if applied more frequently, would raise considerably the general level of public relations practice in this country).

There is another practice—though far less prevalent than the one above—that should be adopted by the public relations man. He should use survey research to ascertain the needs and interests of his relevant publics *before* he has decided upon and developed his program. Ideally, a practitioner should strive for balance in his use of survey research. He first researches his publics in order to discover and understand their attitudes, motives, needs, and so forth. Next, he designs a program, keeping in mind the needs of both the organization and the relevant publics (look back at our definition of public relations). Lastly, he employs research once again to find out how effectively he has achieved his public relations goals.

[4] Apropos of this point, the writer first intended this book to describe the various research methods, from the social and behavioral sciences, utilized by public relations practitioners. However, after extensive efforts to uncover some examples of this, it devolved that almost the only type used was survey research. The title of the book then had to be changed to reflect the fact that it would contain examples of survey research alone.

2 | Public relations: the need for research and the quest for reliable knowledge

IN OUR first chapter we presented a definition of public relations and examined several of its implications for public relations practice. We argued that the practitioner in effect functions as an applied social and behavioral scientist, and that some knowledge of research is necessary to his job. Also, we felt that the *form* most frequently used was survey research. Let us now examine the term research and consider a perspective which relates this definition to public relations practice.

In simplest terms, the word research sums up the methods used to obtain reliable knowledge. Thus, in a carefully conducted scientific research project—be it in chemistry or psychology—the scientist undertakes a systematic effort to learn something new, and, at the same time, to assure himself that his information is not spurious. Hence, research is really a *process,* or *method.* The person who obtains his knowledge scientifically follows certain rules and introduces controls that help him to evaluate his information—what phenomena cause what other phenomena, or what event correlates with what other event. It follows that any particular discipline can engage—at least, theoretically—in scientific efforts to obtain reliable knowledge. Some of the steps, such as the data collection phase, may present greater difficulty to a sociologist than to a chemist. For instance, the sociologist is at a distinct disadvantage when he tries to collect data during a riot or during the confusion that takes place when an audience panics in the face of fire. He is less able than the chemist to define the phenomena (panic, for example) he wishes to measure, and hence study; and he cannot claim that his findings are completely accurate. By contrast, the chemist can usually identify the phenomena clearly (a chemical process, for example) and thus analyze his data with more precision. In other words, it is more *difficult* for some disciplines than it is for others to live up to the scientific method; but it is always *possible* for a discipline to seek pertinent knowledge scientifically.[1]

If one accepts the definition of research as essentially a method by which we obtain reliable knowledge, it follows, if we give it some thought, that *all of us* need reliable knowledge, scientists and nonscientists alike. Knowledge about human behavior is essential to sound relationships with our family, our neighbors, our bosses—in short, with everyone we encounter in our daily lives. We need reliable knowledge to pursue a livelihood, be it as businessman, professional man, or farmer. In every occupational category one can name, the doer needs a certain level of knowledge in order to function adequately. We need reliable knowledge to drive to work, cross a street, fly a plane, make a telephone call—in short, in order to function every moment of our waking lives.

It should be clear from the above that the difference between a scientist and a nonscientist is not logically in their need for reliable knowledge. In fact, what a scientist does while functioning as a scientist reveals a remarkable amount of overlap with what a nonscientist does while functioning in his everyday life. The following quote will elaborate this contention:

To demonstrate the overlap, let us take a hypothetical example of a public relations practitioner arising in the morning and wondering what the weather is going to be like for that day. For our purposes, let us assume that he does not pay attention to the weatherman's report. What is he likely to do? He may look out the window, quickly make an observation of the skies, and apparently very simply come to a decision to wear a raincoat and rubbers. To bring out the overlap between research and everyday life, let us delve a little deeper into this apparently simple behavior.

For our starting point, we ask, "Why does he look out the window and look at the sky?" Asking this slightly ridiculous-sounding question enables us to bring out several very important aspects of research that are hidden in it. They are:

[1] This last point is generally discussed in books on research, under the heading of the unity of science, along the following lines: all sciences are alike from the standpoint of how they go about obtaining reliable knowledge; the difference lies in their *content*, not in their *method*. Thus, because the areas of study of a psychologist and a physiologist are so dissimilar, on the surface and to a layman, their research activities appear to be completely different. This sometimes causes the layman to confuse *content* with *process*. In fact, the process of obtaining reliable knowledge in their respective fields is the same for both scientists—one field is just as "scientific" as another. The difference is in the *precision* with which one field can predict outcomes and explain phenomena. A higher degree of precision is now possible for the physiologist because of fewer problems in defining and measuring (and hence studying) the subject matter. In psychology, however, with greater problems even in defining terms (for example, what is thinking?), less precision is possible at the present time. These differences in degree of accuracy must not mask the underlying similarities of the two fields, and of other sciences as well. Leaving aside subject matter definitions and measurement problems, all scientists in all fields must proceed to reliable information by the same rules. Hence the notion of the *unity* of the sciences—unity with respect to how we obtain knowledge in our respective fields.

THE NEED FOR RESEARCH 11

1. *Our public relations practitioner has at least an idea of what problem he is trying to solve.* That is, he wants to be able to tell what the weather is going to be for the coming day. As simple as this sounds, it is not always an easy goal to know exactly what it is you want to solve.
2. *Our public relations practitioner knows what information he needs to solve his problems.* He knows that he must have some information about his present cloud cover (or lack of it); what it "looks like" outside—threatening, dark, and so forth.
3. *Our public relations practitioner knows where to look for his information.* Half the battle in solving any problem is knowing where to go to obtain the necessary information. In our illustration, we must not overlook the fact that the public relations practitioner knew that he had to look outside and observe the sky and the general environment. Because this step is so simple and obvious in this instance, it should not mask the fact that knowing where to look for the pertinent information to solve a problem is of paramount importance.

With this step of the overall process still in mind, our next question may run something like this: "What led our public relations practitioner to the conclusion that he had better dress for rainy weather?" (assuming, for purposes of our illustration, that this is the conclusion he comes to). This question helps us to bring out some other hidden processes in this apparently simple bit of behavior.

4. *Our public relations practitioner applied some of his previous experiences to the present problem.* He related the information he had obtained on the outcome of similar days in the past to this particular day.
5. *With the past and present before him he came to a decision.* In short, he decided to dress for rainy weather.

This examination of a typical, everyday act in the life of a hypothetical person serves to highlight our central theme. It's this: *Much of what we do in our everyday life has its counterpart in the research process.* Naturally, not all of the important elements of research can be brought out in such a simple example. However, a surprisingly high percentage of the research processes can be found in everyday life.[2]

THE PROBLEM-SOLVING CONTINUUM: A LINK BETWEEN SCIENTIST AND NONSCIENTIST.

Perhaps the most effective way to bridge the gap between scientist and nonscientist is to view the work of both as problem-solving efforts—the scientist coping with areas of ignorance about a given phenomenon and the nonscientist trying to change attitudes and behavior. Figure 2-1

---

[2] Edward J. Robinson, *Communication and Public Relations* (Columbus, Charles E. Merrill Books, Inc., 1966), pp. 469–470.

consists of a *problem-solving continuum,* which should clarify for us similarities in the need for reliable information. In addition, it should enable us to understand better the role of research in general in helping scientists and nonscientists solve their problems. After we have examined this figure, we will be able to see in proper perspective the relationship of research to public relations.

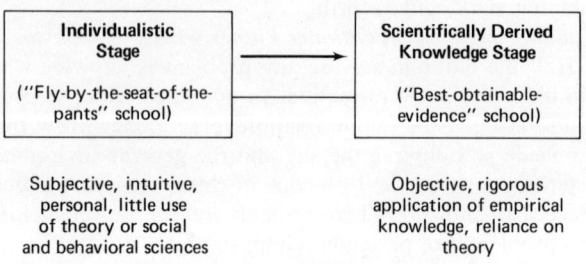

Figure 2-1. Problem-solving continuum

Source: Edward J. Robinson, *Communication and Public Relations* (Columbus, Charles E. Merrill Books, Inc., 1966), p. 48.

On the left side of the continuum we see what has been called the "individualistic stage," which has been further described as the "fly-by-the-seat-of-the-pants" school. This portion of the continuum suggests that in some problem-solving situations (primarily applicable to the nonscientist) the individual has to depend on his own judgment in making a decision, realizing full well that his reliable knowledge is extremely limited at this point, and that he must do the best he can in spite of it.

Another characteristic of this end of the continuum is that there is no available body of knowledge that the practitioner can call upon to help solve his problem. The nonscientist, as a rule, cannot turn to some literature and read research data that have bearing on the problem he is trying to solve, because such data do not exist. He must depend upon his own tools —intuition, hunches, previous experiences, and the like—which by definition are highly personal and nontransferable.

The "scientifically derived knowledge" end of the continuum represents an entirely different situation with respect to problem solving. This end, also called the "best-obtainable evidence" school, stands for circumstances in which the practitioner is able to turn to a body of reliable knowledge that will guide him in deciding how to solve his problem. This body of knowledge represents the best to be had at that particular time, and has been collected through the combined efforts of many different researchers working within a given field. Problem solving at this end of the continuum means utilizing available reliable knowledge as a basis for a deci-

THE NEED FOR RESEARCH 13

sion. Let us compare public relations with a completely different sort of practitioner to complete our understanding of the continuum presented in Figure 2-1.

THE PROBLEM-SOLVING CONTINUUM RELATED TO TWO APPLIED DISCIPLINES

First, let us take medicine. Several hundred years ago, the field of medicine was at the "individualistic stage," in the sense that physicians in those days approached their problems on the basis of personal knowledge. They had their own notions about what caused certain illnesses and what remedies would cure them. For a variety of reasons, they were not able to benefit from the work of other physicians or of persons in related health fields, and this placed them pretty much on their own, so to speak. How a physician became a physician was also a rather personal matter. He worked with another physician and learned from him all that he knew, as there were no schools to go to and practically no books to read.

Gradually, this situation started to change, and the problem solving began to shift from one end of the continuum to the other. More and more research was being conducted in such fields as biology, physiology, and chemistry, and slowly there began to emerge a relationship between these allied disciplines and the field of medicine. This meant that the body of reliable medical knowledge continued to expand and further the shift from the personal to the scientific end of the continuum.[3] Likewise, the education of a physician underwent drastic changes. Schools took the place of on-the-job training of one physician by another. With all of the reliable knowledge in related fields collected in a single place, the physician-to-be had at his fingertips all the information that was available to him to help solve his patients' problems.[4]

This brief examination of physicians can be applied to the practitioners in any related field with respect to problem solving. We could have used engineering or dentistry. Each of these fields could have been seen first as functioning at the individualistic end of the problem-solving continuum, and then gradually moving toward the right-hand end. Naturally,

---

[3] Naturally, such developments were aided greatly by progress in other areas—such as printing, travel, communication systems, and the like. We are not trying to spell out all the factors that make knowledge more general and more widely available. Rather, we want to illustrate in simple fashion how the problem-solving functions of practitioners in a wide variety of fields changed in relation to the type of knowledge made available to them.

[4] Just in passing, it is interesting to note that a serious problem facing physicians and medical students today is how to keep up with the avalanche of research information that increases year by year. This is, of course, also true of many other fields. For example, research knowledge in the broad field of engineering develops so rapidly that one becomes "obsolete" within a very few years of graduation.

the starting point in time on the individualistic end, and the degree of progress toward the scientifically derived end, will vary for each applied field considered. The point is that *every* applied discipline can be examined against this continuum; and based on the analysis, important generalizations can be derived about its present state and its prospects for the future. We will return to some of these generalizations after an examination of public relations practice in terms of this contiuuum.

From our discussion thus far, it is clear that public relations practice is at the extreme left-hand end of the problem-solving continuum. Its practitioners, like our physicians of old, go about their work pretty much on the basis of their own theories and their previous experiences in similar circumstances. Not too long ago, physicians argued that you couldn't teach medicine—that the only way to learn was by the individual tutorial method, which consisted mainly of a period of apprenticeship with another physician. There was many a practitioner who thought that all this talk about teaching medicine in schools was foolish, and for this reason, the development of medical schools was resisted for some time. We hear the same thing about public relations today; it is said that one cannot learn public relations in any way other than at the "school of hard knocks," working along with an established practitioner in the field. We also hear that knowledge from logically related fields, such as psychology and sociology, is neither necessary nor helpful, and that a period of working as a reporter on a good newspaper will do more to produce a public relations practitioner than a lot of longhair theory about communication or human behavior.[5]

Because the practice of public relations is now at the individualistic end of the continuum is no indication of what can or will happen in the future. Theoretically, at least, it *can* move toward the right-hand end in that the problem solving (decisions and corrective steps) will become increasingly based on reliable knowledge derived from research. It is feasible that practitioners will eventually be able to analyze their public relations problems in terms of the attitude and behavior changes (or maintenance) required and then apply toward their solution the best knowledge available from the social and behavioral sciences. In this respect, the public relations practitioner can, in theory, function like the engineer or dentist.

There are a number of factors, however, that determine *when* any particular point toward the right-hand end of the continuum is reached, and not all of them are within the control of the public relations practi-

---

[5] It should be pointed out that the writer has deliberately overstated the case to make a point. There are practitioners who do not subscribe exclusively to this apprenticeship point of view. Many are strong advocates of training development at any appropriate level, particularly graduate training in public relations at the university level. A number of schools in the last twenty years have begun to offer instructional and degree granting programs in public relations. They also contribute to moving public relations practice toward the right-hand end of the continuum in Figure 2-1.

tioner. For example, the rapid development of physiology and biology over a relatively short span of time thrust the practice of medicine ahead very quickly. Physicians themselves had little or no control over the rate of such development. The same relationship exists between public relations and the fields of psychology and sociology. If in the next decade or two psychologists make breakthroughs in their understanding of human behavior, then the public relations practitioner will be that much farther along toward the right end of the continuum. If no such advances occur, he will not be so far along as he might like.

A number of other contributory causes influence how quickly the right-hand end of the continuum is achieved in public relations. For instance, the sophistication of the training provided for aspiring practitioners, the amount of research money made available for research on problems peculiar to public relations practice, and so forth. It is not our intention, however, to give a long list of these various factors at this point in our discussion. Suffice it to say that all of them have a bearing on how rapidly the practice of public relations will become based in research knowledge as contrasted with hunches, guessing, untested previous experience, and so forth.

More to the point at this time is that although one cannot specify how rapidly an applied field will move from the left-hand end of the continuum toward the right, one *can* make the statement that such a direction of development is imperative. What we have in effect shown in our brief tracing of the practice of medicine is the progression of an "art" toward a profession. The same sort of thing has taken place in dentistry, engineering, and a number of other applied fields. If this progression takes place, then the discipline emerges from weakness into strength, from guess work to precision, from quackery to respectability, from rejection by society to full acceptance. Obviously, these are all desirable developments for the practitioner and society alike, but such objectives can be gained only if the practitioner solves his problems in the light of a reliable body of knowledge obtained scientifically.

As pointed out, one cannot be sure that such a change of events will take place within any applied field, or if so, at what rate it will happen. In any organization, be it profit-making or nonprofit-making, government or private, the author is convinced that the *activities* now subsumed under the heading of public relations are unquestionably here to stay, and there is little chance of their being minimized in the future. However, we are not yet able to predict what sort of person the practitioner will be. What kinds of training will he possess? What will be his departmental affiliation at college, and what level of graduate training will he reach? These questions are unanswerable at this time. In any case, it is the author's conviction that the practitioner will, among other things, be well enough trained in the social and behavioral sciences to be able to function as an applied social and behavioral scientist. In addition, with a good foundation in research methodology, he will feel at home with research data and be able to apply them readily to his day-to-day problems.

SURVEY RESEARCH AND THE PROBLEM-SOLVING CONTINUUM

We are now in a better position to relate survey research to the practice of public relations and our problem-solving continuum. Let us take as an illustration our fourth case, which describes the cholesterol scare and what the American Dairy Association did about it.[6] The public relations practitioner with the ADA had certain intuitions, hunches, or even hypotheses, and he believed, for example, that there was far less awareness of the cholesterol controversy outside than inside the dairy industry, and that there was not nearly the "scare" involved that one might think. He also believed that eating habits were patterns of behavior quite resistant to change. Consequently, he felt it highly unlikely that any substantial modification of eating habits had taken place as a result of the general public reading about the dangers of cholesterol. Although we do not plan to go into the case in detail now, we would like to bring out that the practitioner's views can be thought of as a product of his previous experiences with the ADA.[7] Faced with the problem of what to do about all these articles on cholesterol, he might decide to disregard them entirely and continue with his public relations program as usual. In fact, this was indeed his inclination—that the situation did *not* call for any special counterattack to "prove" that foods high in cholesterol need not be avoided in one's daily diet.

If our public relations practitioner had decided to do nothing solely on the basis of previous experience, he would have been operating at that moment from the left-hand end of the problem-solving continuum. He decided, however, to have a survey conducted in order to either confirm or reject his experience-based conclusions. By deciding to obtain research data *before* planning what to do, the practitioner in effect moved toward the right-hand end of the continuum with respect to his problem-solving efforts. In other words, he replaced his hunches and educated guesses with decisions made in the light of knowledge obtained by means of survey research.

[6] Case 4 (pages 182–204) concerns the long-term controversy among medical experts about the role of cholesterol in the bloodstream—and deposited on the walls of arteries—in inducing heart attacks. Some foods, and certain dairy products are among these, have higher amounts of cholesterol than others. It is understandable that the dairy industry would view with some concern the recommendation that foods high in cholesterol content be discontinued from the diet.

[7] For purposes of simplicity, we will ignore the fact that some of these views—for example, that eating habits are patterns of behavior resistant to change—are not completely a function of previous experience. This knowledge could have been partially derived from research on the general topic of resistance to change.

THE NEED FOR RESEARCH 17

To continue our example, he found, as he suspected, that the general public was far less aware of the cholesterol controversy than others in the dairy industry had imagined. With his judgment thus confirmed through survey research, he no longer had to rely on educated guesses and could now proceed with greater confidence. By the same token, he also found out that the industry's advertising of "fat free" milk (skimmed milk) was contributing to an undesirable interpretation by the consumer that milk was to be avoided because of its high fat content. The advertising was in some ways more damaging than the articles on cholesterol; and in this respect the dairy industry was acting as its own worst enemy. This situation might not have, and in this case did not, come to light as a result of common sense or previous experience.

To summarize briefly, we have tried to establish a context into which to place research and then relate it to public relations practice. We have illustrated, by means of a problem-solving continuum, what happens when an individual practitioner in any applied field tries to solve his day-to-day problems. We see that he may work from either end of the continuum—or from a point somewhere in between—making a decision from knowledge based on scientific research (which is more reliable), or from one based on hunches, previous experiences, or guessing (less reliable).[8] This same range of possibility is found in public relations practice, in that occasionally certain decisions or certain portions of an overall program can derive from either extreme—scientific knowledge or intuition. We see how the public relations practitioner for the American Dairy Association went about his problem solving when faced with an undesirable situation—from hunches, intuition, and tentative conclusions (left-hand end of continuum), to research, reliable knowledge, and decisions (right-hand end of continuum).

Hopefully, we have now managed to move one step closer to the main focus of this volume: the use of survey research, as one form of research, in solving public relations problems. However, in order to round out the *relationship* between research and public relations, we should develop one more perspective—the communication context in which public relations practitioners always operate, and how research, communication, and public relations practice go hand in hand. This will be our task in Chapter 3.

---

[8] There are many ways in which a public relations practitioner can increase his reliable knowledge—"in-between" points on the continuum that do not qualify as scientific research. The writer calls these "do-it-yourself" efforts—or "researchettes"—and they are discussed in detail in Robinson, *op. cit.,* Chapters 17–20. In this same vein, Fred P. Frutchy ("Evaluation, What Is It?" in Darcie Byrn, ed., *Evaluation in Extension,* Washington, D.C., U.S. Department of Agriculture, Federal Extension Service, Division of Extension and Training, n.d.), suggests the concept of "degrees of evaluation," as shown in the following scale:

| Casual everyday evaluations | Self-checking evaluations | Do-it-yourself evaluations | Extension studies | Scientific research |

3 | Public relations: relationship to the process of communication

THE public relations practitioner, no matter what else he may be, is first and foremost a communicator. Practically all the problems he encounters in his daily work can be translated into a communication context; to achieve his goals, the practitioner ultimately uses some form of communication—be it the spoken word or written word, or both—in his attempts to persuade, motivate, inform, and inspire. Although the emphasis of this book is on the relationship between survey research and public relations practice, we would be remiss if we did not look at public relations from the additional perspective of communication. In addition to the enormous part it plays in the work of a public relations practitioner, it has an equally important role as a function of the research process; the use of survey research to help solve public relations problems illustrates one way by which an essential dimension of communication is attained. This dimension is called *feedback of information,* or *feedback,* for short.

As we will soon learn in more detail, information acquired by an individual for the purpose of gauging the effectiveness of his communication efforts can be thought of as feedback. Thus, when a person frowns following some remark that we make, and we hasten to explain what was meant by the remark, the communicator is making use of feedback of information. The frown is an item of information (whether correctly or incorrectly interpreted is beside the point, for the moment), that serves as a guide to his subsequent communication efforts. Similarly, in a public relations program, one form of feedback might be a survey research project that measures the attitudes of a particular public toward some aspect of the program. It is an integral part of the communication process and must be considered as a normal part of public relations work, as well. We will want to consider this further after we have examined public relations practice from the point of view of a communication theory model.

THE PROCESS OF COMMUNICATION

A COMMUNICATION THEORY MODEL

Figure 3-1 depicts a communication theory model that we will use to develop our communication perspective. We will not examine it in as much detail as we might, since our major objective is to demonstrate the relationship between the communication process in general and the feedback of information in particular. Following this we wish to emphasize the link between feedback and survey research, and then their relationship to public relations practice.[1]

In Figure 3-1 the communication process is depicted by four "boxes," which are usually referred to as *stages*. This particular version of the model identifies the four stages as sender, message, media, and recipient.[2]

Sender stage

The *sender* stage symbolizes the person or the group responsible for instigating a particular communication. The sender as an individual might be Mr. A conversing with Mr. B, or Mr. A addressing a large audience, either in person or via radio or television. The sender as a group might be a company, a government, a club, or the United Nations—the size does not matter. Sometimes the recipient perceives the sender as an "institutional" sender, so to speak, despite the realization that the message must have been constructed by an individual (or group of individuals) on behalf of the organization.

In a public relations context, the sender in the particular communication situation is generally the practitioner. In Part III, each of the cases will show that the practitioner (as a sender or representing his organiza-

---

[1] We could spend considerable time on how communication takes place in a given social structure. All the constituents (country of travel, particular subcultures, etc.) of any social structure are important for a complete understanding of the process in any given communication situation. The communication model in Figure 3-1 is enclosed within the boundary "total social structure" in order to show that communication does not take place in a vacuum. These details, plus many others inherent in such a model as depicted in Figure 3-1, are taken up in detail in Edward J. Robinson, *Communication and Public Relations* (Columbus, Charles E. Merrill Books, Inc., 1966). The reader is advised to refer to this material if he is interested in a fuller exposition of this particular version of a communication model.

[2] It should be noted that there are many different versions, or models, of the communication process. They are intended to help one visualize the communication process, just as chemists use molecular models to help them visualize chemical processes. The models may vary in form, but this is probably due to the particular points each writer wishes to stress in his analysis of the communication process. Or, he may wish to apply his model to something else (in our case, to public relations). Most models do consider the "essentials" of the process—factors such as accounting for the source or the sender—though these may be presented in different ways or at different points in the structure.

Figure 3-1. A communication model

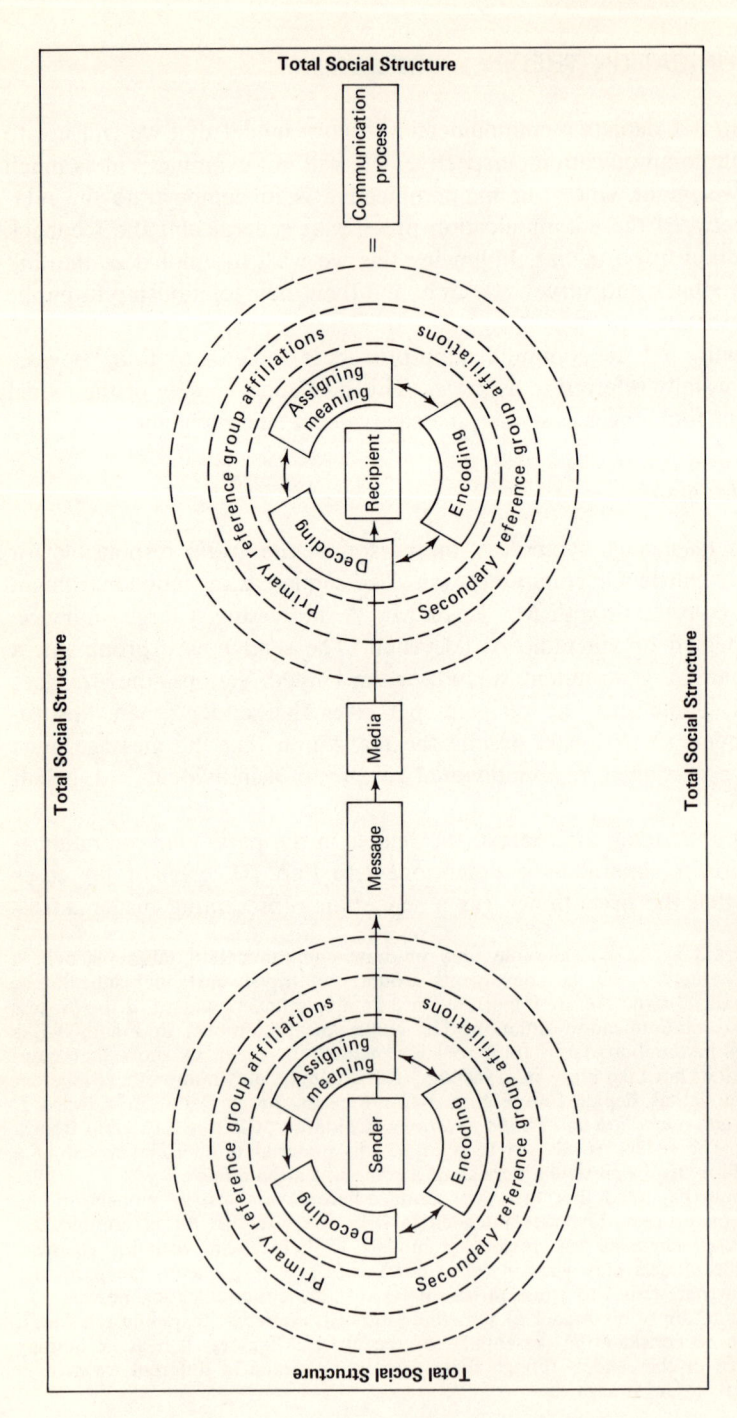

Source: Edward J. Robinson, *Communication and Public Relations* (Columbus, Charles E. Merrill Books, Inc., 1966), p. 122.

THE PROCESS OF COMMUNICATION

tion as a sender), planned some particular public relations program which would involve the use of various media, and that he subsequently modified his plans in the light of research results.

Message stage

The *message* stage symbolizes that which the communicator wishes to transmit to the recipient. Clearly, messages may contain information of any sort that the sender wishes to transmit, and may consist of literally anything intelligible to a recipient. They may be piled-up stones arranged in certain patterns in order to convey a particular idea or concept. They may consist of puffs of smoke, dots and dashes, pictures, configurations on paper called words, or movements of the hands, arms, and fingers as in the case of sign language among the deaf.

Central to the message stage is the notion of *overlapping fields of experience*. For a message to be truly intelligible the experiences of both the sender and the recipient must overlap to some extent. An example of extensive overlap would be communication between two friends who have known each other for many years. For our purposes, let us assume that these two friends grew up together. They share the same language, many of the same friends, many of the same previous experiences (such as football games, dances, parties, and so forth), many of the same values, goals, aspirations, and so on. Under these conditions, the degree of comprehension is likely to be very high; there will be relatively few occasions when one will not understand the other because of the high degree of overlap in their lives.

At the other extreme, let us consider two individuals communicating in the United Nations. For the sake of contrast, let us assume that neither individual speaks the other's language and that they must communicate by means of a translator. They do *not* share the same language; they very likely grew up in two entirely different cultures; and they probably differ widely in their values, goals, and aspirations. Under these conditions, the likelihood of misunderstanding each other's message is very high; their fields of experience hardly overlap at all.

This idea of overlapping fields of experience is one that the public relations practitioner faces constantly. He must contrive some means of ascertaining what degree of overlap exists, and what steps can be taken to increase the amount of overlap to insure effective communication between himself and the recipient. The use of research is one of the most effective methods of accomplishing this, as we shall see later in more detail.

Media stage

The *media* stage embraces all of the means by which we transmit a message. Obviously, these would include media of all kinds—print, radio, television, recordings, and so forth—or anything else that enables a sender to place a message before a potential recipient. The reader will note that we used the word potential. To simply make a message available through some particular medium does not insure that the recipient will pay attention to it. Thus, placing an ad in a newspaper makes the advertisement available to the buyer of that newspaper; but we do not know if he will actually read the ad. The availability of the message does not necessarily infer attendance to it.

Public relations practitioners often feel at home with the media stage as many of them have previously worked in the field—particularly on newspapers and magazines.[3] This stage of the communication process is the most visible part of a practitioner's work. One can see a brochure, a news release, a book full of clippings, and the like. A "clipping book" is often made of the total number of column inches (comprising articles and stories from newspapers and magazines) obtained by a practitioner. This can be used to determine the extent of his activity over any period of time or on behalf of a given organization. In fact, one of the dilemmas that practitioners face is being measured by the "column inch."[4] Clients and superiors alike are often prone to measure the effectiveness of a public relations practitioner in terms of the number of column inches he can garner in a year. Unpaid newspaper space has become so associated with his work that it is almost the trademark of the public relations practitioner. Naturally, a great deal of this emphasis on the clipping book is due to the public relations practitioner himself; like the artist with a portfolio, he frequently uses it to demonstrate his worth, whether to a client or to an employer.

One concept that should be mentioned in connection with the media stage is the *seduction quality* of this particular stage in the communication process. As was noted earlier, it is difficult to demonstrate what a public relations practitioner does all day long. His activity, like certain portions of administrative work, is sometimes hard to "show" to someone else. An administrator can spend hours talking with different people who report to him and who, at the end of the day, appeared to have done nothing. His frustration with the apparent lack of tangible results is applicable to the public relations practitioner, as well. Because so much of what he does

---

[3] It is interesting to note that the frequent use of print (particularly the newspaper) by present day public relations practitioners can be attributed to their previous experience with the medium. As a result, the majority of public relations practitioners feel less at home with other media which have yet to be fully implemented to serve public relations communication goals to their best advantage. In the future we can expect to see a more balanced practitioner, in the sense that he will be as familiar with the use of radio and television as he now is with newspapers and magazines.

[4] The expression "column inch" stems from the practice of measuring the length of any topic or series of topics contained in a standard column of newspaper print. An article which takes five inches of space in a column would be said to take up five column inches.

THE PROCESS OF COMMUNICATION

cannot be easily demonstrated to someone else, the visible portions of the media stage—the brochures, pamphlets, stockholders reports, employee newspapers, newsletters, newspaper articles, and magazine stories—can become a tremendous source of reinforcement for the public relations practitioner; either he can toss an attractive stockholder report before the boss and say with pride, "That's what I have been working on lately"; or he can come home worn out from a hard day at the office and show some pamphlets to the little woman as evidence of a hard day's work.

What we have said thus far might be thought of as stating the obvious. What is not so obvious is that the energy devoted to translating messages into some media form can be confused with successful communication. With a company newspaper, for example, one can become so busy with the actual process of publication that the communicative effectiveness of the paper can become completely forgotten. It is assumed that because the newspaper exists, it *must* therefore, be helping us to communicate. Even worse, in time we can lose sight of whom it is that we are supposed to reach—what people receive the publication, why, and how they were placed on the mailing list in the first place. This is what is meant by the term *seduction quality* of the media stage. Because it is the most visible portion of the overall activities of a communicator such as a public relations practitioner, it can become an end in itself. We can "seduce" ourselves; or, in other words, we can make ourselves believe that we are effectively achieving our communication goals—when, in fact, we are not.

It should be clear that the seduction quality concept applies to *any* communicator, though more generally to professional communicators. Thus, an advertising man can seduce himself into thinking that he is effectively reaching a given audience. The same thing can be said for teachers, radio and TV people, or for anyone who tries to communicate to certain recipients via a medium or a combination of media. Some fields have what might be called "built-in" devices to minimize the effect of the seduction quality. An advertiser has sales figures that can tell him whether he is not reaching his recipient with the message, in spite of a lot of activity at the media stage. Teachers have quizzes and examinations that can tell them how effectively they have been communicating.

There are certain situations, however, that preclude the operation of these built-in devices to minimize the seduction quality of the media stage, and public relations practice is particularly vulnerable to this difficulty. Many communication objectives are hard to specify or measure: "What do we mean by good community relations? How do we know when we have good community relations? How do we know when we have lost it? How do we know which communication efforts will help maintain good community relations?" This is why a public relations practitioner must always be aware of the seduction quality of the media stage, and must always be alert to ways of measuring the effectiveness of his communication efforts.

Obviously, research is one excellent means of counteracting this weakness, and we will return to this point later.

Recipient stage

The *recipient* stage, in one sense, represents the whole point of communication. Specifically, it stands for all the various "objects" of communication efforts. Rarely, if ever, is communication nonpurposive, and generally the object of the effort is another individual or group of individuals.

Like the sender, the recipient of a communication can be a single person—as in a face-to-face conversation—or it can be "everyone out there in radio land"—as in the case of a disc jockey broadcasting his particular version of a record program.

As any public relations practitioner knows, one of the most perplexing problems associated with this stage is how to cause the recipient to respond to and be affected by the communication effort. The whole point of a sender's effort is to change or maintain certain behavior. If no impact or impression can be discerned, then the sender inevitably concludes that he has failed to get the message across. At the present time there are no formulas or panaceas for avoiding this sort of failure, particularly in view of the tremendous competition in the field for the attention of a recipient or recipients.[5] The best one can do to reduce the contingency of failure is to learn as much as possible about the recipient—psychological factors, sociological factors and the like. Thus, for example, it is imperative for a public relations practitioner to find out what the attitudes of his intended recipients are toward what it is he intends to communicate about. This can help him to anticipate their reactions accurately and avoid the pitfalls of incorrect assumption. By now, the reader has probably noted for himself that this is yet another situation in which survey research can be helpful to a public relations practitioner; we will see the process in action in several of the cases in Part III.

COMMUNICATION AS A PROCESS

The last "box" to consider in our communication model is labeled *communication process*. This final addition is designed to prevent a common error that is often made—that of referring to a problem or to a misunderstanding as merely a "breakdown in communication." This statement

---

[5] Although any guess as to the average number of messages received by an individual in any one day is subject to error, the daily volume of commercial messages directed toward the single consumer has been estimated at 1,500. (See Murray Blumenthal, ed., *The Denver Symposium on Mass Communications Research for Safety*, Chicago, National Safety Council, 1964.)

THE PROCESS OF COMMUNICATION 25

implies that a communication problem connotes a singular disorder instead of plural, when, in fact, a breakdown generally is the result of a number of elements. It can occur at any point or points over the enormous range of the various stages that comprise the *communication process;* this is why the four stages in the model are linked together to form the whole. The model structure should help illustrate the concept of communication as a dynamic process consisting of many parts[6]—one that should be viewed in its *entirety* when used as an aid in analyzing problems in public relations.

To underscore the use of the model as a whole, let us consider three generalizations that one might make:[7]

[6] It might be useful here to point out that analyses of the communication process —of which our model is only an example—are comparatively arbitrary and can be broken down into many more stages than four. A number of years ago the writer was associated with the director of a research laboratory. He made an analysis of the communication process involved when aerial photography is used to obtain intelligence about enemy activity. Starting with the target as the first stage, he was able to generate a long string of boxes—or "stages"—that linked the target to the eventual intelligence report (based on aerial photographs that had been analyzed by a photo interpreter). The process—or string of stages—might be illustrated as follows:

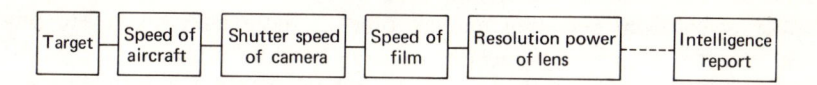

| Target | Speed of aircraft | Shutter speed of camera | Speed of film | Resolution power of lens | | Intelligence report |

The point of this example is not to count how many stages were used, but to show that an individual may employ any number of stages in his analysis of the communication process. Generally, this multilabeled breakdown is for purposes of highlighting some particular part of the overall process that might otherwise have been overlooked.

To apply this thinking to our four-part model, one could, for example, subdivide the media stage into a number of parts, thereby making additional stages. The new model, with a newspaper as the medium, could appear as follows:

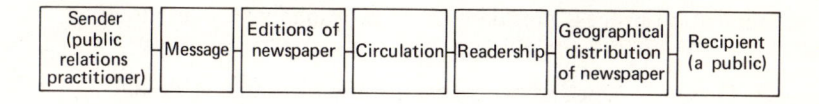

| Sender (public relations practitioner) | Message | Editions of newspaper | Circulation | Readership | Geographical distribution of newspaper | Recipient (a public) |

With this illustration, we have made a more detailed analysis of the media stage, just as our earlier example made a detailed analysis of the steps between photographing enemy territory and the intelligence report based on the photography. This sort of specialized analysis might be made if one wanted to focus on obscure aspects in the publication of a newspaper that might have adverse effects on how well a public relations practitioner (the sender) is able to communicate with a given public. For instance, the readership and geographical distribution might not "fit" the public that the practitioner wishes to reach, just as in our previous example the intelligence report of aerial photograph (or series of photographs) is hindered or facilitated by the resolution capability of the lens and the shutter speed of the camera.

[7] These generalizations are paraphrases of a more detailed analysis made by the author of the communication model under consideration. (See Robinson, *op. cit.,* pp. 90–105.)

1. Comparison of the communication process to a chain

We have long heard the old saying about a chain being no stronger than its weakest link. An analogy can be made to communication in that regardless of the amount of effort expended at any or all of the stages, the communication effort will fail if even *one* stage is operating at below minimum efficiency. Thus, we could be strong at the message and media stages (a campaign via the mass media urging people to give blood), and yet fail to achieve our goal because of weakness at the recipient stage (lack of research into the reasons for resistance to the idea).

2. Stress of one stage to the exclusion of another

In our earlier discussion, we noted that the public relations practitioner feels most at home with the media stage of the communication process and that efforts connected with it are more visible than at other stages. In fact, the attractiveness of this stage can be summed up in the concept of its "seduction quality"—an attraction that tempts the practitioner away from spending enough time at the sender stage. He might neglect entirely to investigate what *assumptions* he brings to the problem situation, what interests, knowledge, and background the recipients have, and whether these assumptions are valid. Also to be examined at the sender stage is the question of motive. What are the ethics involved in his particular communication goal? If he succeeds in modifying the behavior of the recipients in question, will he or his organization benefit at their expense?

We could continue to spell out some of the considerations that are associated with the sender stage, but this is not our purpose at this time. Rather, we wish merely to emphasize that if one becomes preoccupied with either the message or the media stage, or both, then the other stages in the communication process are likely to receive inadequate attention.

3. Different types of problems are peculiar to each stage

Somewhat akin to our first generalization is the fact that each stage has problems peculiar to it alone, and that remedial efforts in communication should reflect an awareness of this. Examples of problems at the message stage might be the readability of the copy produced or the intelligibility of the graphs or charts employed. At the recipient stage, they might be certain prejudices on the part of the recipient toward the subject of persuasion, or an intelligence level that requires special steps to insure their understanding of the message. Disregard of problems such as these often results in unnecessary waste of time and money. For example, an organization might issue a stockholder's report more elaborate and expensive than the previous year's (in order to make a dramatic impact), only to discover that the reading comprehension of the audience was not sufficient to meet the level of difficulty of the copy.

Decoding, encoding, and assigning meaning

There is one last portion of our communication model that should be discussed at this time: the three processes of *decoding, encoding,* and *assigning meaning.*[8] They are equally important to the sender and to the recipient stage.[9]

Our first point about these three processes is that they occur simultaneously and with intricate interaction. Once again our analogy to chemistry is applicable: a chemical process takes place rapidly and complexly, whereas the *analysis* of the process is a slow series of steps completely out of pace with what goes on in the test tube. The same is true with the processes of decoding, encoding, and assigning meaning. They can be analyzed separately, but as a course of action cannot be isolated from one another. It would be extremely difficult to identify exactly which of the three steps an individual was engaged in at any given moment.

The process of decoding embraces the things that we do to understand the various communications directed to us—we try to make sense out of what is being said, written, televised, and so forth. Obviously, our ability to decode will vary as a function of our familiarity with the message: an article written in our mother tongue is easily decoded; on the other hand, an article written in a less familiar language[10] reduces our decoding ability considerably.

We *assign meaning* at practically the same instant that we decode. In addition to translating the words contained in a paragraph and letting it go at that, we also interpret what the writer intended to evoke by the words, such as emotional reactions, feelings of hostility or friendliness, or an

---

[8] The other concentric circles that surround the sender and recipient stages—*primary and secondary reference group affiliations*—are outside the scope of our treatment of the model in this book. They are discussed, however, in *ibid.,* and the reader is encouraged to examine the material.

[9] From one point of view, the process of communication *is* decoding, encoding, and assigning meaning. This is true especially when they are linked to the concept of feedback, as we will see later in this chapter. In the opinion of the author, however, this does not preclude the value of our breaking down the communication process into the four stages, as well. By doing *both* types of analyses, we are less likely to overlook certain details (such as the seduction quality of the media stage), which are more applicable to one analysis than to the other.

[10] The reader has probably recognized that the process of decoding is not limited to languages in the usual sense (English, Spanish, French, etc.). The concept is equally applicable to mathematical languages or to any unusual notations that might require special understanding. In addition, such things as slang, colloquialisms, or any other "in group" terminology will affect the ability of an individual to decode a communication.

understanding of the writer's motives. We even "read between the lines," teasing out meanings that are not immediately obvious or reading meanings into the writer's words when no such meaning was intended.

The term *encoding* represents the process of taking what we wish to communicate to someone else and translating it into a "language" that he will understand. Naturally, our knowledge of the recipient is vital here. If we are not thoroughly aware of what *he* is able to understand, we may encode our message in a language that is incomprehensible to him.

Now let us relate these processes directly to the public relations practitioner, who is bombarded daily by a variety of communications that he must decode. In addition to decoding the messages the public relations practitioner must assign meaning to them and relate them to various portions of his overall responsibilities for the organization or for the client. To illustrate his course of action, let us assume that each day a practitioner reads one in a series of newspaper articles on the general theme of "Why are our electric rates among the highest in the country?"[11] He must first *decode* these articles with any and all associated material, such as letters to the editors, editorial comment, and so forth. He must then *assign meaning* to them—that is, figure out their impact upon the readers (consumers of electrical power, public officials, and other pertinent groups)—and then decide what, if anything, he should do. If some form of communication is indicated, he must then *encode* his message in a manner that is appropriate to the recipient or recipients in terms of the particular communication he plans to use.

The concept of feedback

A great deal of what we have seen about the processes of decoding, encoding, and assigned meaning is summed up by the term *feedback*. With it, we have the best chance to react effectively toward achievement of our goals—particularly if we are professional communicators. Without it, we run the risk of failure, which for the professional is fatal.

Let us look at a passage which illustrates this in more detail:

If we are attempting to "sink a basket" with a basketball, we generally can do this successfully in a very few trials if we have any degree of eye-hand coordination at all. If, however, a barrier is placed between us and the basket, such that we can still shoot but cannot see the results of our shooting, then we take much longer to sink a basket. The reason: we have considerably reduced the

[11] Such a series recently took place in one of the Boston daily newspapers. Simultaneous with the series was an advertising campaign run by the local electricity company to the effect that electric power was one of the best buys available to the consumer because its cost continued to go down while all other consumer costs continued to rise. The author does not know whether the campaign happened to be purely coincidental, or whether it was anticipated by a public relations man and planned as a reaction to the newspaper series.

THE PROCESS OF COMMUNICATION

available feedback. We can't see what we are doing and we now have to rely on hearing how well we are doing—something that we are not used to, as you can readily find out by closing your eyes and relying on hearing instead of sight. Take away any cues of sound, and we might never learn to sink a basket consistently. Only by chance would the ball go in now. This example illustrates the principle of feedback.

Let us now examine another simple example, this time emphasizing communication a little more. Let us assume that two gentlemen meet for the first time at a cocktail party. Let's identify them as Mr. A and Mr. B. From the moment they meet and begin to talk, the process of feedback is operating for both of them. Mr. A may refer to a football game that was played that day. Mr. B may be completely uninterested in football and make only some polite, perhaps even trite reply. If he is halfway perceptive, Mr. A immediately detects the lack of interest in football on the part of Mr. B. This behavior of Mr. B now has served as feedback for Mr. A, and Mr. A may drop the subject, defend the sport, or what have you, depending upon his personality, the amount of spirits he has imbibed, and so on. In short, for both men, such things as gestures, facial expressions, implicit and explicit verbal statements, all serve as feedback for both of them—feedback that they both will use to guide their subsequent behavior, particularly their communication behavior, which is our interest in this example.

What is true for an individual (our first example of trying to sink a basket) or two individuals interacting (Mr. A and Mr. B at a cocktail party) or any other possible combinations of individuals (such as an individual communicating to an audience in a lecture situation) is true for any communication situation. There will be feedback, however extensive or limited.[12]

Clearly, feedback is an indispensable portion of the total communication process. Any communication effort, regardless of the method used, will suffer from lack of feedback and benefit by its availability. The relationship of this concept to public relations practice is clear; *it is the responsibility of the public relations practitioner to make provisions for as much feedback of information in his work as is humanly possible.* Without adequate feedback—like the basketball player—he won't be able to see (or worse, *hear*) the effects of his shooting and will have to trust to chance in achieving his goal.

[12] Robinson, *op. cit.,* pp. 71–72. At the risk of redundancy, we might point out that *both* Mr. A and Mr. B are undergoing the process of decoding, encoding, and assigning meaning. In this sense, too, both are utilizing the feedback from their interaction to shape their subsequent behavior—both verbal and nonverbal—toward each other.

Summary of Part I

We are now ready to pull together some of the main ideas that have been generated in this and in the previous two chapters. In addition to listening, reading, and observing the behavior of others in order to obtain feedback of information, another major means by which it is achieved is through scientific research. Feedback obtained through this method is more reliable than that achieved via human alertness because scientific research currently represents the most dependable method we know of obtaining reliable knowledge. This broad statement, of course, embraces the feedback obtained from *any* form of scientific research; but what we have chosen to focus upon in this volume is that obtained from *one* particular form of scientific research—survey research. From all that has been said thus far, it follows that *we are viewing survey research as a means by which a public relations practitioner obtains feedback in order to function more efficiently in solving his public relations problems.* It also follows that the more the public relations practitioner utilizes survey research—assuming, of course, that this is the appropriate form of research to use—the more he will be moving away from the left-hand end of the continuum in Figure 2-1 toward the right-hand end—which, as we have already seen, is the direction in which he *must* move in his daily practice.

Now that we have considered 1) the perspectives that are necessary to understand our way of viewing public relations, 2) its relationship to research in general and to survey research in particular, 3) a communication theory model, and 4) the concept of feedback of information, we are ready to consider the topic of survey research. Our objective is a limited one—to provide enough background for the reader to become conversant with this prime public relations tool. This material will constitute Part II of this volume.

Following our examination of survey research we will then be ready to look at the seven cases in Part III. These have been selected to illustrate the use of survey research in obtaining feedback of information, so that the public relations practitioner can function at the "best obtainable knowledge" end of the continuum and spend a minimal amount of time flying by the seat of his pants. Finally, by viewing public relations practitioners in action, we should come away with a better understanding of what it means to be one.

PART II
Survey research in a nutshell

4 | Survey research: relationship to other means of obtaining reliable information

IN Chapter 2 we defined research rather broadly as means of obtaining reliable knowledge. This definition was developed within the context of a problem-solving continuum, in which we noted that anyone—be he scientist or nonscientist—needs reliable knowledge in order to cope with problems that confront him. We also pointed out that scientific research, as one process of obtaining reliable knowledge, was the most dependable method of accomplishing this yet devised by man.

Obviously, there are *degrees* of reliable knowledge. Some approaches will generate information about which we can be quite certain; others will produce results that are highly suspect—and, of course, there will be degrees of reliability in between.

Besides the question of the *degree* of certainty, there are other dimensions of reliable knowledge that we should consider. We need, for example, to look into the distinction between descriptive research and experiments that are *causally* oriented—those which are designed to help the researcher understand how phenomenon Y is caused by phenomenon X. These other dimensions are important to us for a number of reasons:

1. We need to understand more of the *terminology* used in the social and behavioral sciences—for example, in connection with the broad activity called research. There are a number of terms which identify a variety of different approaches to obtaining reliable knowledge. It is easy to become confused in trying to differentiate between *field research, laboratory research, scientific research, ex post facto research,* and so on, and we need to develop a perspective that will enable us to see these distinctions.

2. We need to understand how survey research, as one member of what might be called a "family" of efforts, is different from and similar to its "relatives."

3. We must know exactly what survey research can accomplish for the public relations practitioner; we should not attribute to it capabilities that it does not possess; but, equally important, we must not be ignorant of what it *can* do as a tool for the practitioner.

EXPLORATORY, DESCRIPTIVE, AND EXPLANATORY STUDIES

Before continuing with our examination, we should recognize that research studies vary with respect to the objectives of the researcher. This point is expressed by Selltiz, among others, and reads as follows:

Each study, of course, has its own specific purpose. But we may think of research purposes as falling into a number of broad groupings: (1) to gain familiarity with a phenomenon or to achieve new insights into it, often in order to formulate a more precise research problem or to develop hypotheses; (2) to portray accurately the characteristics of a particular individual, situation, or group (with or without specific initial hypotheses about the nature of these characteristics); (3) to determine the frequency with which something occurs or with which it is associated with something else (usually, but not always, with a specific initial hypothesis); (4) to test a hypothesis of a causal relationship between variables.[1]

Following along with the above distinctions, we shall identify as *exploratory studies* those which fall into the first category. Research work that can be characterized by categories (2) and (3) we will label as *descriptive studies*. Lastly, those designed to test hypotheses of causal relationships between variables, category (4), we shall designate as *explanatory studies*. Let us examine each category in turn, relating it to public relations practice whenever appropriate.

Exploratory studies

Exploratory studies are research efforts designed to accomplish exactly what the title implies—designed to look into some relatively unfamiliar topic or problem area in order to gain sufficient understanding to permit further exploration and allow the researcher to intelligently design a thorough study or program to test a particular hypothesis.

One point should be emphasized with respect to this type of study; the investigator should do all that he can to remain open to any insights and observations that might prove advantageous to his exploration. For example, one important method used in conjunction with exploratory studies

---

[1] Claire Selltiz, *et al., Research Methods in Social Relations,* rev. ed. (New York: Holt, Rinehart and Winston, Inc., 1965), p. 50. This chapter has been considerably aided by the authors' excellent material on research design in their Chapters 3 and 4.

is the *case method*. The investigator makes a thorough examination of one or two persons, groups, or organizations. With persons, this may consist of long, unstructured interviews covering as many topics as possible; and the information obtained may be supplemented by various tests or personality inventories. The exploratory work might also be carried out by interviewing a number of persons in a group or organization and subsequently watching them at work.

The attitude with which the investigator should approach his exploratory work can be described by the seemingly contradictory phrase *planned naïveté*. In this context, the term *planned* means that an investigator has to decide what it is he has to know and how to go about it in the most intelligent way. If he is going to make a "literature search" about what others have done, he has to think about what he plans to read and where he can find the material. Likewise, if he is going to examine an organization *à la* case method, he must think about things such as who should be interviewed and which processes within the organization should be observed. Naturally, the examiner should not be so rigid in his planning that he fails to take advantage of new approaches that may present themselves. There must be planning, but it should include an attitude of serendipity; otherwise, the whole point of exploratory study is defeated.

The other term, naïveté, is used to convey an attitude of open-mindedness in exploratory studies. The investigator must try to observe what is going on with as few preconceptions as humanly possible; in other words, he must attempt to overcome the effects of familiarity (the opposite of naïveté), which tends to dull one's sensitivity to his surroundings. For example, we have all experienced the inability to remember a sign or the location of a store that we pass frequently, or even daily, to and from work. We look at these landmarks—in the sense that our visual system intercepts light from the objects—but we do not "see" them in the sense of noticing details, changes in the store front, and so on. Moreover, a husband often completely misses a flower arrangement, a new lamp, or a new set of drapes, merely because they are located among the very familiar objects he no longer really sees. It is when we are naïve that we have the best chance of seeing things with the least prejudice. So it is in exploratory studies; the investigator who tries to maintain a posture of naïeveté is more likely to catch the small detail that may prove very important to his understanding of his subject.

Some form of exploratory study is frequently used in public relations work. This is particularly true if the practitioner happens to be a consultant with a wide range of clients; he encounters many different problem areas with which he is totally unfamiliar, and he must, of necessity, engage in some exploratory work. Like his scientist counterpart, he must take steps to learn more about his problem areas in order to move efficiently toward more definitive work.

Let us take a specific public relations example to convey the sense of exploratory work. The author once had as client a research and development company, most of whose employees were scientists and whose main activity was scientific research. The client was curious about the general public's understanding of science and scientists, and about the attitudes of the public toward scientific work and the people who engaged in it for a living (in this connection, see the introductory material to Case 5).

The starting point, as is the case in any exploratory study, was to look into the literature on the topic. What previous studies had been done? Had any related work been carried on? If so, what were the findings? In addition to researching literature, the author engaged in a practice which is a standard phase of his own exploratory research; he informally asked questions of friends, acquaintances, tradesmen, and so forth: "When you hear the word *science,* what comes to mind? What do scientists do in their daily work? How interested are you in the work of scientists—any scientists?" After querying thirty or forty odd persons along these lines, the author began to get some idea of the obstacles that might confront him in his further exploration; he reached tentative conclusions about the difficulty of a formal study, and he began to develop some general ideas about possible approaches to the problem of obtaining more information. He also developed some tentative hypotheses[2] about people's attitudes toward science and scientists. In this case, there appeared to be a gap between the nonscientist and the scientist. The laymen felt that they really did not understand what scientists did, nor could they comprehend many of the scientific theories. Because the generalization seemed to apply to a rather wide cross section of those interviewed, we could not attribute this lack of comprehension to the intelligence or occupational level of the respondent—professional people were as prone to this feeling as nonprofessionals. A second hypothesis which emerged during the exploratory work was that people had a great deal of respect, even awe, for scientific research. In fact, there was a hint that the halo effect surrounding research work even spread to the company supporting the work. Incidentally, this latter, tentative hypoth-

[2] The term *hypothesis* simply means the statement of an assumed relationship. Thus, if one assumes that people who are fearful and generally anxious are likely to perceive or discriminate events going on around them more acutely than those who are not fearful and anxious, one has made a statement of an assumed relationship between fear, anxiety and discrimination. The hypothesis is that anxious people tend to pay better attention to their environment than those who are more relaxed. The next step would be to develop an experiment that would either support or reject the hypothesis.

Let us take another example. A four-color annual report with a high ratio of pictures to words (half the page is taken up by words, the other half by pictures) will be read and understood more than an annual report in one color with a low ratio of pictures to words. Here the assumed relationship is between color and pictures and their effect on the potential reader. We will return to the topic of hypotheses in the section on explanatory studies.

esis to the effect that research might be a particularly good theme around which to build a large part of the company's communications proved to be one of the most valuable findings later confirmed by more substantive research work.

Descriptive studies

Our second major category of studies embraces all research efforts that describe or summarize the characteristics of the public or publics under investigation.

An enormous number of descriptive studies have been conducted; in fact, most of the survey research carried on in private research agencies, in business, and in nonprofit institutions of all descriptions falls into this category. An example of a descriptive study might be a public relations practitioner's investigating the employees for whom he publishes a company newspaper. Such a study typically would collect the following types of information: what proportion of the total employee group reads the paper regularly, frequently, infrequently, never? How many of the readers take their copy home to their families? Are those who read the paper frequently more likely to take it home than those who read it less frequently? Does formal education have any bearing on frequency of readership? What portions (or features) of the paper do the readers like or dislike? Are likes and dislikes in any way related to the length of service of the employee, his status within the organization, or his age? In short, any reasonable combination of factors can be studied. This is true whether they be socioeconomic factors (age, income, or occupation), attitudinal dimensions (pro- or anti-big business), or the interrelationship of these variables (what bearing age, income, and occupation have on attitudes toward bigness in business).

One of the cases in Part III illustrates the descriptive research category. Case 3 concerns the Kennecott Copper Corporation and its television program, "Kennecott Neighborhood Theater." The company wanted to know what age groups watched the program and how frequently they saw it. Clearly, many of the data collected *describe* the type of audience that "Kennecott Neighborhood Theater" attracted (see Table 13-2, p. 166). However, age, sex, income, and so forth, were not the only factors that the researchers had in mind. They attempted to measure the *impact* of the program with respect to the viewers' attitudes toward the company's responsibility as a corporate citizen, its reputation as an employer, and the institutional message associated with the program. In this case, the viewing audience was described in terms of personal characteristics and demography as well as with respect to certain attitudinal dimensions.

It should now be clear to the reader why the bulk of survey research conducted each year falls into the *descriptive* research category.[3] The public relations practitioner, in this connection, needs to describe his various publics in as much detail as possible. The more he knows about the age, income, occupation, and so forth, of his various publics, the easier it will be for him to communicate effectively with them.

He will be in an even better position if he can extend the process to include their attitudes. In fact, if a practitioner's most sophisticated knowledge were descriptive in nature, and if it were detailed, up-to-date and included attitudinal dimensions, then public relations practice would probably be at a very refined level today. Unfortunately, at present comparatively few practitioners design and conduct their public relations programs on the basis of detailed descriptive studies. More often than not, because of the dearth of descriptive information, we rely on the ability of the experienced practitioner to make educated guesses about his various publics.

Explanatory studies

Explanatory studies immediately usher us into an exceedingly complex phase of the whole area of research. While they are comparatively simple to

---

[3] Although this generalization is certainly accurate, there are exceptions. For one thing, there is a category of research closely related to survey work (some would classify it within survey work) called the *field experiment*. Essentially, this is a laboratory test conducted in a natural setting, in which an experimenter manipulates independent variables and ascertains their effect upon dependent variables—just as we described the process of explanatory type studies. Thus, if one is interested in experimenting with how what one person says to another reinforces the other's behavior, he can do it in an artificial setting, such as a laboratory, or he may try to conduct the study in a normal, everyday situation where the people may not even be aware that they are participating in an experiment. Consequently, *a field experiment, unlike a typical piece of survey research, is an example of an explanatory study, not one of the descriptive type*. How closely field experiments live up to all the controlled situations normally associated with a laboratory study will, of course, vary from situation to situation; the difference between the two types is a matter of degree. The important point is whether there are independent and dependent variable relationships involved and under the control of the experimenter.

Another point we might make here is that the distinctions between descriptive and explanatory studies are not always so obvious as we might like them to be. Furthermore, many technical details are not included in our presentation of descriptive and explanatory studies, such as how research designs relate to these two main categories, the use of "tests of significance" (statistical significance), and so forth. The research oriented reader may wish to read further in this area (see, for example, Margaret J. Hagood and Daniel O. Price, *Statistics for Sociologists*, rev. ed. (New York: Holt, Rinehart and Winston, Inc., 1962); F. Stuart Chapin, *Experimental Designs in Sociological Research* (New York: Harper and Brothers, 1955); Hanan C. Selvin, "A Critique of Tests of Significance in Survey Research," *American Sociological Review*, 22 (1957), 519–527; Robert McGinnis, "Randomization and Inference in Sociological Research," *American Sociological Review*, 23 (1958), 408–414; and Leslie Kish, "Some Statistical Problems in Research Design," *American Sociological Review*, 24 (1959), 328–338.

describe in terms of their overall objectives, they are difficult to execute, and they can also generate considerable philosophical discussion.[4]

Explanatory studies are executed to test a hypothesis—which, as we learned in footnote 2, is a statement of an assumed relationship between two variables, one *independent* and the other *dependent*. There are literally an infinite number of hypotheses that one may wish to develop and then test by means of an experiment.[5] For example, a practitioner may wish to test the hypothesis that the informed employee is a more effective employee —in terms of productivity, loyalty, or any other characteristic he chooses. This hypothesis logically reflects many of the "in house" communication efforts that practitioners undertake within a company. In this instance, the various communications used to inform employees about their company may constitute the independent variable which is assumed to cause the improved effectiveness, or the dependent variable.

A study designed to test this hypothesis becomes an illustration of our explanatory study category. Naturally, there are many additional factors associated with the design of experiments to test hypotheses about causally related variables[6] but this brief statement should make it clear to the reader how explanatory studies differ from the other types already discussed.

[4] Philosophical overtones enter the picture because in an explanatory study the experimenter has presumably identified what phenomenon or phenomena (*independent* variable X, or $X, Y,$ and Z) cause, produce, or bring to pass some other phenomenon or phenomena (*dependent* variable X, or X, Y, and Z). This can easily lead to questions such as why these phenomena are causally related—a complicated business indeed. Consider the topic of the motivation of human behavior as an illustration. Ultimately, we would like to be able to conduct explanatory studies that would enable us to see which variables cause one individual to be a delinquent, mentally ill, successful in business, or an outstanding scientist, and which variables cause another individual to exhibit a different set of behaviors. It is generally not sufficient to merely make the statement that one or a combination of variables produces a given set of behaviors. Immediately, one is asked why this happens. Any attempt to answer this question opens a veritable Pandora's box and causes the boundaries between science and philosophy to become blurred indeed. While we cannot even touch upon this whole aspect of explanatory or causally oriented studies —searching for the "why" behind a given phenomenon—it is important to realize that such a relationship between science and philosophy exists.

[5] There is a degree of arbitrariness to hypothesis formulation and testing. Although, in practice, hypotheses are usually based on personal experience and the findings of related studies, this does not preclude the development of hypotheses based on hunch, intuition, educated guessing, or sheer inspiration. Indeed, it is often difficult to trace the genesis of a given hypotheses.

For example, during some research work conducted by the author in which he examined the eye movements of individuals as they looked at visual displays (in this case, a series of ads), it became apparent that certain individual scanning patterns persisted regardless of the visual display viewed. Gradually, the notion of a "visual fingerprint" was generated as a tentative hypothesis for some of the data collected. The author would find it hard, however, to explain just exactly how and when this particular hypothesis came into being.

[6] We have overlooked such factors as how one goes about "proving" hypotheses and the relationship of such terms as truth, fact, law, and so forth, to tests of statistical significance. Likewise, we have said nothing about the various types of experimental design, how we obtain the samples to be studied, and the importance of con-

Explanatory studies probably typify the layman's notion of what scientific research is all about. Because they are often conducted in laboratories, and because they require precise controls and procedures that must be carefully executed, it is easy to become confused about what is essential to a typical experiment. The following material lliustrates this confusion:

In the laboratory context, whether you are doing a psychological experiment or one in physics, the step-by-step procedures that you follow tend to be highlighted. Even persons completely unacquainted with research associate standardized procedures with laboratory experimentation. Unwittingly, the reader may make an unnecessary assumption concerning the steps in the research process—that you need to have a laboratory, or something close to it, to do research. In short, laboratories, research, and the necessary steps in the research process all appear to go together naturally. The fact is, of course, that they do go together; but what may not be so apparent to the reader is that a laboratory is not the *only* place where research can take place. *Research is essentially a process and, as long as this process is followed, it can take place in any context.*[7]

From what we have said about explanatory-type studies, it should be obvious to the reader that they are seldom conducted by, or for, practitioners in specific public relations problem situations; we have seen that public relations research is almost always descriptive or exploratory, but seldom explanatory, in character. This is not to say that benefit would not be derived from explanatory studies. To the contrary, as would be true for any applied communicator, there is a vital need for verification of the enormous number of untested hypotheses that guide the practitioner. At almost every turn in his day-to-day work, the public relations practitioner, either consciously or unconsciously, makes a decision based on an assumed relationship between variables. To return to our earlier example, any number of practitioners are guided by the implicit assumption that the informed employee is a better employee, at least in some respects. Although this generalization should not be challenged automatically, there are limits to how often an implied hypothesis such as this[8] can be accurate; and there

---

trols in executing sound research experiments. We have not touched on the relationship between causally oriented studies and correlational studies, nor have we discussed the limitations of this latter type of research effort. All these additional ramifications must eventually be understood by public relations practitioners; but this is not the proper place to go into them. The reader is urged to seek out appropriate sources for further readings on scientific research. (See, for example, William S. Ray, *An Introduction to Experimental Design,* New York: Macmillan Company, 1960; and Fred N. Kerlinger, *Foundations of Behavioral Research,* New York: Holt, Rinehart and Winston, Inc., 1964.)

[7] Edward J. Robinson, *Communication and Public Relations* (Columbus: Charles E. Merrill Books, Inc., 1966), p. 477.

[8] For example, (1) an employee who understands something about the economic system of which he is a part will be a better employee; (2) a public informed about the needs, goals, and accomplishments of an organization will be more positively disposed toward that organization; (3) being informed is tantamount to changing attitudes; and (4) an employee with a large package of fringe benefits will

OBTAINING RELIABLE INFORMATION 43

are contexts or situations in which accuracy is not even possible. The more aware the practitioner is of such limits or contexts, the more precise his work becomes. Moreover, to the extent that these hypotheses could be tested scientifically, the practitioner could move more toward the right-hand end of the problem-solving continuum introduced in Chapter 2.

RELATED TERMINOLOGY

Now that we have looked at the three major categories of research studies, we are equipped to examine any research work we wish and to come to a conclusion about the sort of study it involves. There are several reasons why this classificatory schema is important to a public relations practitioner; if he is clear on what sort of study he is reading about, conducting himself, or arranging for, he is less likely to attribute more precision to the study than it deserves; or, he will be in a better position to recognize and be more critical of overgeneralization in studies written by others.

For example, any generalizations made in an *exploratory* study must be regarded as extremely tentative, because the very processes involved do not permit a high degree of certainty. Similarly, with respect to *descriptive* studies, a systematic description of the attitudes of a given public based on survey research conducted with this public, does not allow one to begin making statements about the *causes* of these attitudes. There is a great temptation to say that the reason such-and-such a person has certain political or educational views is linked to his previous education, the effects of his greater than average income, and so forth, even though such data do not permit these generalizations. *To jump from describing a particular state of affairs to explaining why such a state of affairs exists is a very simple step indeed, and one that is often taken by practitioners.*

Let us look at a portion of the data reported in Case 4 to illustrate how easy it is to go beyond the limits of a study, in this instance a *descriptive* study. In the section on the "dimensions" of awareness about the link between diet and heart disease (including the generalizations about cholesterol), Tables 14-3 and 14-4 on page 188 summarize the types of individual most aware and least aware of the issue. It is clearly indicated that persons with more education, those on the professional and managerial level, and those higher in the socioeconomic hierarchy are considerably more aware of the diet-heart disease controversy than those with less education, those in the blue collar category, and so forth. It is tempting to talk as if one knew *why* people with one set of characteristics are more in-

---

be a better and more loyal employee. The author has deliberately tended to stick to hypotheses that concern employees, although long lists of explicit and implicit hypotheses could obviously be developed for any facet of a practitioner's work.

formed than those with another. It is easy to slip into the error of saying that the *reason* college graduates are more aware of the diet-heart disease relationship is that better educated people are usually more intelligent and more literate.

The tendency in overstating data is to ascribe to descriptive studies generalizations that are appropriate to explanatory studies; that is, as soon as one starts to insert interpretative statements about *why* a certain finding is obtained, *one has essentially moved over into the type of statement normally associated with the explanatory type.* Another element in the overlap of descriptive and explanatory studies is that many people do not understand the research process known as *correlation* and how it relates to the three research categories. This whole procedure is important to practitioners and we will go into it in detail in the next section.

The question of the limits of generalization also applies to *explanatory* studies. Even if, for example, an individual who has done a controlled experiment concerning a certain drug is permitted to make causal statements regarding the effects of this drug upon, let us say, the driving ability of a patient, these statements or generalizations must be limited to the dimensions of the study itself. First of all, generalizations about the effects of other drugs, however closely related, cannot be inferred from this one study; or if the subjects employed were adults, we could not necessarily assume the same effects for children. In short, just as both the other types have limits imposed upon them because of the nature of the research work involved, explanatory-type studies, too, have their own limits concerning generalizations.[9]

THE RELATIONSHIP BETWEEN DESCRIPTIVE STUDIES, EXPLANATORY STUDIES, AND CORRELATION

It is comparatively simple to state the procedures involved in an explanatory study. Essentially, the experimentor selects an independent variable (often identified as a stimulus, or S) and manipulates it according to some preconceived pattern or study design. He tries to hold constant all

---

[9] The reader must not confuse limits of generalization in our three main types of study with the hypothesis-generating character of all research. The difference is that by classifying a given research study we are better equipped to interpret this study. On the other hand, one of the by-products of any research—be it exploratory, descriptive, or explanatory—is that the researcher thereby obtains insights into the problem area. Consequently, he may go beyond the limits of his data and speculate about a relationship he might not have studied directly. This process of extending the findings is generally identified as hypothesizing, and it is clear that the statements in question actually have gone beyond the confines of the particular study. What we have been discussing thus far have been overgeneralizations by the researcher (and at times the reader) that he is unaware of and that he incorrectly believes to be statements supported directly by the data rather than hypothetical extensions of the data.

OBTAINING RELIABLE INFORMATION 45

other variables that would in any way confound the effects of the independent variable that he is manipulating.[10] Much the same procedure is followed with a dependent variable; that is, the particular response (or R), that is presumed to be elicited by the independent variable. With the S (or S's) identified and other relevant variables isolated (held constant or excluded), and with the R (or R's) likewise established, we have stated in simple terms the basic experimental design that qualifies as an explanatory-type study.

Clearly, the possibilities are practically limitless for manipulating and measuring the specified S's and R's to see what sort of causal relationship exists between them. If we use people as our point of departure, the S's can be literally anything whose effects can be discerned and measured.

At this point we should discuss the term *manipulate*, which is often a stumbling block in an explanatory-type study. Any independent variable, the effects of which a researcher may wish to identify, must be introduced *in some amount or degree*. If the researcher is interested in ascertaining the effects of electric shock on the learning of certain prose passages, he must expose the subjects to varying amounts of the shock (or manipulate the independent variable). The reason for this is simply that without variation the effects of any particular S cannot be isolated, at least not to a very helpful degree; if the researcher could not increase or decrease the amount of electric shock, and note carefully the effects of this manipulation upon the R's of the subjects, then his knowledge of the relationship of electric shock to certain aspects of human behavior would be very limited:

We now come to the notion of a correlational study. There are many, many times when an experimenter is *not* able to vary the stimulus conditions in which he is interested. . . . Consider the sociologist. He would like to study the effects of panic on large aggregates of individuals, such as in the case of earthquakes or fires. Certainly he is not able to induce earthquakes of any degree or severity in order to study their effects. Even if he *could* vary panics, perhaps by engaging the services of a pyromaniac, certainly this would not be tolerated by society.

. . . One way out of such a situation is to resort to a *correlational* study. The term *correlation* means to co-relate, and this is exactly what the researcher attempts to do. He tries to see how one variable (or set of variables) co-relates (*i.e.,* correlates) with another variable (or set of variables). Take a simple example, but one which is gaining more attention all the time these days: college entrance exams. To establish cut-off scores (that is, scores below which an applicant is rejected), we first give our tests to a large number of applicants, and then follow their careers through college. After doing this for a number of years, we are able to establish the correlation between our entrance exams and college

---

[10] It should be noted that the method of holding variables "constant" is only one of several ways a researcher can keep the relationship between independent and dependent variables free of the confounding effects of extraneous (or "unwanted") variables.

success (college success defined, for example, in terms of grades obtained and whether the individual eventually graduates). If the correlation is a high, positive one—that is, if a high scorer on the college (entrance) exams almost invariably receives high grades (in college) and nearly always graduates—then we can make use of the exams as a selection device for admitting candidates to college.[11]

How has our correlational study differed from the experimental one that we described earlier? For one thing, we did not manipulate any variables with respect to the subjects (*i.e.*, college applicants) in any way. We merely measured them by a tool that we had, a college entrance exam, which gave us one sort of measure. In other words, we did not manipulate any stimulus conditions. We merely gave the candidates the college entrance exam and scored their performances. Likewise, we did not control any other variables that might be operating at the time that individuals were taking the exam, nor did we try to isolate our stimulus. Lastly, we subjected our individuals to a gross and complex stimulus situation. The test itself, the test conditions, the persons administering the test, the type of day—*all* of these things operating.

What are we able to say as a function of this type of study? First, let us assume that we obtained a very high, positive correlation between the college entrance exam score and college success. This would mean that the higher the exam score, the more certain we can be that an individual will successfully complete college. And *this* would mean that we could, with confidence, require candidates to take the exam and either admit or reject them on the basis of their scores. Now comes the sixty-four dollar question: Can we make any causal statements on the basis of this study? Can we say that high college entrance exams *cause* an individual to be successful in college? The answer is no. In fact, we are not able to make any causal statements whenever we conduct a correlational type study. All we know is that one *co-relates* with the other. A large amount of one variable is correlated with a large amount of another. We can not say why or how this condition takes place. . . .

Perhaps a slightly facetious example, still devoted to college entrance exams, can make for clarity. Suppose, instead of a college entrance exam, we now required that every candidate have his big toes measured to the nearest millimeter. Suppose, too, as in the case of the college entrance exam, we measured the big toes of thousands of individuals and also kept track of their performance in college. Lastly, grant one more assumption. Suppose that this study revealed a very high, positive correlation between big toes and college success; that is, very clearly, that those with big toes went on to outstanding college careers. What would we be justified in doing with these data? The answer: *exactly the same thing that we did with the conventional college entrance!* The reason is simple. Even though in this contrived example we do *not* have the feeling that the data make sense—that is, we do not see how big toes and college success go together—the fact is that we would have to make the same interpretation. In both instances, all that we have really demonstrated is that one factor correlates with another. In neither instance have we been able to determine any causes. . . .

[11] We should mention at this point that a prime example of a correlational study is the typical opinion attitude survey. We will consider the relationship between correlation and survey research a little later (see pages 47–49).

We are now able to contrast an experiment with a correlational study. In the former, certain S's are isolated and manipulated so that their relationships with certain R's can be ascertained. The whole point of the experiment is *to be able to make causal statements*. In correlational studies, we co-relate the presence of one variable with another. In such instances, all that we need to do is *measure* and *count* variable A and variable B. By a statistical technique known as correlation, we are able to arrive at a statement of the degree to which these two variables are correlated. If the variables are highly correlated, then we can use this correlation to predict events or to make decisions of all sorts. Or we can use the fact of high correlation as an insight and proceed to develop an experimental study to determine how and why variable A and B are correlated.

It may have occurred to the reader by now that the correlational method is inextricably involved in everyday living. We meet a few people in our life with such-and-such a personality and find that those people are the kind we can trust or like to be with. Gradually, we build up sort of implicit correlational data relating personality with certain outcomes. Before long, we use this information to predict how we will like subsequent people who have similar personalities. The only trouble is we do not realize that we have only correlational data. *We believe that we know why this or that person can be trusted.*[12]

At this junction, we might summarize the highlights of our discussion in the previous sections:

1. We have examined a three-part schema which permits us to distinguish between the major types of research studies that one encounters. Specifically, these three categories were identified as *exploratory, descriptive,* and *explanatory*.

2. For each category we noted the limits imposed upon the researcher with regard to the types of generalizations that can be made at the completion of the study. We further noted that one often encounters what we call overgeneralizations, or making statements that go beyond the legitimate limits for any given category.

3. One type of false overgeneralization focused upon was the tendency to make causal (or explanatory) statements based on data obtained in a descriptive study. This error, briefly, consists in taking data which *describe how* one variable appears to be related to another—such as high income to certain attitudes that differ from those exhibited by individuals with low income—and making generalizations as to *why* they are related.

4. This tendency on the part of practitioners to confuse descriptive studies with explanatory ones was suggested to result partially from ignorance of the research technique known as *correlation*. The process was then described and examples were provided to illustrate what is involved in a study of this type.

5. The next step was to point out that correlation is one of the basic tools of the scientist and, perhaps more importantly, that it constitutes the

[12] Robinson, *op. cit.*, pp. 534–538.

process of data collection utilized by all of us in our everyday lives. Furthermore, we were able to understand more clearly why a researcher is so often unable to conduct an explanatory-type study and must turn to a correlational study in order to enlarge his store of reliable knowledge about a particular problem area.

With this summary behind us, we should now be in a position to move on to the final point in this section. We know what a correlational study is, and we know what a descriptive study is. We also realize that survey research studies generally fall into the descriptive research category.

Two additional generalizations based on this knowledge should be made here. First, in all survey research the *process* of correlation is employed in analyzing the data. Typically, in a survey research study the examiner develops a questionnaire and uses it as the basis for collecting data from a sample of individuals. After the questionnaires have been returned, the various replies are exampled. Usually, these are then cross-referenced or cross-tabulated; that is, they are analyzed in terms of certain socioeconomic categories—or any other groupings that make sense—into which the respondents have been placed. In other words, any distinctions among respondents—such as old versus young, high-income neighborhood versus low-income neighborhood, customer versus noncustomer—that might be expected to have a bearing upon the replies to the various questions are used to guide the researcher in how he groups his data. Let us look at Case 1 for an illustration of what we have been talking about.

From page 117, we see a breakdown of responses to question, Number 3, "In general, what is your view of how the people in the country you are serving feel toward the people of the U.S.?" The replies are tabulated in categories that range from positive (very good opinion) to negative (very bad opinion), with provision made for the "don't know" response. The individuals whose replies fall into these various categories are then separated into officers and airmen. This classification of respondents in terms of their replies to questions is the point that we are illustrating. For a number of reasons the researchers had grounds to believe that the officers' responses might be different from those of the airmen. If this turned out to be so, then a subsequent public relations program would have to take these differences into account. In effect, we have correlated officers' replies and compared this correlation with the one obtained for airmen for each of the categories in question 3. Although the information obtained through this survey is useful to the public relations practitioner, he must keep in mind that he cannot draw any conclusions from the responses about the causal relationship between military rank and the expression of certain attitudes.

The second generalization has to do with the *type* of research that one encounters most often in public relations work. As we have noted before, public relations is virtually dominated by survey research. Therefore, practitioners today, when engaging in research of a relatively formal nature, are most likely to work in the descriptive study category and, within this category, to employ the process of correlation, whether they realize it or not.

Now that we have elaborated on the various types of research study that can be identified, and have shown the relationship of survey research to this categorization system, we are ready to devote the balance of Part II to a more detailed examination of survey research.

5 | The survey research process

IN Chapter 2 we defined research as a means to reliable knowledge, and further identified it as a *process* by which one goes about obtaining this knowledge. What each of us does in everyday life to accomplish this differs in *degree,* not in *kind,* from what a scientist does to attain the same objective. We all need reliable knowledge, scientist and nonscientist alike, and the only difference is *how* we arrive at it.

This perspective should remove some of the mystique that is at times associated with science and scientists. To be sure, the research work they perform may be complicated and difficult to understand, and it may require special training, vocabulary, and so forth. However, there should be no mystery as to what constitutes scientific research, which is simply a series of efforts to obtain reliable knowledge according to a set of rules, or steps. These steps make up the scientific research process.

THE NINE BASIC STEPS

One way of describing the research process is to list the nine basic steps it involves: (1) stating the problem; (2) deciding on a manageable portion of the problem; (3) establishing definitions; (4) making a literature search; (5) developing hypotheses; (6) deciding on the study design; (7) obtaining the data; (8) analyzing the data; and (9) drawing implications and generalizations.[1] These nine steps together constitute the scientific research process and, basically, are followed by all scientists in their research work.[2] Let us briefly examine each of these nine steps to be certain that we understand what each of them entails.

[1] These steps are taken from Edward J. Robinson, *Communication and Public Relations* (Columbus, Charles E. Merrill Books, Inc., 1966), p. 478.
[2] It should be pointed out that the particular sequence of these steps and the fact that there are nine (instead of eight or ten, or what have you), is somewhat arbitrary. Another scientist might use a different classification system in a given research project, or he might follow the steps in a different sequence from that

1. The first step, *stating the problem,* is not always a simple thing to achieve. Before he can tackle a problem, the researcher must state exactly what his problem is, and this is often made difficult because of the many dimensions, or sub-problems, inherent in any problem area.

2. This step is closely linked to Step 1. In addition to identifying a problem to be studied, the researcher must go further and *specify what portion of that problem can be tackled* with any given single research effort. Although an investigator may be interested in identifying the causes of cancer or juvenile delinquency, when it comes to doing any particular research study he must plan one that is manageable. He has to take into account the amount of money at his disposal, the manpower available for the research, the time that can be devoted to it, and so forth. These and many other factors serve as constraints to the researcher in formulating his plan.

3. Our third step emphasizes the fact that a *careful definition of all relevant terms* is a prerequisite to intelligent research. The practitioner must clearly spell out any ambiguous word or hazy concept connected with the development, execution, and reporting of his program. He must define carefully what he means by "poor community relations" and how a certain "public relations program" will "improve" the poor relations because of the establishment of a more "effective communication program." All of these words or phrases can have many different meanings, or worse still, can practically defy definition.

4. All of us make use of reliable information that others have provided. It is highly unlikely that anyone interested in a given problem is the *first* person to be concerned with that area of investigation; hence, the notion of the *literature search,* Step 4, in the research process. No self-respecting scientist would ever dream of executing a research project without first finding out what there is in the way of available knowledge, either directly or tangentially related to the problem. By means of the literature search the scientist can benefit in various ways from the work of others; and even negative results—that is, finding out that what someone else learned did *not* help solve the problem—can be as valuable as positive ones.

5. *Developing hypotheses* might require a fuller explanation than some of the other steps, as fewer people understand the role of hypotheses in the research process. As we have noted before, a hypothesis is a statement of an assumed relationship. Thus, if someone says that breathing polluted air causes lung cancer, he has stated a hypothesis, or assumed a relationship between the two conditions.

The formulation of hypotheses as an integral part of the research

---

presented here (for example, generate a hypothesis and then double back and conduct a literature search). What is important is that regardless of the classification system used, or the sequence followed, *all* persons who do scientific research (or who write about it) must touch the same bases, be they physical scientists, biological scientists, or behavioral scientists.

process offers a number of advantages: if the researcher outlines in hypothesis form what he plans to study, he will be able to visualize his objectives more clearly; moreover, he will be less prone to state hypotheses that cannot be tested (how many angels can dance on the head of a pin?); lastly, he will be more likely to focus on the pertinent aspects and not execute a study that has no bearing on the problem.

6. *Deciding on the study design* points to the researcher's need to plan *in advance* all of the parts of the total research project. What will be his independent variable(s), his dependent variable(s)? What variables must he control for? What measurement problems might he face? What group or groups of people (assuming we are not talking about experiments with infrahuman subjects) will he include in his study? These plans for action must be spelled out in detail *before* the research is executed—one cannot go ahead with the research project intending to take care of some of the study design details later—and the only later modifications that should be allowed are those that are unavoidable (or desirable, as when a valuable insight is gained and can be incorporated while the research is in progress).

7. *Obtaining the data,* identified as Step 7, represents the beginning of the final phase of the research process. By this time, the researcher has presumably done all that is required of him in connection with the first six steps. If his project happens to be survey research, his interviewers are now in the field gathering their information (or in a mail survey, his questionnaires have been sent out). If his study design phase has been successful, he will probably pass through this step in the process comparatively smoothly.

8. This step brings the researcher to the point he has been aiming for: the time when he sits down with his data and *analyzes* them to see what reliable information, if any, he has been successful in unearthing. This is the pay-off of the whole effort and is one of the most exciting moments for any researcher. At this point he is able to see whether his hypothesis (or hypotheses) is supported by his research findings or whether he must reject it in the face of the collected data.

9. The last step in the research process highlights the scientist as the final arbiter in the research process. There is the mistaken notion that the research itself will contain the decisions about the *implications* to be derived from the findings. To be sure, in some situations the findings may be so clear-cut or the hypothesis so firmly supported that deriving an implication from the research may be a very straightforward process. Thus, if a vaccine proves to be highly effective in preventing the incidence of a certain disease, the implication that it should be widely used is self-evident. More often, however, the findings are not so obvious, the implications must be "teased out" and the plans for action weighed very carefully. As the reader will observe in the cases in Part III, the findings and the implications

THE SURVEY RESEARCH PROCESS 53

of the findings are two different things. In each instance, the program of action instituted by the practitioner on the basis of the data was certainly not the only course open to possibility. This, incidentally, reminds the author of that old saying that has been around for years, "The facts speak for themselves." This is completely erroneous; in the first place, it takes someone to identify what phenomena are going to be regarded as fact, not to mention their importance and how they are reported.

THE RESEARCH PROCESS RELATED TO SURVEY RESEARCH

We have just examined the research process briefly and in broad terms for several reasons. We wanted, first of all, to highlight the major parts of what is known as the research process. Secondly, we wanted to convey the generality of the research process in the sense that these nine steps apply to *all* research regardless of the scientific content—it could involve the work of a chemist, physicist, biologist, psychologist, or sociologist. In any of these areas scientists have to follow the same process: they all need to define their problem, develop hypotheses, establish definitions, spell out research designs, and so forth. Lastly, we wanted to prepare the reader to see the relationship between research in general and research in particular, as typified by survey research.

The next step in our examination is to suggest a "checklist" which, when taken as a whole, covers the major considerations associated with any typical survey research project. As the reader will readily discern, this checklist is nothing more than our nine basic steps modified to fit our interest in this book: survey research.

A SURVEY RESEARCH CHECKLIST FOR PUBLIC RELATIONS PRACTITIONERS

Just as we found it useful to break up the scientific research process in general into steps, it would also be a good idea to use the same approach to survey research in particular. Accordingly, we have developed a *survey research checklist* consisting of the following seven steps: (1) defining the purpose; (2) identifying the population and sample; (3) utilizing the data collection instrument(s); (4) training the data collection staff; (5) preparing raw data for analysis; (6) analyzing and interpreting the data—the survey research report; and (7) planning the public relations program based on survey research. We shall examine the checklist from the point of view of a public relations practitioner, whose goal is to make intelligent use of survey research as a public relations tool. Our study will be sufficiently detailed so that we can come away with an appreciation of what is involved in each step, an understanding of the usual terminology or vocabulary associated with each step, and a comprehension of why the procedures involved are necessary. Throughout our examination of these steps we will jump back and forth from the perspective of the survey researcher to that of his client, the public relations practitioner. This two-fold context is necessary for our study of the checklist, because we are interested in the use of survey research as a tool to help solve problems rather than as an end in itself. Also implied in this approach is our thought that the bulk of survey research is, and will be, conducted *for* rather than *by* the public relations practitioner.[3]

One further point: some of the items on our checklist are more visible than others, and are therefore more easily questioned or examined by the public relations practitioner. Even if a research project is being conducted for him, the practitioner is nonetheless intimately concerned with establishing the purpose of the survey itself, and it is he who defines (or should define) its objectives. He has to be involved in identifying the population and sample involved, and he must be directly connected with the data collection instrument itself. In contrast, he will have little, if any, contact with the data collection staff, the preparation of raw data for analysis, and so forth. Because of the variation in how closely concerned the public relations practitioner is with the various checklist items, our examination of the items will vary as well. We will devote one chapter each to the first three items on the checklist, the other four will only receive cursory attention.

[3] This generalization should not mask the fact that some practitioners (or public relations departments) conduct their own survey research; but, in the opinion of the writer, at the moment this is the exception rather than the rule. Also, it should not imply that the writer does not advocate the public relations practitioner's becoming more of a researcher in his own right. In fact, in Robinson's *op. cit.,* Chapters 17–20 are devoted to a thorough examination of research as it applies to public relations; and the concept of "do-it-yourself researchettes" is advocated in the last chapter.

6 | Survey research checklist: step one

DEFINING THE PURPOSE

AS WE have learned, one fundamental requirement of any research is that the researcher know what problem(s) he is trying to solve; another is that, at the outset, he identify the objectives of the survey research program. As seen in our context, this is the responsibility of the public relations practitioner and cannot be delegated to the survey researcher, although further clarification or emendation may emerge during the initial conferences when the survey researcher is apprised of the practitioner's objectives. Thus, the survey man may ask questions which reveal purposes that inadvertently were overlooked. Or, refinements of objective may be generated in the discussions held before the actual survey work begins. This does not obviate the point made earlier, however; the public relations practitioner must think through his problem clearly and decide why he feels a survey will help him solve his problem.

Let us look at one or two of our cases from the point of view of the purpose step in our checklist. In Case 2 (pp. 137–154), we see stated the main reason behind the work done in connection with speech reprints for U. S. Steel. What good does our program of speech reprints do? Is this part of our public relations program to achieve the goals we want? What exactly are these goals? Could they be met more effectively by other methods?

Case 5 (pp. 205–236) illustrates this first step more elaborately. Not only is the general question posed, "What is our reputation among the members of the scientific community?" but we see spelled out a number of specific dimensions of this reputation that the public relations men at Petroil Development and Research Corporation wished to have detailed.

To many people, the requirement of spelling out the public relations objectives of a survey brings on an almost perceptible "Ho hum." They often react to this first step as if it were extremely easy, obvious and consequently hardly worth mentioning. The fact is that the statement of purpose can be very deceiving—particularly for problem areas in public relations. Let's examine this contention a bit further. Perhaps the most common reason given for wanting a survey is to find "what good" a given public relations program (or portion of a program) is doing. But translating this objective into explicit terms is often quite difficult. For example, let us assume that a practitioner wants to find out "what good" his company newspaper is doing. What measures are implied in this question? Does the newspaper serve to inform its readers about company events, policies of the management, and so on? Normally, in a readership survey, we would then try to find out how aware the regular readers are of various issues that have been included in previous editions of the paper. So far, this sounds quite simple. However, if we begin to examine our purposes more closely, we can come up with some disquieting observations: How can we separate what the person learns from the newspaper from what he learns through the company grapevine. And even more perplexing, how much emphasis has been placed on the information function of the newspaper? Has each item in the survey quiz been given equal treatment in the paper? Has roughly the same number of column inches been devoted to each item of information? If not (and this is nearly always the case), how do we account for this in the survey when interviewing the respondent? If we shift our focus to the questionnaire or the interview guide sheet, we must apply the same careful scrutiny to the questions themselves. Can we properly measure what is meant by "information about issues contained in the newspaper" by asking the respondent what he remembers having read in the last few issues? In other words, we must, as public relations practitioners, press for specific details with regard to the relationship of each survey research question to the purpose of the survey.

So far, we have only addressed ourselves to one dimension of "what good" the company newspaper does: the information or informing function. Suppose, however, one argued that the more important measures of "what good" must be determined by means of attitude testing. For example, what changes in reader attitude—toward the organization, his work, his fellow workers, his community, and himself, to name a few—can (and should) be attributed to the reading of the newspaper? Even more to the point, what changes in attitude is the public relations practitioner claiming for his newspaper? Obviously, it is more difficult to measure attitude changes by means of a survey than it is to measure information. However, the onus on the public relations practitioner remains unchanged. He must examine the survey instrument the same way, regardless of what is being measured. What questions should be asked to elicit the response he needs, and how confident can he be that they reflect the impact of the company newspaper?

THE CHECKLIST: STEP ONE 57

In one respect, we have only scratched the surface of the details that are actually embodied in establishing the purpose(s) of a survey. In other words, the first step is not simply a matter of stating the objectives in high-level, abstract terms that sound as though they are communicating but which, in fact, are not. The author has repeatedly seen purposes that included such phrases as, "We must ascertain the communicative effectiveness of our public relations program," or, "We must ascertain the communicative effectiveness of our annual report." It is certainly not very clear what "communicative effectiveness" was supposed to mean. Even worse, how certain questions in the survey were supposed to measure this communicative effectiveness was left undefined. Hence, it sounds impossible—or certainly unlikely—that a survey could be conducted without carefully defined purposes—purposes that clearly and explicitly relate the survey research to the public relation problem. Unfortunately, the "impossible" happens quite frequently.

This, then, is what Step 1 of our checklist is all about. It is hoped that the reader can now appreciate just how much work and careful thinking are involved in accomplishing this step successfully. It is often difficult to translate public relations purposes into manageable survey research; but it is seldom really impossible. As he looks at the various cases described in Part III, the reader should ask himself repeatedly how the various survey questions relate to the stated objectives of the public relations practitioner.

To return to Case 2 for a moment, Table 12-5 (page 148) is relevant to this question of relationship. How strongly does the reader feel that the image of U. S. Steel, which was rated according to customer treatment, corporate leadership and so forth, is acceptable as a measure of "what good" the speech reprint program happened to do?

Obviously, in most instances of this sort of examination, it is not that the decisions made by the researcher and practitioner are either right or wrong; rather, it is a question of how one defines his purposes and decides what should stand as a measure of his purposes. The point here is not to differ with those responsible for the research, but to be aware of how important it is to a meaningful survey that purposes be specified and carefully defined.

7 | Survey research checklist: step two

IDENTIFYING THE POPULATION AND SAMPLE

WHENEVER a research project is conducted, regardless of the *type* of research involved, the investigator is seldom interested in characterizing *only* those persons or phenomena directly involved in his study. Almost invariably he is interested in generalizing to a larger, but presumably identical, group that he did not study directly. He studies a *sample* in order to be able to generalize to a *population*. A definition of these two words offers an excellent starting point for an examination of what is known as sampling.

A *population* is defined as the total of any phenomena that conforms to a particular definition describing that population. Thus, we may wish to define as a population all cross-eyed, left-handed, blonde women between the ages of 19 and 29 who are enrolled in four-year colleges in the United States. *All* women in the United States who fit these specifications become our *population*.[1] One point that should be emphasized is that a population can be defined as anything we wish, and in that sense the definitions can be arbitrary. For some purposes our population might be relatively unspectacular, such as comprising all Boy Scouts in the United States between the ages of 9 and 12. On the other hand, for certain other purposes, we might have to define our population in such a manner that unusual criteria must be met to conform to the population specifications. A second point we should make is that the usual connotations of the term *population* do not hold. Thus, we might speak of a population of nuts and bolts defined in a certain manner; or, it could consist of certain types of seeds, fertilizers, galaxies, drugs, or what have you. The term is not linked to human beings;

[1] In the literature, the reader may encounter the term *universe* instead of *population*, and from the standpoint of statistics the terms are synonymous.

THE CHECKLIST: STEP TWO

except that, of course, one can have populations of humans defined in a certain way.

The term *sample* refers to a certain proportion (usually quite small) of a given population. Let us say that there are 100,000 blonde women enrolled in four-year colleges in the United States who are cross-eyed, left-handed and between 19 and 29 years of age. If we were to select 50 or 100 or 500 of these women from this population, we would then have a sample.

POPULATION, SAMPLE, AND SURVEY RESEARCH

We are now able to discuss an exceedingly important aspect of survey research—or of all research, for that matter. One reason that defining the population to be studied is so important is that it enables us to make clearer generalizations when we have finished analyzing our survey research results. As public relations practitioners, do we want to be able to talk about *all* adults over the age of 21 residing in the United States? Or, is our target all the employees of a given company, or all of the alumni of a particular university? Defining our population keeps us from forgetting the relationship between our survey research effort and the ultimate *applications* we have in mind for the data. All too often a research study is conducted with a group of individuals because they are available (the classic example is the researcher who took a sample of college sophomores because he had access to a group of them), and not because they fit a carefully defined population. Unfortunately, it is not rare for a study to be conducted with a sample of individuals *without* the population being specified. What generally happens in such cases is that the readily available group is studied, but the generalizations that are made at the conclusion of the study apply to types of people who were not included in the sample itself.

The application of the above to the public relations practitioner is that, after he has decided the purposes of his survey research, he must then carefully identify the population to which he ultimately wishes to generalize. Thus, for example, if a practitioner wants to find out more about how clearly people understand the objectives of his health-welfare organization (the reader can insert any *particular* health-welfare organization he wishes), his starting point is to define *what people* he is talking about. Does he mean all adults (defined arbitrarily as over 21 years of age) who live in the community in which his organization is located? Does he mean all adults in the greater metropolitan area in which his organization is located? Or, does he mean only *certain* groupings of individuals, regardless of where they happen to reside, broken down by profession, occupation, or income? To put it into public relations terminology, the particular public or publics must be clearly identified. *As soon as the public is identified, the population has been specified.*

In essence, then, the practical value (to say nothing of the scientific necessity), of identifying the population that one wishes to deal with, generalize to, and design public relations programs for, is that the practitioner winds up with data that truly permit him to make the generalizations he wishes to make. With the population clearly specified, he can turn intelligently to how he will obtain a *sample* of the population, what size sample is necessary, and how to evaluate its representativeness.

WHY USE SAMPLES?

It may be useful to examine some of the more important reasons for using samples. Why not just study the entire population? Wouldn't the knowledge obtained be more reliable? The reader can undoubtedly think of a number of reasons why not. For one thing, there are the questions of time, money, and professional staff. To conduct a survey with all the members of a given population, such as the Boy Scouts, would be prohibitive on all three counts. There are just too many Boy Scouts in the United States to be interviewed feasibly either personally or by mail; so, by limiting the number of individuals to be studied, the costs can be reduced considerably.

Another reason for using samples is that in many situations a study of the entire population would be self-defeating. In a program of stress-testing of the output of a given factory, for example, if *all* the production (of whatever part or unit is involved) were tested until the product broke, pulverized, or otherwise failed, there would be nothing left to sell. In other words, whenever the research itself adversely affects what is being studied, we need to limit our study to a workable sample rather than extend it to the entire population.

There is still another reason, and in one sense a more important one, for using a sample instead of a population; it is possible today to get such a high degree of precision that there is seldom, if ever, justification for studying the entire population, regardless of the population involved and the study problem at hand. The following quote elaborates this point of view:

Perhaps the most convincing reason of all for using samples is that a properly obtained sample will provide information so accurate that there *is very little increase in accuracy to be obtained by studying the entire universe.* To put it another way, once the researcher has established the level of precision or accuracy he needs in his study, this requirement shapes the size of sample that he will need. Obtaining more and more cases or items beyond a certain point, thereby enlarging the sample, the costs, and the likelihood of human errors, adds very little to what the researcher already knows. In sampling, as in many other situations, the so-called law of diminishing returns sets in and does so quickly. The curve in Figure 7-1 depicts this point. What it illustrates is that the amount of information one derives from a study of a sample or the precision with which predictions can be made based on sample information (such as average income

THE CHECKLIST: STEP TWO 61

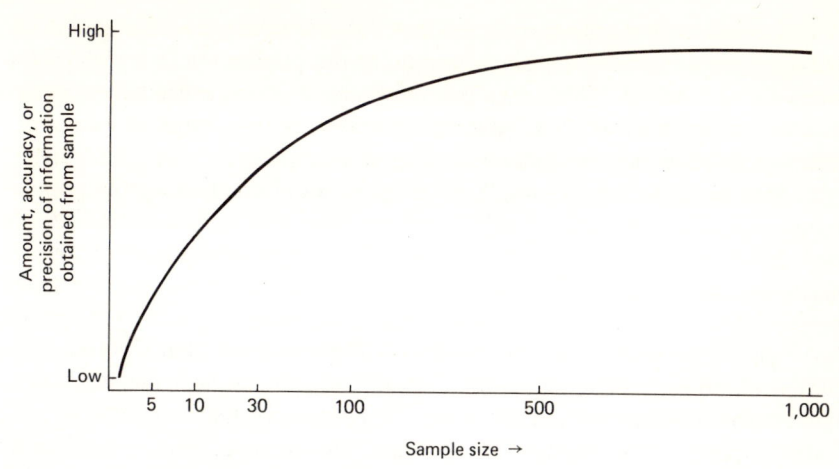

Figure 7-1. Relationship between sample size and precision or accuracy of knowledge obtained

of a given population) increases very sharply at first, while the sample sizes are comparatively small. However, as sample size increases, the increase in precision or amount of information obtained begins to level off markedly. Hence, the information to be derived from a sample of 1,000 is not much more accurate than was obtained from a sample of 500. Twice as many cases in the sample is likely not to be worth the extra time and money, to say nothing of increasing the likelihood of what Deming called "persistant errors." Twice as many cases when the increase in sample size is from 10 to 20 or 50 to 100 is another matter, however. Here the increase in precision is more marked and generally worth the extra effort and money, assuming, of course, that the researcher needs greater precision in the first place. . . .

Once again we are simplifying in order to make a point. Naturally, there are many factors that enter into sampling. Studies in which the population concerned is the entire eligible voting populace of the United States are based on samples of between 2,000 and 3,000 persons. These sample sizes have gone beyond our illustrative curve, which stopped at 1,000. In such cases, other sampling considerations dictate that the sample size must be larger. The principle of rapidly diminishing returns as sample size increases still holds, however. Even so, it is interesting to note that with sample sizes of between only 2,000 and 3,000 we are able to predict, with remarkable accuracy, certain behaviors of a population of over sixty million. The effectiveness of small numbers, properly sampled, is supported by such studies.[2]

REPRESENTATIVENESS OF SAMPLES

Earlier we made the point that the researcher (and also the practitioner) is rarely interested in talking only about the sample he has studied.

[2] Edward J. Robinson, *Communication and Public Relations* (Columbus, Charles E. Merrill Books, Inc., 1966), pp. 525–526.

Almost always he wants to extend—that is, generalize—the findings he has obtained from a study of a given sample to the population from which the sample was selected. This raises two questions that are exceedingly important to the practitioner, (1) How representative is the sample of the population? (2) How do we estimate the degree of representativeness involved?

Whenever we take a sample for purposes of characterizing the population these characterizations will *to some extent* be representative of the population; thus, the representativeness of a sample is a matter of *degree*. When we take a sip from a full pot of soup cooking on a stove, we make generalizations on the basis of that sample: too salty, not salty enough, or just right. If we wished, we could ask how representative that sip (the sample) is of the soup (the population). Was it taken from near the surface? Is it therefore atypical of the rest of the pot because of the difference in consistency between the top and the bottom? Had the pot been stirred sufficiently to allow the ingredients (including salt) to be mixed in thoroughly? The same questions on sample-population-relationship can be asked about a sample of employees quizzed on their acceptance and utilization of the company newspaper. Are their views representative of those of all the employees? Or, as in the case of the soup from the top of the pot, might their views differ (widely or moderately) from those of the rest of the employees because of certain constraints or biases involved in their selection? In the sense that a sip of soup can be atypical, were these employees atypical and not representative of the entire employee population?

We have juxtaposed two very different examples in order to make the point that all samples of population must and can be examined with respect to their degree of representativeness. The trouble is that this is not done so often as it should be. Of course, one should not just go around sipping soup or sniffing the air in order to make generalizations about the populations. We do need to raise these questions, however, when public relations decisions and programs are likely to be based on the generalizations. When survey research must guide a practitioner the question becomes critical indeed. But before he can know how representative a sample is of the whole population, the practitioner must consider the question of *how* the sample was selected. Statisticians distinguish between *nonprobability* and *probability* samples, and we shall now consider these two broad categories in some detail.

Nonprobability sampling

In our everyday life we make constant use of samples of other people's behavior. Without being conscious of doing so, we sample the behaviors of others, and on the basis of these samples we come to conclusions about the individuals in question. For example, when we meet someone for the first time and if we happen to talk with him for a half-hour or so, we have, in effect, sampled both his verbal and nonverbal behavior; we sample how he talks and base our inferences about his attitudes on this sample; we sample his gestures, his habits of dress, and so forth. In short, we generalize from the sample behaviors to the whole population of possible behaviors. This type of sampling, where we are unable to specify the probability that a given element (in this case, of behavior) will be included in the sample, is known as *nonprobability sampling.*

A key point should be made here. Although we might not think of it in these terms, we could question how representative our sample is of the behaviors of the individual. How safely may I draw conclusions from this half-hour about the type of person I have been talking with, his personality, strengths and weaknesses, and so forth? The answer, of course, is that it is risky indeed. First impressions can be quite incorrect, particularly when based on a very small sample of behavior. We know a very close friend—by definition, we have sampled his behavior many, many more times and in a great many more situations—because we have had greater exposure to him.[3]

Let us now link this feature of nonprobability sampling to the definition that we used earlier. As we sample the total behavior of others, there are a variety of factors operating *that prevent us from specifying the probability* that a given element (of behavior) will be included in the sample. A hundred and one factors, ranging from our prejudices to poor eyesight and hearing, prevent certain of the behaviors of the person under observation from being included in our sample.

What is true in our everyday process of sampling applies to some survey research efforts as well—we very often make use of nonprobability samples upon which to base our generalizations. Once again, we are not able to specify the probability that each item or element in the population will be included in the sample. The main varieties of nonprobability sampling are *accidental samples, quota samples* and *purposive samples.*[4]

Accidental sampling refers to the practice whereby the researcher takes advantage of whatever situation he may be in to obtain his sample for study. If the person responsible for a company newspaper asks the first dozen people he happens to meet in the halls or in the cafeteria their views about the paper, this is an accidental sample. Another instance is the col-

---

[3] There are interesting implications concerning sampling in the behavior of a boy and girl during the courtship phase leading to marriage. If for a period of a few weeks or months the only samples they have of each other's behavior are in settings of no particular stress, in which they are having fun and giving in to the other's wishes, it is not surprising that after marriage they find out things about each other that they never suspected before. After the honeymoon is over, both literally and figuratively, the couple usually realize that the samples they obtained during dating were quite unrepresentative of the total behavior of their spouse.

[4] Claire Selltiz et al., *Research Methods in Social Relations,* rev. ed. (New York: Holt, Rinehart and Winston, Inc., 1965), pp. 516–521.

lege professor who uses his classes as his subjects (see p. 59). In short, accidental samples are those for which the researcher took the path of least resistance and used as his subject for study whatever persons were most readily available.[5]

It should be obvious to the reader that the likelihood of error in generalizing from accidental samples is bound to be high. An even greater problem is that we really have no way of guessing the nature of the biases that have been introduced by this form of sampling.[6] In other words, not only are our generalizations in error, but there is the additional difficulty of our inability to anticipate the sorts of errors that might be encountered. All one can do is trust to luck that the generalizations won't be too far wrong.

In *quota sampling,* the researcher imposes on his selection process a form of a sampling plan that presumably insures a more representative inclusion in the sample of various key elements in the population. Suppose a public relations practitioner has reason to believe that a critical factor in determining the reaction of an employee to an impending relocation of his company is the number of years he has been with the company. With access to employee records, the practitioner is able to ascertain how many employees have been with the company say, two years or less, three to five years, six to ten years, and so forth. In view of the importance of longevity, he might impose *quotas* (in this case, percentages of persons to be interviewed) that would enable him to wind up with a sample that closely resembled the population of employees with varying amounts of longevity with the company (or, he might include a higher proportion of long-term employees in his quotas). He would then instruct his interviewers (or use the guide himself) to select employees that were easily accessible, but always only doing so with the quotas in mind. Let's say for the purposes of illustration that he needs a quota of five employees who have been with the company two years or less. After he has found five who fit the specifications, he will not interview anyone else in that particular category. This

---

[5] The reader has undoubtedly recognized that what we have just described here as an accidental sample probably constitutes a large portion of the samples that public relations practitioners use in their daily work. Accidental samples are, in this sense, a mainstay of many public relations practitioners.

[6] We have introduced another statistical term with specific meaning and with connotations that are different from those generally associated with it. The word is *bias.* Simply stated, it refers to any variable that causes the generalization based on a sample to be incorrect with respect to the population. To put it another way, bias is the favoring of some alternatives over others in the sampling process. Thus, if one obtained an accidental sample that comprised individuals with college degrees, and it later turned out that having a college degree happened to be related to having a different attitude toward a given topic, then this would be a biasing element in our accidental sample. While under certain circumstances the bases for the error in an accidental sample might be that certain individuals were biased (prejudiced, as in the everyday meaning of the term), the word as used by statisticians would embrace any and all factors that would cause a sample *not* to be representative of the population from which it was selected.

procedure would be used for all longevity categories until the various quotas had been filled.

As the reader can imagine, quota samples *can* be an improvement over accidental samples insofar as the bases for establishing the quotas correspond to important differences that one might find among individuals. Thus, to the extent that length of stay is a significant factor in how employees will react to a company relocation, to that extent will this factor be more effectively measured in the survey. In turn, the public relations practitioner should be able to provide his management with more reliable information about employee reaction to the relocation than had he not used that particular sampling plan.

In spite of its potential improvement over accidental sampling under certain circumstances, the fact remains that quota sampling is still a variation of the accidental type. In any of the longevity categories—the three- to five-year one, for instance—the sample of employees interviewed is still an accidental sample within that particular group. *We still cannot specify* the likelihood that all significant factors will be included in that particular sample; and, therefore, statistically speaking, we have no way of making rigorous inferences from the sample to the population. For example, some employees might have been sick or on vacation and thereby missed the chance to be selected when the quota for their particular longevity period was being filled.

Other hindering factors might be mentioned in connection with quota selection. Suppose an individual is instructed to obtain 50 percent men and 50 percent women in his sample, again assuming that he is selecting employees to be interviewed. Such variables as *friendship* (I can count on someone I know to give me the time), *appearance* (He appears to be grumpy and will probably turn me down), and *status* (He is a big wheel in the company and can't take the time) can influence *how* the interviewer fills his quota. So despite the fact that the quota sampling might help detect significant differences among respondents, this in no way avoids the accidental feature that is built-in, so to speak, within each of the quotas.

One last point, we have been focusing on situations in which the particular variable used as the basis for the quota sampling happens to be relevant. There is nothing to prevent an individual from using a variable that has no bearing upon the subject of his study. Thus, longevity might turn out to be unrelated to attitudes toward relocation, in which case the quota sample might be less representative of the population than a straight accidental sample would have been.

Our third variety of nonprobability sampling is *purposive* sampling. Essentially, it involves the use of selective judgment as a guide to arriving at a sample that is representative of the population in question. Querying "thought leaders," or "opinion leaders," in a community or group would be an example of purposive sampling. It can be illustrated as follows. Suppose a practitioner wanted to get some idea about the reaction of his local community toward a particular public relations program planned by his company. Let's say that the company wanted to stimulate the citizens, both private and corporate, to become more concerned about local water pollution. Furthermore, the company planned to take steps (through a variety of communication methods), to press local government officials to inform the community of their intention to help reduce local water pollution. Before launching an elaborate program (or during its formulation), the public relations practitioner might have called a number of leading local citizens to obtain their views about what his company planned to do.

In effect, the practitioner is sampling the citizenry in order to get a feeling of what the reaction of the community at large might be. The fact that he selects *certain* individuals to talk with beforehand reflects the *judgment* factor inherent in purposive sampling; in the judgment of the public relations practitioner, these "thought leaders" represent a better sampling of the whole than would a random selection of citizens. Whether the practitioner is right or wrong in this instance is irrelevant. The point is that he selected a sample from a total population along certain guidelines which, in his judgment, would give a better estimate of community reaction than would a different sample of individuals made up along other judgmental lines. This is purposive sampling.

We have now considered the more common forms of nonprobability sampling.[7] In each instance, we have tried to provide the reader with the highlights, the main limitations, and the relationship of these procedures to what a public relations practitioner does in selecting a sample for generalizing to a population.

In the next few paragraphs we shall look at probability sampling and will come to the conclusion that it seldom pays (nor is it defensible in day-to-day public relations work) to base estimates of population on nonprobability samples. The main point of this generalization provides us with a summary statement as to why it should be avoided; with nonprobability samples we cannot know the nature or extent of the errors in our

[7] There are other procedures that we have not considered which would qualify as nonprobability sampling. An illustration would be the process whereby samples are obtained and studied, their number dependent upon the stability reached in the findings obtained. For example, suppose a public relations practitioner was curious about the reaction of company employees to a special newsletter (or issues of the regular paper) designed for their *families* rather than for themselves. He could select a sample to be interviewed and question them concerning their reactions to the idea. One way to determine how many people to interview is to continue the questioning until *no new ideas or objections are encountered*. After the same ideas and objections have come up again and again, the public relations practitioner then discontinues the interviewing. Obviously, in this form of sampling the practitioner cannot know if he just happened to select a sample of employees that became repetitious as he interviewed the last five or ten; nor can he tell if some other form of sampling procedure would have produced different results. The use of repetition as a guide to representativeness has its limitations, as do any of the nonprobability sampling methods.

THE CHECKLIST: STEP TWO

sample, and *we are, therefore, unable to specify the degree to which the sample is representative of the population.* Thus, it is *not* that nonprobability samples are not representative of the population from which they are selected—they may be highly accurate, but they can also be highly inaccurate, or somewhere in between. There are various sources of bias which make the nonprobability sample a more or less inaccurate representation of the population; but we can neither tell what they are, nor tell how they contribute to the inaccuracy of the estimate. By contrast, probability samples *do* enable us to specify the degree of representativeness of the sample to the population, and therein lies the significant difference between the two major categories.

Probability sampling

To understand probability sampling, we need to reintroduce into our discussion the term *bias* and present some additional terminology: *random sample, nonsampling errors,* and *sampling errors.* The following extract defines these terms while spelling out the basic reason for using probability samples in research work:

The *main* use of samples is to learn something that can be generalized to the total population. To do this, a sample must be representative of a population. For a sample to be representative of a population, it must be a *random sample.* A random sample is one that is selected in such a fashion that each element, score, or observation has either an equal or a specifiable opportunity to be selected.[8] If this condition is satisfied, we can generalize about the total population, and, through certain statistical techniques, estimate the likely degree of error in our estimates.

When we obtain a *random sample,* we have a sample that is obtained without bias. That is, we have removed from the selection process all sources of bias that would affect the representativeness of our sample. There is one source of error that remains, however. That one remaining source is *chance.* A chance event is one that has an unpredictable (thus, no known) cause. A chance event is one which occurs randomly, and this is why we speak of a random sample as one which has no bias; that is, no *cause* other than the factors which cause it to behave randomly.

Although chance events, taken singly, are unpredictable, if we take a *large number* of chance events, we *can* make predictions. This is why we were careful earlier to define chance events as those without any known cause. This is not the same thing as saying *no* cause. A chance event is one which has some causes, but we do not know what they are. But if you take a large number of these chance events and study them, the combined effects *can* be predicted. This is known as the study of *probability* and is a part of that special branch of mathematics known as *statistics.*

[8] As the reader has probably noted, the definition for the term *random sample* is essentially the same as was presented for *probability sampling.* The reason, of course, is that probability sample *is* a random sample.

Authors always run the risk of inaccuracies in making simplified presentations of complex subject matter. From our discussion of the desirability of random samples, it is possible that the reader has concluded that there are really only two categories of error in a sample: sampling error and, in the case of a nonrandom sample, certain unknown inherent biases that produce error. There is another source of error that the experimenter must always cope with: *errors that crop up because of mistakes made by the researcher himself or his assistants in recording data, making measurements,* and so on. In short, errors that crop up because researchers and their colleagues are human. Deming makes this point when he suggests that the following triangle of errors be kept in mind:

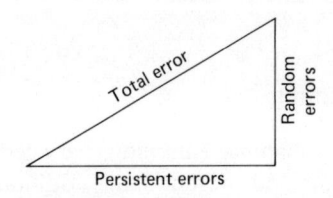

One leg of the triangle represents persistence. The other leg represents the random errors, which include the sampling variation. The hypotenuse is the sum of the uncertainties, or the total error. When the nonsampling errors are large, it is uneconomical and ineffective to waste funds on a big sample, as a big sample will decrease the sampling error but leave the total error about the same. One must face the fact that the *overall usefulness and reliability of a survey may actually be enhanced by cutting down on the size of sample* and using the money so saved to reduce the nonsampling errors. *In the sampling of records, this might mean tracing and correcting wrong and missing information. In a survey of human populations, this might mean more time and money on the questionnaire, hiring fewer and better interviewers, providing better training and better supervision in the field, and making more recalls on people not at home on a previous call.*[9]

In this excerpt from Deming we may translate *persistent errors* to mean the same thing as *nonsampling* errors. What this triangle brings out is that there are all sorts of errors that can be made in the execution of an experiment (nonsampling or persistent errors) that will affect the accuracy of predictions of data based on samples. Of course, these same sorts of errors will persist even if the entire population is studied! In fact, one of the advantages of sampling is that the likelihood of nonsampling errors is *greater* if one tries to study an entire population simply because there are that many more chances for error to occur. By and large, these nonsampling errors are known. That is, we *know* that we must check for the accuracy when people are asked to take measurements or readings. We *know* that we must take pains to train interviewers and check out questionnaires very carefully. We *know* that in spite of our carefulness we must double check our data and run "spot checks" all of the time in order to weed out these nonsampling errors. However, in our discussion of errors we will be focusing on errors *due to bias* introduced by nonrandom selection of samples.

[9] W. Edward Deming, *Sample Design in Business Research* (New York: John Wiley & Sons, Inc., 1960), pp. 61–62. Italics added.

THE CHECKLIST: STEP TWO

This type of error we are not able to anticipate and correct because we do not know what it is. Or, if we find out (as in the case of the Literary Digest Poll situation) we are not able to do anything about it. To put it another way, errors due to nonrandom sampling can be avoided by using random samples. Thus, our total error is reduced. The errors that have a nonsampling basis (carelessness, misplaced data, incorrectly tabulated data, or, in short, all human errors) must be constantly combated by the researcher. However, there is no comparatively simple step that he can take to rid himself of such errors as in the case of errors due to nonrandom sampling.

Now let us return to what we said about a random sample being a selection process that removes all bias and leaves only chance as the source of error. Because statisticians have evolved very precise estimates of *errors* inherent in samples *because of chance,* a randomly selected sample is one in which the experimenter can estimate the error in his predictions. This error is commonly known as *sampling error.* Thus, although he cannot remove this last source of error by resorting to a randomly selected sample, at least he can estimate what it is. This is almost as good as removing it entirely.[10]

It should now be clearer to us why nonprobability sampling is not easily defended in the light of all the advantages of probability sampling. To be able to estimate the degree of error in a given statistic is in itself more than enough justification for whatever additional efforts are required to select an appropriate probability sample. Also, we have probably reinforced the generalizations made previously that properly drawn samples can be remarkably accurate and that a study of the entire population is seldom justifiable.

HOW LARGE DO SAMPLES NEED TO BE?

One of the most common questions asked by practitioners is how large a sample is required in order to study a given population adequately. Though seemingly simple, this question can require several chapters for a thorough answer, and it represents a distinct challenge to attempt an intelligent discussion in the limited space allotted to us here.

As the reader will remember, we noted earlier that the size of the sample needed bears little relationship to the size of the population; as the sample size increases from 10 to 50 to 100, for example, the information obtained therefrom increases sharply; as the sample size increases further, however, the amount of information levels off. Consequently, as one gets into sizes of 500, 1,000, or beyond, the amount of information obtained decreases sharply as the sample increases. Although it seems to run counter to common sense, the fact is that the sample size required for a given level of accuracy remains amazingly constant as the population increases. Thus, for example, when the size of the population is 200 to 300 persons and we

[10] Robinson, *op. cit.,* pp. 519–521.

want estimates of the population to be accurate to within 2% (in 99 out of 100 samples drawn), the sample size required is close to 50%, or approximately 100 for a population of 200. On the other hand, as the universe or population increases to 50,000 or 100,000, the sample size grows by only slightly more than 100 additional cases and in fact remains virtually the same, a little larger than 200, for *both* populations. From this illustration we can see that while the *population increased by 98,000 cases* (from 200 to 100,000), the *sample size* required for the same level of precision *increased* only by a few more than 100. This bears out the statement *that the sample size required for a given level of precision is comparatively unaffected by increases in population size.*

Let us take the following example to round out our discussion about sample size. Suppose a public relations practitioner planned to have an open house at his organization and he wished to obtain an estimate (by means of a survey) of what the male attendance might be. (Perhaps the handouts and types of participation planned for the guests in some way depended upon whether they were males or females.) Let us assume that another open house had been given a couple of years back and that the predecessor's records showed about 70% males in attendance. This statistic, which can be considered an estimate based on previous experience, would be used as a guide by the practitioner.[11]

With this information let us now look at Tables 7-1 and 7-2 and see how they can be used to estimate the sample size required.[12] Table 7-1 shows the sizes that allow us to be very sure, and Table 7-2 is expressed in terms of "fairly sure." The difference between these levels of accuracy means that for a given error limit (for example, no more than 4%), the size of sample required will be greater if we want to be "very sure" (99 chances in 100), than if we want to be "fairly sure" (19 chances in 20).

[11] It should be noted that the formulas used for estimating sample size include some sort of *estimate* of the statistic under research. Usually there exists some basis for making an intelligent *estimate,* such as previous experience. Two points might be made here. (1) If the practitioner has *no* basis for making an estimate, he can take the most conservative path and call it chance—in this case 50% women versus 50% men in attendance. (2) *After* he has conducted his study and has obtained the latest statistic, he can compare his findings with his estimate and interpret accordingly. If the pre-study estimate was correct, he can then interpret the findings in the light of the 70% estimate made. If his pre-study estimate was incorrect, he can adjust his interpretations to take this into account.

[12] As Mildred Parten points out in the book containing these tables, the following formula is used for determining sample size and is a variation of the standard error formula:

$$Ns = \frac{p.c.\,(100 - p.c.)z^2}{T^2}$$

Ns is the sample size needed, *p.c.* is the preliminary estimate of the percent, *z* is the number of standard error units to be employed, and *T* is the required precision, or tolerance of error. Instead of having to use this formula each time a sample size estimate is required, researchers have developed tables to reflect the various factors involved. Tables 7-1 and 7-2 illustrate how the process can be simplified.

THE CHECKLIST: STEP TWO 71

Returning to our example, if the practitioner in question wanted to be accurate to within 4% in his estimate of how many males were attending, and he wanted to be "very sure" of his estimate, he would then require a sample of 871. The complete statement would now read that if a public relations practitioner wants to be sure 99 times out of 100 that his estimate of male attendance is correct to within plus or minus 4%, he needs to include 871 persons in his survey.

With this basic observation in mind, let us go on to a number of additional observations, all of which have important practical implications. They are all linked with the question of *precision;* that is, how precise does the practitioner have to be, or more correctly, how precise does the information have to be for the situation that prompted the research?

1. First of all, note the difference between being "very sure" and "fairly sure" with respect to how repeated samples can often produce essentially the same results. Looking at both tables and using the same level of accuracy ($\pm$ 4%), we see that to be "very sure" requires 871 cases, while being "fairly sure" requires only 504 cases. In terms of time and costs, interviewing *367 fewer respondents* represents a considerable saving.

2. Suppose that being wrong were not too serious and that the situation could be saved by a few additional brochures or a couple of tour guides standing by. In this case the practitioner might well settle for a $\pm$ 8 or 10% error in his estimate, rather than 4%. Translated into the number of individuals required for the sample survey, this means a reduction either to 218 or 139 persons (to be very sure), or to 126 or 81 (to be fairly sure). In a great many public relations situations, estimates that are accurate within $\pm$ 10% are quite acceptable. Moreover, the difference in costs is sizable—in some cases large enough to make the survey prohibitive at the higher levels of accuracy and quite feasible at the lower levels.[13] It cannot be stressed too strongly that choosing the level of accuracy is the responsibility of the public relations practitioner; the researcher does not know the situation well enough to make this decision.

3. Our third point applies to the relationship between the pre-survey estimate and the finding. Suppose, for example, the survey finding was that 50% men would be likely to attend the open house. This means that the 70% estimate the practitioner used as a guide was in error, and that he really should have selected a sample of 1,037 respondents. (Read down the 50–50 column in Table 7-1, using the same 4% level of error. All the

---

[13] This is a good time to reinforce a point made earlier about the relationship between sample size and population size. The reader will note that in neither of our tables is there a column for population size. We arrive at estimates of the sample size required *without* plugging in, so to speak, the population size from which these samples are to be selected. This is because the critical variables that affect the size of the sample are such things as the precision and accuracy desired, and whether the factor being identified is evenly distributed (in the 50–50 range), or markedly skewed (as in the case of our 70% proportion of males attending the open house).

SURVEY RESEARCH IN A NUTSHELL

Table 7-1. Size of sample necessary to be very sure (99 chances in 100) of accuracy to within specified limits

Limits of error in % + and −	1 99	2 98	3 97	4 96	5 95	6 94	7 93	8 92
.25	15,510	20,807	30,892	40,765	50,425	59,875	69,109	78,133
.50	2,627	5,802	7,723	10,191	12,606	14,968	17,277	19,533
.75	1,168	2,312	3,432	4,529	5,603	6,655	7,679	8,681
1	657	1,300	1,931	2,548	3,152	3,742	4,319	4,883
2		325	483	637	788	936	1,080	1,221
3			215	283	350	416	480	543
4				159	197	234	270	305
5					126	150	173	195
6						104	120	136
7							88	100
8								76
9								
10								
15								
20								
25								
30								
35								
40								

Source: Table 3 (p. 314) *Surveys, Polls, and Samples* by Mildred B. Parten. Copyright © 1950 by Harper & Row, Publishers, Incorporated. Reprinted by permission of the publishers.

practitioner would have to do in this case is merely interpret his results with a slightly larger margin of error, such as ± 4.5%. This could be obtained by interpolation, as a sample size of 871 cases would fall very near the 4.5% accuracy point in the 50–50 estimate column (specifically, between 1,037 and the next lower number, 663).

SUMMARY OF CHECKLIST STEPS ONE AND TWO

Let us now complete our discussion of the first two items of our survey research checklist by stating some generalizations that are useful rules of thumb for the public relations practitioner.

1. The steps that a scientist goes through to conduct a piece of scientific research consist of necessary procedures that must be followed in

THE CHECKLIST: STEP TWO

Table 7-1 (Continued)

9	10	15	20	25	30	35	40	50
91	90	85	80	75	70	65	60	50
86,944	95,543	135,352	169,853	199,047	222,933	241,510	254,780	265,396
21,736	23,886	33,838	42,463	49,762	55,733	60,378	63,695	66,349
9,660	10,616	15,039	18,873	22,116	24,770	26,834	28,309	29,488
5,434	5,971	8,459	10,616	12,440	13,933	15,094	15,924	16,587
1,358	1,493	2,115	2,654	3,110	3,483	3,774	3,981	4,147
604	663	940	1,180	1,382	1,548	1,677	1,769	1,843
340	373	529	664	778	871	943	995	1,037
217	239	338	425	498	557	604	637	663
151	166	235	295	346	387	419	442	461
111	122	173	217	254	284	308	325	339
85	93	139	166	194	218	236	249	259
67	74	104	131	154	172	186	197	205
	60	85	106	124	139	151	159	166
		38	47	55	62	67	71	74
			27	31	35	38	40	41
				20	22	24	25	27
					13	17	18	18
						12	13	14
							10	10

order that the data obtained be as reliable as is humanly possible. These steps can be thought of as a *process,* and the scientific process is what defines a scientific effort at obtaining reliable knowledge.

2. This process is the same for all sciences, and it varies from one discipline to another only in respect to the *content* of the discipline in question. Behind these content differences, however, lies the requirement that all scientists follow the rules of the scientific method or process.

3. Survey research is a special case within the scientific process. The seven steps of our checklist (from defining the purpose to building the public relations program based on survey research), represent a modification of the research process to fit the survey research context.

4. To conduct an intelligent and useful survey, the public relations practitioner must first clearly state the purpose of the survey—that is, the *application* of the survey findings he has in mind. The writer has seen it happen that a final report, summarizing what has sometimes been an expensive project, has not been utilized by the practitioner in question. For a

Table 7-2. Size of sample necessary to be fairly sure (19 chances in 20) of accuracy to within specified limits

Limits of error in % + and −	1 99	2 98	3 97	4 96	5 95	6 94	7 93	8 92
.25	6,085	12,047	17,886	23,602	29,195	34,665	40,013	45,237
.50	1,521	3,012	4,471	5,900	7,299	8,666	10,003	11,309
.75	676	1,339	1,987	2,622	3,244	3,852	4,446	5,026
1	380	753	1,118	1,475	1,825	2,167	2,501	2,827
2		188	279	369	456	542	625	707
3			124	164	203	241	278	314
4				92	114	135	156	177
5					73	87	100	113
6						60	69	79
7							51	58
8								44
9								
10								
15								
20								
25								
30								
35								
40								

Source: Table 4 (p. 315) *Surveys, Polls, and Samples* by Mildred B. Parten. Copyright © 1950 by Harper & Row, Publishers, Incorporated. Reprinted by permission of the publishers.

variety of reasons, the data were not reflected in any *subsequent* public relations program.

5. The second major requirement of an intelligent survey is that the practitioner know just what population or populations he is dealing with and wishes to generalize to on the basis of the research conducted. There is no room for ambiguity here; if he does not know his populations, he cannot hope to execute a useful survey.

6. The study of entire populations is seldom necessary for most public relations problem situations, because present knowledge about sampling and statistics makes it possible to generalize from the sample to the population.

7. The samples themselves should be of the probability type, and any departure into nonprobability sampling must be carefully supported or documented.

THE CHECKLIST: STEP TWO

Table 7-2 (Continued)

9 91	10 90	15 85	20 80	25 75	30 70	35 65	40 60	50 50
50,338	55,317	78,366	98,341	115,244	129,073	139,829	147,512	153,658
12,585	13,829	19,591	24,585	28,811	32,268	34,957	36,878	38,415
5,593	6,146	8,707	10,927	12,805	14,341	15,537	16,390	17,073
3,146	3,457	4,898	6,146	7,203	8,067	8,739	9,220	9,604
787	864	1,224	1,537	1,801	2,017	2,185	2,305	2,401
350	384	544	683	800	896	971	1,024	1,067
197	216	306	384	450	504	546	576	600
126	138	196	246	288	323	350	369	384
87	96	136	171	200	224	243	256	267
64	71	100	125	147	165	178	188	196
49	54	77	96	113	126	137	144	150
39	43	60	76	89	100	108	114	119
	35	49	61	72	81	87	92	96
		22	27	32	36	39	41	43
			15	18	20	22	23	24
				12	13	14	15	15
					9	10	10	10
						7	8	8
							6	6

8. Information reliable enough for most, if not all, public relations situations can be based on small probability samples. The size of the population in question has little bearing on the size of the sample.

9. The degree of accuracy or precision required from any given sample survey must be determined by the public relations practitioner in question, as it is outside the experience of the external survey research expert.

10. Generalizations based on sample survey results must always be examined in the light of the relationship between the sample and population involved. Conclusions arrived at from outside these confines should be clearly labeled as speculations.

We have now considered in some detail the first two items on our survey research checklist, (1) *definition of purpose,* and (2) *identification of population and sample.* We should now know what information (broadly speaking) that our survey research project is supposed to produce. We know what population or populations we wish to generalize to, and also how both checklist items relate to the public relations problem situation that generated the need for survey research in the first place. We are now ready to consider the next step in the checklist.

8 | Survey research checklist: step three

THUS FAR in our discussion of what we call a survey research checklist, we have examined two items: purpose and sampling. Presumably, by now, the researcher knows what purpose(s) his research is supposed to achieve, and what population will be involved in his generalizations. To put it another way, he knows whom he wants to survey and why.

UTILIZING THE DATA COLLECTION INSTRUMENT

The next item on our checklist is what we have identified as the *data collection instrument*. This heading embraces all the ways in which information is obtained from respondents in a survey research study. Before taking this item in detail, however, let us consider for a moment the more general question of measurement.

How well the phenomena can be measured is the essence of any scientific study. In fact, the degree to which a given science can measure the subject(s) under study determines, in large part, the precision of that science. Closely linked with progress in measurement is the degree to which scientists can predict and understand the phenomena normally studied by them. For example, physics and chemistry are two sciences that have made tremendous strides toward understanding the phenomena they deal with. By the same token, measurement accuracy in these two fields has become remarkably precise—even involving differences as small as one wave length of light. Great progress has been made in the biological sciences, but our understanding in certain areas is not as precise as in the case of physics and chemistry. In physiology, for example, our measurements of many bodily functions are comparatively crude when compared with measurements of accuracy at the level of wave length differences. The same is true in such fields as sociology or psychology, where our ability to understand, predict and ultimately measure human behavior is far from exact.

Survey research falls within the general category of the social sciences and embraces sociology and certain work within psychology. It follows that we would expect measurement in survey research work to be relatively crude and inexact; indeed, such is the case. Some of the more critical variables that affect the accuracy of such measurements will be studied in succeeding sections, including an examination of the concepts of reliability and validity and how they relate to measurement.

THE INTERVIEW: BASIC MEASUREMENT TOOL OF SURVEY RESEARCH

In survey research, the basic measurement tool is the interview. By means of a series of questions asked of the respondent by the interviewer, we collect a variety of replies which constitute the basic data upon which to base our interpretations and generalizations.

There are two major categories of interviews: *remote* and *face-to-face*.[1] In a *remote* situation the interviewer and the respondent are separated physically from one another, as is the case in a *telephone survey*. Certain features of the richness of the face-to-face interview situation are necessarily lost or modified when the interviewer is unable to see the facial expressions of the respondent. Is he confused? Is he bored? Uneasy? And so forth. The interviewer also has less control over the interview situation —it is much easier for the respondent to hang up the telephone than close the door or walk away from the interviewer. *Mail surveys,* which are essentially interviews on paper, represent another variation of remote interviewing designed to permit useful measurement to take place without the presence of the interviewer. The questionnaire is worded in such a way as to simulate a dialogue between the interviewer and the respondent. Obviously, particular attention must be given to a number of special details (instructions, covering letters, and so forth) in order to obtain useful information in the absence of the interviewer.[2]

---

[1] Applied to survey research, this simple categorization system focuses on the relationship between the two major ingredients of any survey: interviewer and respondent. Certain other distinctions encountered in the literature related to survey research, such as *panel surveys, field experiments,* and so forth, will not be discussed here, as they fall within the framework of the remote and face-to-face categories. For example, in a panel interview a certain sample (or number of samples) of individuals is questioned (either individually or as a group) and requestioned possibly a number of times. The panel member generally is made aware of his role in the process. This variation in survey research is useful under certain circumstances where change in attitude occurs over a period of time as a function of the operation or with the introduction of certain variables.

[2] There are many other nuances of difference between the remote and face-to-face interview situations which have implications for the data collected, the difficulty of collecting the data, and so forth. We are not going into the pros and cons of various interview methods in this volume. Our intent, rather, is merely to spell out the major variations found under the general heading of survey research.

THE CHECKLIST: STEP THREE

In a face-to-face situation the interviewer and the respondent are in close physical proximity to each other. This type of interview has become practically synonymous with the term *survey research;* it affords, potentially, the richest source of data for the researcher. For example, in addition to obtaining answers to questions asked, the interviewer can measure other aspects of the respondent such as his appearance and emotional state, thereby reducing the likelihood of misunderstanding between them. In the face-to-face situation the trained interviewer has the greatest opportunity to establish rapport with the interviewee to explain or clarify and to probe for further details or nuances of answers. Lastly, the face-to-face interview approach enables the interviewer to obtain probability samples as he has the option to select the interviewee desired (rather than having the interviewee "select" himself by choosing to respond to a mail questionnaire).

We are careful here to use such words as "potentially," "opportunity," and "option" in connection with the various advantages of the face-to-face interview situation as it applies to survey work. Just because a given piece of survey research happens to be based upon face-to-face interviews is no assurance that all advantages of this variation will be automatically forthcoming; this approach only affords the researcher the potential of benefiting from these advantages. He must still take the many necessary steps to insure that he actually achieves them.

One final point about face-to-face interviewing is that, generally, the interviewer has with him what is often referred to as an interview guide sheet. This consists of a list of the questions to be asked, and it shows the desired wording of the questions and the sequence to be followed in interviewing a particular respondent. The reader can appreciate what chaos would result if interviewers were given free rein along these lines. In addition, the interview guide sheet is quite explicit with regard to what questions require further probing (additional questions an interviewer will ask following the so-called primary questions), what supplementary materials (such as checklists and pictures) are to be employed, and so forth. The only time a guide sheet is not used is in connection with exploratory interviews, in which the researchers are still formulating views about what they want to find out, the best way to word the questions, and about the particular type or format of question to use. Assuming that the study moves on to a survey proper, the standard interview guide sheet is then developed and used by all interviewers in that given study.

TWO BASIC QUESTION APPROACHES

After the decision has been made whether to question the respondent by remote interviewing or by the face-to-face method, the next question is

SURVEY RESEARCH IN A NUTSHELL

how to go about it. The approach, or combination of approaches, used is reflected in the manner in which questions are put to the respondent.

The direct approach

The *direct* approach is based on the assumption that needed information can be obtained simply by asking for it. Whenever a survey researcher feels that the data he seeks is available to him through a question or a series of questions that solicit specific information, feeling, plans, or intentions, he is, in effect, *utilizing the direct approach*. Because the answer to the question, "Can I elicit the information I seek simply by asking for it?" is often "yes," it is safe to say that the overwhelming preponderance of survey work falls into this category.

|—————————————————————————————|
Comparatively structured   Comparatively unstructured

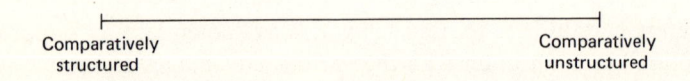

Figure 8-1. Direct question approach as a continuum

One way of examining the direct question approach is to visualize it as ranging along a continuum from *comparatively structured* to *comparatively unstructured*. At the left-hand end, we are concerned with the various questions normally asked in surveys—those which seek personal or socioeconomic information from the respondent, such as his age, name, address, income, marital status, formal education, and so forth. The reason that these are called comparatively structured questions is obvious; the respondent has little, if any, latitude in his reply with, presumably, only one correct answer possible. Every survey contains at least some questions that qualify for the comparatively structured end of the continuum. The data obtained from these are generally analyzed in order to measure such breakdowns as the attitude of the young versus the old, wealthy versus poor, and educated versus uneducated respondents.

The other end of the continuum is typified by the so-called *open-ended question*. This type of question raises some topic or issue with the respondent who is free to answer the question as he wishes, usually in a fair amount of detail and with a number of subquestions (or probes) from the interviewer. A few examples of open-ended questions are shown here, as selected from different cases in Part III:

Case 3: Would you mind telling me anything you can remember about the sponsor's commercials on "Kennecott Neighborhood Theater"?

Case 4: Some people have been concerned that diet and the kinds of foods people eat may be associated with heart disease. Have you heard anything about this?

THE CHECKLIST: STEP THREE

Case 5: Do you think that industrial research organizations are doing a good job of telling you about their research activities and goals?

As is obvious from the question format, the topic that the interviewer wants to hear about is supplied to the respondent. How the interviewee replies—what he chooses to emphasize, criticize or elaborate on—is left up to him. Because the respondent is given no indication as to how he should reply, such open-ended questions are regarded as *unstructured*.

In the middle range of the direct approach continuum are found the so-called multiple choice or fixed-alternative questions.[3] Following are some examples of this format, also taken from cases in Part III:

Case 1: What is your opinion of the people generally of the country you serve in?

Am now overseas or have served overseas since 1 Jan '59:
a. Very good opinion
b. Good opinion
c. Neither good nor bad
d. Bad opinion
e. Very bad opinion
f. Don't know

Served overseas prior to 1959:
a. Very good opinion
b. Good opinion
c. Neither good nor bad
d. Bad opinion
e. Very bad opinion
f. Don't know

Case 2: Do you think that a company like U.S. Steel should or should not try to make the company's views known on subjects of this kind?

Subject	Should	Should Not	No Opinion
1. Government control of prices			
2. Union negotiations			
3. Tax legislation			
4. Problems of inflation			
5. Social legislation			
6. Political issues			

[3] It should be pointed out that while the far ends of this continuum are fairly definite, the area between these extremes are not. Thus, while we would place the multiple-choice question somewhere along the middle of the continuum, someone else might argue for a slightly different placement. The specific location of any form of the direct question is unimportant; what is important is awareness of the different formats that do exist within the category and how they vary with respect to the constraints (degree of structuredness) placed upon the respondent. These remarks about the continuum of direct questions should be kept in mind when we consider the continuum of indirect questions later in the chapter.

Case 5: As far as your particular field of science is concerned, where do you feel the most significant research is being done today—in government, in industry, or at colleges and universities?

The reader has undoubtedly noted the "in-betweenness" of the multiple-choice approach and why this format is placed in the middle portion of the direct question continuum. A question with a number of responses from which to choose imposes less constraint than does one with only a single correct answer, such as age, income or marital status. In this sense, multiple-choice questions are comparatively less structured than those at the extreme left-hand end of the continuum. On the other hand, because the respondent can pick only one category and is limited to its particular wording to convey his feelings, multiple choice questions are more structured than the open-ended questions at the right-hand end of the continuum.

We have not considered all of the variations in questioning that can qualify for the in-between portion of our direct question continuum. There are questions which provide the respondent with adjectives to choose from, numbers to circle or select, scales of some sort to use in grading his reply, and all these variations are readily identified. With his understanding of the continuum described above, together with the examples of the two extremes and of the midpoint, the reader should now be able to look at any questionnaire or interview guide sheet and figure out for himself what types of direct questions are employed. If necessary, he should now be able to judge whether the question types are appropriate for the information desired, and also whether the direct question approach is the proper one to use.

One final word. If we include all of the possible variations of the direct question approach which can be spelled out and placed somewhere on the above continuum, we have, in effect, categorized an exceedingly high proportion of all the survey work that is being or has been conducted. The reader can take this continuum and apply it to any questionnaire he comes across; he should, of course, begin with the cases described in Part III of this book.

The indirect approach

There are times when the answer to the rule of thumb on whether or not a question can be asked directly turns out to be "no." The researcher is forced to conclude that he would be unable to elicit the information desired by means of direct questioning. Among the many possible reasons for this, three of the more important ones are as follows:

First, we have the simple refusal to answer because the question is considered an invasion of privacy. The respondent feels that the interviewer

THE CHECKLIST: STEP THREE 83

has no right to the information he seeks because it is too personal, or perhaps because it deals with a sensitive area of some sort involving social taboos. Naturally, the range of topics likely to be considered too personal will vary with the individual, but a number of areas are fairly common to us all—personal fears or phobias, family matters, income, sexual relations, business or professional secrets, and so forth.

A second major reason has to do with the respondent himself. He may be evasive or suspicious and attempt to withhold information or refuse to cooperate. This second category can be closely linked with our first, in that the reason for the individual's evasiveness is that he feels the question to be too personal. However, in this second category the individual's suspicion is based not so much in the subject matter as in his own personality makeup.

The third main reason that might be pointed out is that there are times when the person is apparently perfectly willing to cooperate but is unable to do so. This happens most frequently when the individual is unaware that he is exhibiting certain behavior. Hence, it might be a fruitless approach to ask a parent, "Why are you overprotective with your child?" if the parent is completely unconscious of the fact that he is. Naturally, there are other subtle variations in this category, but the net result is the same: the interviewer is unable to obtain the information he needs.

When the researcher realizes that the direct question approach will not work, he can either decide to drop the question area or attempt to devise other methods to get the information he seeks. These other methods are those that fall into our indirect questioning category.[4]

Just as we were able to visualize the direct question approach along a

```
|─────────────────────────────────────|
Comparatively                    Comparatively
 structured                       unstructured
```

Figure 8-2. Indirect question approach as a continuum

---

[4] In clinical psychology these indirect approaches are known as *projective techniques*. We will return to this term in more detail a little later in our exposition of the indirect question approach. The problem of overcoming resistance to questions was noted many years ago in clinical work with disturbed patients; consequently, over the years many devices have been developed for both children and adults to circumvent this problem, in a clinical setting. They all have one thing in common—they are designed to elicit information not available to the clinician by direct questioning. In the past decade these projective devices have been used in business and industrial settings in a number of ways, including, of course, survey work. Furthermore, they have been modified especially for survey work and are called, among other things, "structured disguised tests." The point is that while not utilizing one of the classical clinical projective devices, industrial researchers have embraced the *indirect approach* inherent to the projective methods and have applied it to business-type problems, often in the context of survey work. This whole movement has become better known as *motivation research*.

continuum from structured to unstructured questions, we can do the same with the indirect approach. Once again, let's regard the left-hand end as the comparatively structured one and the right-hand end as comparatively unstructured. This time, however, we will begin with the right-hand end of the continuum, which embraces the classical projective techniques used in clinical psychology. What we have in mind here are such devices as the Thematic Apperception Test (TAT) and the Rorschach Ink Blot Test. The TAT consists of a series of cards depicting persons, places, or things about which the individual is asked to tell a story. Generally, he is asked to tell what events have led up to the scene shown in the particular card and what is going to happen in the future. One of the cards constitutes virtually the most unstructured device possible, as it is nothing but a blank white card. Usually he remarks, "But there's no picture here"; to which the interviewer might reply, "That's all right, just make up a story, anyway." The Rorschach Ink Blot Test is quite different from the TAT, but the principle of exposing the respondent to an almost completely unstructured stimulus situation to which he has to respond is common to both techniques. The Rorschach was originally developed by placing ink on white sheets of paper and folding them, causing the ink to blot. This process produces a series of nondescript black (with all shades of grey) configurations on a white background, and the individual is asked to give his impression of what the pattern might represent.[5]

At this point the reader may think that he understands what projective techniques are, but he may not see their relationship to the indirect methods of obtaining information from a respondent. We will make a modest detour into the topic of perception, after which we will relate it to the projective techniques and, incidentally, to all the other techniques that are embraced by the indirect category.

The term *perception* refers to how an individual organizes the world around him into various categories. Thus, we speak of visual perception, auditory perception, and so forth. If we make even such a simple statement as, "He perceived me as a threat," we have actually summed up a great many different components—visual, auditory, and olfactory components—into one complex whole. The inference in this short sentence is that "he" has organized his world around him in such a way that we are viewed as dangerous to him in some manner.

One way of thinking about the process of perception is to say that it consists of *structural* and *functional* factors. *Structural* factors refer to all phenomena *external* to an individual, such as other people, noises, lights, buildings, cars, and so on. The functional factors, on the other hand, refer

[5] It is important to note that the instructions or requests made of the respondent in a projective technique situation be unstructured; otherwise, the unstructured nature of the stimulus would be partially or wholly lost and the value of the device seriously, if not unalterably, affected.

THE CHECKLIST: STEP THREE   85

to all variables *internal* to the individual, such as his previous experiences, moods and motivations, which will affect the way he perceives (or organizes) the world around him. The relationship of these factors in perception is usually expressed as follows: structural (factors) times functional (factors) equals perception ($s \times f = p$).

In some perceptual situations the structural factors play such a dominant role that the functional factors have almost no effect. *Illusions* are an excellent example of this. We have all witnessed the sort of trick that causes us to perceive things in a comparatively uniform way, though perhaps incorrectly. In the desert, for example, nearly everyone has experienced the optical illusion that he can see water not too far ahead when there is, in fact, none there. Under these extreme circumstances the structural factors dominate, with the functional factors—such as motivations[6]—only minimally involved in determining what an individual perceives.

By contrast, we can also find situations in which the structural factors play a minimal role in determining a given perception while the functional factors are dominant. An example of this would be the person who thinks that he is Napoleon, or who believes that he is the victim of some international plot and that he does not have long to live. Under such circumstances the structural factors (reality, as well as the behavior of others in the world) are at such variance with the individual's thinking that we conclude that his perceptions are almost totally determined by functional factors (processes going on within the individual himself). In other words, structural factors (Napoleon is dead) have little or no effect here upon the mentally ill "Napoleon."

We have described two extreme situations where, on the one hand, structural factors were the primary determinants of perception and where, on the other hand, functional factors played a dominant role. Obviously, there are practically unlimited in-between combinations. With this simple formula we are able to sort out the determinants of perception and arrive at some estimate of what factors might be operating and to what degree.

What has all this to do with indirect questioning, particularly as regards the projective devices? A useful way of looking at the various projective methods and the modifications of this approach (included in the term *structured disguised tests*) is that they all represent efforts to minimize the contribution of the structural factors in perception in order to highlight those functional factors. Let's relate this comment to the projective devices we have discussed thus far. In the case of the TAT where an individual looks at a picture and is asked to tell a story about it, the picture actually plays a very minor role in determining what will be said. If the

---

[6] In our example we are assuming that the individuals involved have plenty of water and that thirst (which would be a functional factor) is not operating to affect their perceptions. If there were no water, thirst would probably contribute to the perception of "seeing" water in the distance.

respondent tells a story full of hostility, sadness, interpersonal frictions, or misunderstandings, the impetus for such content does not lie in the picture but in his perceptions. The same thing is true, of course, with the Rorschach Ink Blot Test. The configurations are such that people can "see" anything they wish, once again minimizing the structural factors in order to bring out the functional factors. All indirect questioning approaches—including, particularly, the devices that make use of the projective techniques—are deliberately geared to the principle of emphasizing the functional factors by disguising (minimizing) the structural factors. As a result, when the responses obtained are analyzed, what was not available to the researcher through direct questioning becomes available through some variation of the indirect approach.

It is sometimes difficult for those not familiar with the classical projective techniques, or with the variations based on these clinical approaches, to visualize how the stimulus presented (the picture or inked paper) can be interpreted in a variety of ways. They do not quite grasp that most of the impetus lies in the perceiver and not the objected perceived. Let us illustrate this with an example of picture interpretation, using one of a

Figure 8-3. An example of a modified projective device (structured disguised test) used in a business context

THE CHECKLIST: STEP THREE

number of pictures which, several years ago, were included in a depth study of people's attitudes toward bankers and banking.[7] (We will not consider one of the pictures from TAT or Rorschach tests, because there is an understandable reluctance to let pictures from established clinical projective devices become widely distributed. It would be like handing out the questions used in standardized intelligence tests. To the extent that they become common knowledge, the tests would lose their usefulness as measuring devices.)

Figure 8-3 is one of several specially developed pictures designed to obtain people's attitudes toward a number of basic customer contact situations normally involved in banking work. The teller-customer relationship is one type of common interaction between the bank and the public. Another area of interest (chosen as the subject of Figure 8-3) is the officer-customer relationship which takes place in connection with applying for loans, opening checking and savings accounts, and so forth. In the preliminary stages of the bank study, the author and his associates found it difficult to draw out people's feelings about this area of customer contact by means of direct questions; sample questions (developed during the pilot study) which tried to elicit respondent's reactions to bankers were only partially successful; those designed to get at an individual's feelings regarding loans also proved unsatisfactory. In short, there was good evidence that the indirect approach might be a fruitful one to take. The picture shown in Figure 8-3 was eventually developed and used as part of the total interview.[8]

To convey to the reader how the same picture can be interpreted in more than one way, let us consider some of the different perceptions reported by a few respondents.[9] One respondent reported that this was "obviously" a woman applying for a loan and that she was definitely quite nervous, "because she was sitting on the edge of her chair." Another person reported that this was definitely a man—a lawyer—who was arranging for a loan in order to take advantage of a wise stock investment. Accord-

---

[7] "Attitudes of Framingham Residents Towards Local Banks and Their Practices: A Motivation Research Study" (Framingham, Mass.: Framingham National Bank, May, 1958).

[8] The reader may be interested to know that this figure was the result of close work with an artist, and the version here was the last of several previous ones that proved to be unfruitful. They were unfruitful in that these earlier versions were too structured and the resulting interpretations were more a function of what was in the picture than what the individual contributed to it. The picture was finally unstructured enough so as not to dictate the interpretations of the respondent, but structured enough to make it a plausible banking business context.

[9] Our purpose in giving these examples of possible interpretations is merely to show that people can "project" into a stimulus situation if it is sufficiently unstructured. We are not going into the area of the themes themselves, which revealed what the researchers felt was a number of common sets of feelings and attitudes of the respondents toward banks and bankers.

ing to this respondent, he was "clearly" used to taking out a loan and it was old hat to him. Still another said that the banker (person behind the desk) was definitely "uninterested" in the applicant, that he was a very busy man, and that one could tell this from the fact that his desk was all "cluttered up with papers."

As indicated in footnote 9, we are ignoring for a moment how widely or repeatedly the above themes occurred in the sample of individuals interviewed. Our emphasis is on the fact that the same picture evoked quite different interpretations from each individual and that each person felt that the basis for his interpretation lay in the picture itself. This feeling was revealed in such expressions as "obviously" a woman "sitting on the edge of her chair," "uninterested" in the applicant and working at a desk that was "cluttered up with papers"—and was substantiated in each case by probing from the interviewer. The reader can compare these statements with the picture and see for himself that these interpretations are not "in the picture"; rather, they are in the respondent—in the sense that he is bringing to the picture and projecting into it his own perceptions of customer-banker relations. This tendency to "project" forms the basis for the term "projective device" found at the unstructured end of the indirect question continuum.

This is the essence of the indirect approach: *a minimally structured stimulus situation is presented to a respondent in order for him to project into the situation and thereby reveal feelings and attitudes presumably not otherwise (as a rule) obtainable through direct questioning.* Despite the significant advantage of the indirect approach, there is a great hazard to obtaining reliable information by indirect methods—they require more interpretation on the part of the researcher and, in fact, enable *him to project* as well as the respondent.[10]

Hopefully, we have been able to convey to the reader the right-hand end of the indirect approach continuum, which embraces the various methods that qualify as being highly unstructured, and which, by definition, facilitate projection on the part of the respondent. Let us now examine the left-hand end of the continuum, the comparatively structured indirect approach.[11] This end is perhaps best depicted by the *sentence completion* technique.

---

[10] While this book does not go into the various details of the measurement problems involved in indirect questioning (as well as in the direct approach), we will return to this point later in the chapter when we examine modifiers of information accuracy and the concepts of reliability and validity in data collection.

[11] The reader has undoubtedly noted that the same language has been used to describe both ends of both the indirect and direct question approach—comparatively structured and comparatively unstructured. Within the context of each continuum, this distinction is correct; thus, in the direct question situation, "What is your age?" is a much more structured question (and places more response constraint upon the interviewee), than "What do you think of the work of the Peace Corps?" Likewise, in indirect questioning, the sentence completion test (to be examined next) is much

THE CHECKLIST: STEP THREE

Essentially, this indirect approach consists in asking the respondent to complete a series of incomplete sentences with the first thing that comes to his mind. For example, he might be given the following: "The first thing I think of when I hear the term public relations is _____." "Public relations practitioners are generally _____." "The main reason I would never recommend a career in public relations for my son or daughter is _____." "The difference between public relations and advertising is mainly _____." "The future of relations is _____." "The main reason I would recommend a career in public relations for my son or daughter is _____."

The respondent is required to complete the incomplete sentences as quickly as possible. A series of 15 or 20 of them is often quite effective in eliciting feelings or views that cannot be obtained by the more structured direct questions which give the respondent an opportunity to think out his answer carefully. However, as with all of the indirect approaches, there is the need for interpretation of results. There is also the danger (normally greater than with direct questions) of misinterpretation on the part of the researcher. Let us look at the following examples of the sentence completion technique:

In all social-research techniques and in sentence completion in particular, the effects of context should be kept in mind. For instance, if a respondent has been asked a lot of questions about his smoking habits and had been given a series of incomplete sentences dealing with cigarettes, he would be inclined to complete the sentence "If only . . ." with some comment about smoking. In this way contextual influence can be a help or a hindrance, depending on our

more structured than are the classical projective devices (the TAT or the Rorschach) or the modified projective devices such as the one we examined in Figure 8-3. In fact, both the direct and indirect question approaches can be visualized as segments of one overall continuum ranging from structured to unstructured, as depicted in Figure 8-4.

```
        Direct question          Overlap         Indirect question
          continuum                                  continuum

Comparatively          Comparatively    Comparatively         Comparatively
 structured             unstructured      structured           unstructured
    (a)                     (b)              (c)                   (d)
```

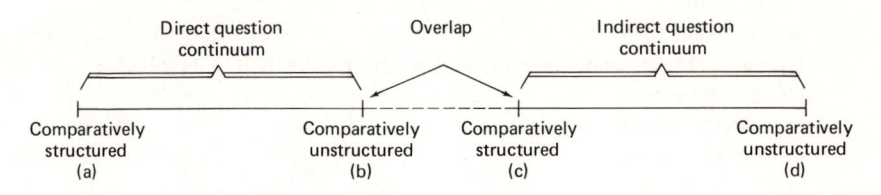

Figure 8-4. Direct and indirect question approaches in a single continuum

When viewed this way, the open-ended question (b) is more *unstructured* than some question concerning the age, income, or occupation of the respondent (a). On the other hand, it is more *structured* than the picture depicted in Figure 8-3 (d), in that an open-ended question restricts the respondent to talking about the topic or issue contained in the question, whereas in the picture he is free to range over a wider spectrum of possible responses in his answer.

intent. If we had wanted to explore the respondent's more general worries and regrets not only those with a relationship to smoking then the context would have produced a rather misleading restriction, making it appear as if his chief concern was with cigarettes and smoking. On the other hand, we can sometimes utilize contextual influences of this kind to guide the responses into certain areas, but this will have to be taken into account when we interpret the results.

In sentence completion techniques we are looking particularly for spontaneity. When we seek to test a particular hypothesis or explore a certain problem, we tend to have greater confidence in a set of responses given to items that do not reveal our purpose. For instance, suppose we were conducting an investigation into the fears and worries of hospital patients undergoing surgery and that one point at issue was the patient's attitudes to anesthetics. We might give them a sentence such as the following to complete: "When I see them coming to give me the anesthetic. . . ." Here are some of the responses:

I would like to get under the bed
I get frightened
I was not conscious of them approaching me
I was a bit nervous
Glad I know I will be all right when I wake up
I think to myself: it won't be long now before I get rid of my pain
Relieved that the worst is over
I'm relieved
Ten horrible seconds of sheer panic
I twitch, become nervous, although I feel this unnecessary
I am very pleased
I feel very frightened and sick, and hope I may wake to see daylight again
I get butterflies in my tummy
I just accept it
I hope to wake up again
I'm glad that the waiting has expired
I feel afraid
A very good idea
I hope they give enough—and not operate before it has its effect
I feel a bit scared
I wonder if I will wake up again
I am glad

It is obvious that these responses can be classified quite easily into such groupings as "fear," "extreme fear," "acceptance," "gladness," and so on. However, the item is highly directive, and its purpose is clear to the respondent. A skeptical surgeon would point out that the wording of the item is rather suggestive. We ourselves might feel that the results tell us little about the feelings or attitudes behind the fear or the acceptance of anesthetics and how such feelings compare to the respondents' attitudes to other frightening events in hospitals. Preceding that, therefore, but within the same context, we might set a much "wider" item: "My worst fear is . . . " with the following results for the same group of respondents:

THE CHECKLIST: STEP THREE

Being treated roughly
Mostly undressing in front of women
Waking before the operation is finished
Will I have to come back to have another operation?
Injections
Arterialgram X-ray
Bedpans
Pain
What of the future?
Being afraid without cause
When I have no one to come and see me
That my graft does not take well
Myself
To fall out of bed
To contract an incurable disease.
In my present case: eating
Injections
Coming into hospital
Death
No fears
When a patient dies
Helplessness

There are two references to injections (which may or may not refer to the anesthetic) and one interesting response concerning insufficient anesthesia (waking before the operation is finished); but, otherwise, there is not evidence that the fear of anesthetics runs high. If there had been many references to fear of anesthesia, it would have seemed more trustworthy, say, to our skeptical surgeon, because here the particular hypothesis being tested is not obvious to the respondent and the results are consequently more convincing.[12]

So much for the left-hand end of the indirect question continuum. As in the case of projective techniques, interpretation is necessary; but with the sentence completion situation there is more structuring than with the classical projective devices or picture interpretation. There are numerous other indirect approaches (the cartoon approach, role-playing techniques, answering "pseudofactual" questions) that would fit somewhere in between the two extremes on the continuum, but their exact location does not concern us at the moment. The point we wish to make is that all these devices represent efforts to obtain information which is deemed (or demonstrated) unavailable by direct questioning and which requires an indirect approach. As such, all these devices share the characteristic of indirect questioning —minimizing the structural factors in order to bring out the functional factors in a person's perceptions.

One final point. In our examination of the indirect approach we have concentrated on providing a definition and some examples of the two ends

[12] Quoted from *Questionnaire Design and Attitude Measurement,* by A. N. Oppenheim, © 1966 by A. N. Oppenheim, Basic Books, Inc., Publishers, New York.

of the indirect data collection continuum; after the particular approach (or approaches) has been decided upon and put to use, the researcher has in hand what is referred to as "raw data" (to be discussed in Chapter 9), and these data need to be analyzed, synthesized, put into table form wherever appropriate, and interpreted. Although the steps involved in making sense out of data collected by indirect approaches differ generally from those used with data collected by direct methods, eventually the two approaches result in the same thing; it is not the ultimate goal of both—the obtaining of data upon which to base inferences about the attitudes of given respondents—that differs, but the technique. In both cases, when the attitudes of the sample respondents have been measured, the researcher may then generalize to the population from which his sample respondents were selected.

In considering both the direct and indirect approaches to obtaining information we have, in effect, examined a schema that embraces all of the particular question variations that the reader will encounter in survey research work. He should now be able to look at any questionnaire or interview guide sheet and classify each question by its proper approach. Secondly, within each breakdown he should be able to estimate roughly where a particular type of question falls along the two continua (comparatively structured to unstructured) and then decide, from the implications in each question, which can be asked directly and which need an indirect approach. The public relations practitioner can later agree or disagree as to whether such data can be obtained by the approach indicated. Furthermore, he is now cognizant of the greater need for interpretation in the case of the indirect approach, on the part of the researcher, and he can tell if the generalizations are justified (see again the Oppenheim quote, pages 89–91, in this connection).[13]

MODIFIERS OF THE ACCURACY OF DATA COLLECTED: THE CONCEPTS OF RELIABILITY AND VALIDITY

Whenever one attempts to measure something, regardless of what that "something" might be, there are always two basic questions—embodied in the terms *reliability* and *validity*—that must be kept in mind. Let us examine these two concepts in some detail before considering some specific factors

---

[13] What we are referring to here is that, all things being equal, the more unstructured the approach used to elicit information from a respondent in a survey, the greater the likelihood of error in the measurement situation. When obtaining attitudes through picture interpretation, the researcher is much more susceptible to errors of misinterpretation because what (and how) he is measuring is more complex and at the same time more vague. On the other hand, it is likely that a high degree of accuracy will be achieved from the measurement of the age, income, and so forth, of the respondent involved.

THE CHECKLIST: STEP THREE 93

which modify (or affect) the accuracy of the data collected. The term *reliability* poses the following: If I were to repeat a given measurement, would I obtain the same value?[14] If the same measurement is obtained under repeated conditions, we say that our measuring instrument is reliable. If the repeated measures vary considerably, we say that our measurement instrument is unreliable.

The importance of reliability is obvious. Suppose a carpenter were working with a tape measure that—unknown to him—fluctuated several inches (or as little as a fraction of an inch) each time he used it. As a result, anything he constructed would be cock-eyed and, in some instances, such as openings for doors and windows, inoperable. Take a survey from the same point of view; if we were dealing with a questionnaire or interview guide sheet containing questions (direct, indirect, or both) that elicited different responses each time they were asked of a given respondent[15] (as in the case of our carpenter's rule), the results of our survey would be just as cock-eyed as our house constructed with an unreliable ruler. Obviously, we must attempt to construct a measuring instrument (regardless of whether it is a tape measure, questionnaire, or IQ test), that is as reliable as we can make it.

Validity raises the question of whether the measuring device measures what it says it does. Does a personality test in fact measure personality? Does a selection test for pilot training in fact select candidates who

---

[14] The expression "same value" should not be interpreted to mean *exactly* the same value; this is rarely the case. There is usually some degree of error involved and, consequently, some factors operating to make subsequent measurements differ from the preceding ones. The variance is usually very slight. Therefore, when we use the expression "same value" we are disregarding the fact that obtaining the exact same measurement the second time is theoretically impossible. From a practical standpoint, the level of repeatability usually obtained makes these smaller variations unimportant. For example, what look like four 18" x 24" plywood frames are probably four plywood frames of different sizes. The home craftsman, in the process of cutting them out, will undoubtedly make errors in each of the measurements. If he is skilled, and equipped with good tools, the errors are small—in the neighborhood of 1/16" or less; if not, the errors might be slightly larger. In any event, the reliability of his repeated measures from a practical standpoint are excellent: to the naked eye the frames look identical. Theoretically, however, he has been in error each time he took a measurement.

[15] In survey work, obtaining repeated measures in order to ascertain the reliability of the measuring instrument provides certain problems not encountered in other measurement situations. One cannot usually ask the same question of the same individual to see if he gives the same answer. Memory and the desire to be consistent invariably affect how the respondent answers the question a second time. This is also true with regard to the reliability of items on a test. There are a number of solutions to this problem; for example, to test the reliability of a mathematics test we might develop a battery of problems (100 for instance) which would then be divided into two groups by means of a table of random numbers. On the assumption that the questions are now equal, the score achieved on one half of the test can be compared with the score on the other half. If the two halves are reliable, the score obtained from a given individual should be the same, or nearly so, in both cases. If the test is not reliable, the scores would be considerably different.

will become pilots? Does an opinion attitude survey actually elicit the opinions or attitudes that it claims to measure? As with reliability, if a measuring device does not fulfill the function for which it was developed, it is not a satisfactory device. It is simpler in some cases than in others to determine the validity (as it is to ascertain the reliability) of a measuring device. For example, the criterion for determining the validity of an instrument that measures length or weight is comparatively straightforward and directly observable. Tests designed to measure such things as leadership or administrative ability or personality are another matter entirely; ascertaining their validity is a much more formidable task. These phenomena are more complex and are exceedingly difficult in terms of evolving independent criteria against which to validate a test.

How do the concepts of reliability and validity relate to our schema discussed earlier concerning direct and indirect data collection approaches? We need to answer these questions in several ways:

1. Whatever is used in survey research work (such as a questionnaire or interview guide sheet) is liable to the requirement of being reliable and valid. This is consistent with the point made in Chapter 2 that the processes of research are applicable to *all* disciplines, and that differences among the sciences are in terms of content and not in the criterion up to which they must live if they are to be called sciences. All sciences make use of different measuring devices in their research work, and these devices, too, must be evaluated in terms of how reliable and valid they are.

2. Another relationship between our schema of direct and indirect data collection approaches and the concepts of reliability and validity is found in the following rule of thumb for public relations practitioners: the more unstructured the data collection approach, the more likely that the requirements of reliability and validity will be more difficult to meet. As one moves toward the unstructured end of either continuum, the phenomena to be measured become less directly observable and more abstract; the more abstract the phenomena, the more difficult it is to measure—and, ultimately, to evolve—a highly reliable and valid measurement device.

In the case of the *direct* approach, such questions as "How old are you?" and "What is your age?" (structured) are more likely to elicit reliable and valid answers than such questions as the following: "From time to time medical advances point to practices that should be instituted or avoided for purposes of the general health of the citizens of a given country. Does an individual have the right to accept or ignore these medical findings, or should some regulatory agency step in and regulate their behavior with respect to these health practices?" (unstructured).

As the reader can surmise, the rule of thumb applies even more to the *indirect* question approach, where the techniques in general will be more unreliable. To be specific, the reliability and validity of projective tech-

THE CHECKLIST: STEP THREE

niques and modifications of the classical projective devices (both unstructured) will probably be lower, and more difficult to ascertain, than for a sentence completion test (structured).

MODIFIERS OF ACCURACY EXTENDED

In our examination of data collection our attention has been focused on certain important features of questionnaire or interview guide sheet construction at a comparatively general level. Although the details will not be dealt with in this book, it is essential that the reader be cognizant of the fact that essentially the same perspective can (and should) apply to any smaller portion of the total process of conducting a survey. For example, we could have devoted several chapters (and some writers have devoted whole books) to the topic of *question wording*. Questions should be presented in such a way that they avoid semantic confusion, do not threaten the respondent, or bias his reply. If the question wording is poor, then the reliability and validity of the survey will be affected (either moderately or seriously); and this will operate in addition to, or on top of, the degree to which the survey contains structured or unstructured questions. This last statement can also be made of the *degree of training* that the interviewers have—assuming, of course, a personal interview situation or a telephone survey. The interviewer who is not skillful and well briefed with respect to his specific survey is likely to reduce his chances of obtaining reliable and valid information.

The point is that there are many, many details that can affect the data collection phase adversely, and they all have implications for how adequately a survey is conducted and how much confidence can be placed in the findings eventually reported. All of these factors can serve to modify the accuracy of the data obtained, and constant vigilance is required to minimize their possible adverse effects on the data collection phase of a survey.

9 | Survey research checklist: steps four through seven

AS WAS brought out in our introductory remarks about the survey research checklist (see pages 53–54), some steps would receive comparatively lengthy attention while others would receive only cursory examination. We have completed our examination of those items that we felt should be considered in some detail, as they directly involve the public relations practitioner. Steps four through seven do not, and we shall express only in brief outline what is involved in each of them.

STEP FOUR: TRAINING THE DATA COLLECTION STAFF

The data collection staff, at least in the face-to-face survey category, are the individuals who go out and obtain the interviews required. If we are dealing with probability samples, well-handled surveys will provide interviewers with explicit instructions on how to "find" their interviewees: where to go (within a city); what blocks to cover; how to select the houses within the block; procedures for selecting interviewees within a given housing unit; and so forth.[1] Before the interviewers are sent out, they are normally provided with two types of training: (1) if inexperienced, they will be given an intensive but comprehensive course on interviewing in general; (2) if practiced, specific training for the survey in question; this generally includes a thorough briefing on the interview guide sheet and some practice interviews for purposes of familiarization. Regardless of the nature of the survey, the reputable organization—whether commercial or noncommercial—does its best to thoroughly prepare its interviewers for their assignments, in order to reduce as far as possible the introduction of errors due to interviewer misunderstandings or inadequacies.

[1] We have in mind here a particular variation of probability sampling known as "cluster sampling."

STEP FIVE: PREPARING RAW DATA FOR ANALYSIS

A survey that has not yet been analyzed consists of interview guide sheets filled in by the interviewer and based on the replies obtained by him from the respondent. Although the field director will check the sheets for completeness (questions missed or incorrectly categorized) as the interviews are turned in, the information is in what is known as "raw data" form—its state as received from the interviewer.

Translation of raw data into analyzable form requires a number of steps, some comparatively simple and others much more complex. Easiest is the straightforward tabulation of the various direct questions (age, income, and so forth) that were precoded beforehand and which require only a checkmark or a circle on the part of the interviewer. The open-ended question and the various indirect data collection techniques require more elaborate procedures. Generally these questions elicit answers that range from a few words to hundreds of words, depending upon the question and the purpose of the survey. In order to make sense out of these thousands of words, they must be analyzed and put into response categories that *reflect* the content of the answer in manageable form. This process is known as *content analysis*. Essentially, it is a technique which permits a systematic, objective, and exhaustive analysis and classification of the responses or "thought units" obtained from all of the interviewees in a given survey into response categories that sum up their replies to a certain question or series of questions. This process was alluded to when we looked at some replies to incomplete sentences on hospitals and anesthesia (Chapter 8). The essence of content analysis was suggested in the statement that certain of the replies could be summarized under the headings "fear," "extreme fear," and so forth. These and similar response categories serve to reflect the content of the replies.

After the raw data have been prepared for analysis (by simple tabulation or content analysis), they are generally expressed in terms of tables, which pull together all of the replies to a given question and enable the researcher to make his interpretations. The cases in Part III will show the variety of forms that tables can assume. They all have one characteristic in common, however: each table represents a synthesis of the raw data according to an analysis plan. In this way, some sense can be made out of the information obtained from the interviewee.

STEP SIX: ANALYZING AND INTERPRETING THE DATA: THE SURVEY RESEARCH REPORT

We would like to highlight three aspects in connection with the analysis and interpretation of the survey data which comprises the final report.

First, the reader has undoubtedly heard the old expression that "facts speak for themselves." Although many people have this attitude toward the analysis and interpretation of data—any data—nothing could be more misleading. There is no such thing as a fact standing alone. The data reported have undergone a variety of organization steps: some of the information has been highlighted, and some omitted or relegated to an appendix; certain breakdowns have been imposed; certain tables have been translated into figures or curves with varying coordinates; some of the differences have been subjected to statistical tests, and others have not; and so on. All of this is as it has to be. Sense must be made out of the data obtained, and it must be conveyed in the final report; but it is impossible not to take a partisan view, at least, to *some* extent, in its preparation. The public relations practitioner, for whom the report was presumably prepared, should therefore assume a slightly critical attitude toward the report as he reads it; he should have to be persuaded that the interpretations and generalizations contained therein are defensible; he should be critical of the support offered so as to sharpen his ability to spot any weaknesses there may be in the data. In short, the practitioner should *not* take the attitude that if it is in print it must be true. In a report, the facts do not speak for themselves.

Our second point stresses *the need to quantify* when summarizing any phenomena—regardless of what that phenomena might be. There are two major approaches to this quantification. One is to report findings in terms of percentages, mean values, frequency tallies, and so forth; this is the approach we normally associate with research reports—and normally expect. The other approach quantifies in terms of adjectives and adverbs, not numbers, and the writer resorts to expressions such as, "The majority attending were in favor of the candidate," or, "Virtually no one agreed with the speaker," or, "The bulk of the community supported the company in its stand against the union." These sentences represent numerical summarizations and generalizations without the use of actual numbers. In this second type of approach the writer is often unaware that he has quantified, that he has *had* to do so in order to summarize. In addition, the writer may not even have any data to support his implied statistics. That is, his use of the expression "majority" conveys a conviction rather than reflecting a statistic that has been obtained by means of some sort of research. This point is particularly important because it is probably safe to say that in summarizing situations most ("most" used here without any numerical data to back it up) public relations practitioners fall into the second category of quantification. They must educate themselves, therefore, to be aware of the distinction between the two approaches, to be sensitive to the absolute need to quantify,[2] and, lastly, to be alert to the fact that most report writing (and any other writing, including this book, for that matter) contains both types of quantification. The importance of this perspective to the report writer cannot be overstated.

Our third aspect is summed up in the phrase *sensitivity to generalizations*. We have already noted that one of the major objectives of any research is generalization. Seldom are we interested in the sample studied as an end in itself; rather, we use the findings based on the sample as a means of characterizing the entire population with which we are concerned. Applying this thinking to our final report, we must be continually vigilant regarding the relationship between the generalizations made and the data upon which they are based. The guiding question is, "Are these generalizations permissible?" (that is, appropriate in terms of the sample). If not—if they have gone beyond the data without suitable precautions noted—we must separate these speculations (or intuitive observations) from our bona fide generalizations that are data based.

STEP SEVEN: PLANNING THE PUBLIC RELATIONS PROGRAM BASED ON SURVEY RESEARCH

Obviously, our perspective in this volume has been that there should be an intimate relationship between survey research findings and subsequent public relations programming. If this is not the case, then the practitioner in question cannot justify the expense of the research.[3] However, many practitioners have been misled with regard to what they think the research findings should do for them in their public relations programming; they do not realize that *a research study, survey or otherwise, seldom tells the practitioner what to do*. It is up to him to interpret the findings and relate them to possible public relations action. This point is made in the following:

To illustrate, let us consider again the hypothesis about the relationship between a certain type of childhood training and adult giving. Let us assume that this study was conducted following all of the research steps so far outlined.

---

[2] The skeptical reader is encouraged to examine any report and verify for himself whether it contains quantification in the verbal sense, or if it is numerically oriented, as is the case with most research reports. Secondly, he might try and rewrite a report *without* resorting to either verbal or numerical quantification.

[3] This statement assumes that there is no distinction made between action or inaction in the light of research findings. "Utilization" of the findings may imply *no change* in programming (see Cases 3 and 4 particularly) just as often as it implies implementing a certain program.

Let us also assume that the statistical tools used enabled us to conclude that there was a very significant relationship between childhood training and adult giving. In terms of our hypothesis, those people who as children received training about voluntary organizations are much more likely to give to such organizations as adults than those who did not receive training. This would constitute a major conclusion (or "fact") derived from the research. (It is worth noting once more that it required someone to marshal the data in a certain way to be able to arrive at this "fact." The facts did not "speak for themselves.")

However clear this conclusion may be, *it does not provide the experimenter with the implications of this finding.* Even more to the point, it does not tell our public relations practitioner what to do next. Should we now devise a way of learning who all of the people who have had this particular type of training are, then seek them out at fund-raising time? Conversely, should we avoid spending too much time with people who have not had this training in the interests of efficient fund raising? Should we be thinking about long-range programs that will help develop this type of training in today's children, so that fund raising in the future will be more certain? One could go on and on developing implications of this one finding. In spite of the fact that one small part of the total picture has been clarified—and the value of this, of course, should not be underestimated—the implications are varied and the research does not help us here. We still need decision making based on the best estimates of the experimenter.[4]

Clearly, the public relations practitioner bears the responsibility for intelligent use of the research findings. This is not an easy task. Unfortunately, it often happens that a survey research study is done, only to wind up in the form of a final report in someone's desk drawer, never again to see the light of day. Indeed, the most frequent single factor in the writer's inability to use a particular research study in this casebook was that when the time came to examine *how* the results of the research were used in a public relations program, subsequent action was nonexistent. Furthermore, utilizing research results in planning such programs will probably continue to be a formidable stumbling block in the future. Why? Because buying the research is one thing, and using it intelligently is another. The former requires only money; the latter requires additional education (or reeducation) on the part of the public relations practitioner; and this is always more difficult to engender, particularly among busy practitioners, on the firing line.[5]

[4] Edward J. Robinson, *Communication and Public Relations* (Columbus: Charles E. Merrill Books, Inc., 1966), pp. 575–576.
[5] This generalization need not, and should not, be limited to public relations practitioners. Medical educators, engineering faculties, and law schools, to name but a few other fields, are continually bemoaning the fact that their practitioners are not keeping up with developments in their respective fields and integrating the latest knowledge in solving their applied problems.

Part II: A postscript

With all the material in this section, plus the contents of Part I, the reader is now prepared to examine the cases contained in Part III. He should now have an appreciation of the research process in general and how the various types and methods of research become modified to guide one specific form: survey research. In addition, we have provided a perspective of the public relations practitioner as an applied social and behavioral scientist and have shown how research fits into this perspective. The writer would encourage the reader to study each of the problem situations described in the cases in Part III as deeply and thoroughly as the material permits. Maintain a posture of, "What would I have done in the same situation?" and, "How might I have done things differently and why?" Take each of the steps in the survey research checklist, relate them to the cases, and come to your own conclusions about how well they were handled by the researcher(s) involved. Pay particular attention to the use that the practitioner made of the research findings and spell out in some detail (preferably in written form, as it is so easy to "talk a good game"), what you might have done differently, what you would have done the same, and what you may feel was unwarranted, and why. In short, use the cases as they are normally designed to be used: as a vignette of real life intended to stimulate thinking and discussion of contrary and consonant points of view. Use them to advance your learning in a controlled practice context, where being "wrong" does not constitute a threat to your livelihood but, rather, should hasten you along the road to being a professional.

PART III

Seven cases:

The use of survey research in solving public relations problems

10 | Introduction to the cases

CASE materials have long been regarded as an excellent means of stimulating the student to independent thinking in a context that comes reasonably close to approximating real life. From what one can judge from the comments of others, as well as from the writer's own experience in using the case method in his seminars, this observation would appear to be justified. However, the reader should emphasize in his own mind the word *approximate*. These cases only approximate what actually happened, since, like all cases, they are the end product of a number of distillations, not the least of which is the author's in translating them into their present format.

This filtering is neither good nor bad; perhaps a more appropriate observation would be that it is inevitable. However phrased, this filtering does not necessarily detract from the use of the case method. In many ways it is fortunate that we can ignore how accurately the write-up of a case mirrors what actually happened, assuming the writer did his best to reflect reality *as he saw it*. As a method of instruction designed to stimulate, involve, motivate, frustrate, and otherwise titillate a student to think in a controlled learning situation, cases are remarkably free from the need to be "the truth and nothing but the truth." The question of how accurately a case reflects what happened is much more germane to the relationship between the case writer and those who provided him with the materials and permission to write the case than it is to the student using the cases in his classes.

In addition to this point about approximation, there are several other features of case write-ups that should be commented upon at this juncture. There is the danger that these cases can overstate a view regarding the sort of research now being utilized by public relations practitioners in their day-to-day work. As was mentioned in Chapter 1, this book started out to be an exposition of how the public relations practitioner makes use of social and behavioral science research methods to help solve his public relations problems. As the months passed, it became quite clear that these methods reduced essentially to survey research. The writer was able to obtain satisfactory (we will see a bit later exactly how we define "satisfactory") case materials in only one other methodology. It appeared certain that the overwhelming majority of research conducted to help solve public relations problems *is* survey research. Although we feel quite sure that this observation is an accurate reflection of reality, it should not cause the reader to conclude that no other types of research are being utilized at the present time.

While on the topic of obtaining cases, we should spell out the criteria used to select the ones included in this book. First, we needed information on the nature of the problem situation faced by the practitioner in question, and a statement on how and why he felt that survey research was called for. Second, we required a copy of the full report of the research results as provided by the researcher (either staff man or outsider) for the public relations practitioner. Third, and this was deemed more important, we asked for as much detail as possible with regard to how the research results were utilized by the practitioner in subsequent planning and execution of public relations programs. *It was a revelation to the writer how much of a filter these apparently simple criteria proved to be.* In situation after situation a given problem appeared quite intriguing and was thought to be suitable for the book, only to be rejected because one or more of the above criteria could not be met. Interestingly enough the factor that proved most frequently to be the stumbling block was the *requirement for evidence of subsequent use of the research results in a public relations program.* The guide used to select the final seven cases from the total number that met all the criteria was diversity. An effort was made to include cases that portray the wide range of contexts and problem situations within which present-day public relations practitioners work.

Case write-ups are probably as varied as the people who author them. For this reason, there is no "correct" way of writing a case. One function that is commonly cited (one that provides for considerable latitude, however) is that they should provide the reader with enough information that he can "put himself in the shoes" of some individual associated with the events depicted in the case.

As he developed the case material, the writer essentially took the position of the investigator reporting the results of the survey research; he tried to convey in brief and concise form the findings and their interpretations as the researcher saw them. This applied primarily to those portions of the cases where data (usually in table form) are reported and interpreted. In other sections of the case, the writer from time to time took the liberty to suggest implications, note limitations, cite data or generalizations from other sources, and so on. He also tried to present the data that were selected in enough detail that the reader could come to his own conclusions about the appropriateness of the question and the interpretation of the findings.

INTRODUCTION TO THE CASES 107

Undoubtedly, the writer has occasionally overstated, understated, or included interpretations not found in the original research report. These errors are, of course, not intentional and, in line with the point made earlier on approximation, should not detract from the usefulness of the case studies.

Perhaps the most significant thing to be said, however, is that these cases *should not be interpreted as value judgments by the author on the importance of the research itself.*[1] Like all casebooks, this volume is intended primarily to stimulate thinking and, as such, aid the student and instructor in the classroom, as well as the individual involved in self-study. Obviously, the writer has his own views and criticisms concerning the way in which the research was conducted; his task, however, was to bring together what was done by the public relations practitioner and the research in each case, and *not* to judge or evaluate how it was handled. That role belongs to the reader (and to the instructor, if the book is used in a classroom or seminar). In this connection we subscribe to the point of view expressed by Cabot and Kahl a number of years ago:

> . . . In addition, it might be useful here to answer a persistent query: why not have a list of questions after each case to stimulate discussion? Although such a list is common in many books of source material, we believe it is out of place in this particular context.
>
> In the first place, it tends to remove one of the most stimulating learning experiences of students: the discovery of the multiplicity of questions that can be asked productively about the same "simple" social situation. When a group of people react spontaneously to the material, their diverse points of view come out to the amazement and stimulation of them all. We would not want to inhibit this process by suggesting that particular questions are "right" and all others irrelevant.
>
> In the second place, a list of questions would necessarily grow out of our conceptual prejudices. Yet the cases are free of those prejudices (except for the selection of what is included); they are direct reports in everyday language of events that have actually happened. They are "true" and not illustrations of any particular theories. Students can read them with their own theories in mind. Teachers whose prejudices differ from ours can use the cases in the context of their own conceptual approaches. Questions formed by us after the cases would only stand in the way.
>
> We recognize that teachers who have not yet taught a class by the discussion method, such as we have outlined in Volume I, justifiably feel that questions would help them get started. Yet we have found that once they plunge into this new activity they find strength in its freedom. When students are allowed (perhaps we should say "forced") to ask their own questions about data, they always prove more observant and more original than either they or

---

[1] It should be mentioned here that case materials are usually footnoted with a disclaimer along the following lines: "These cases have been prepared for class discussion rather than to illustrate either effective or ineffective practices and/or policies." Although such a statement does not appear in this book, certainly it applies to our cases as much as it does to any others.

their teachers had suspected. The teachers will find that the discussion of cases, in the way we have suggested, will raise plenty of "good" questions both in their own minds and in those of their students.[2]

To these sentiments we would only add that if, after considering the cases in Part III, the reader does not raise questions such as the following, then the first two parts of the volume have not served their purpose effectively:

1. Has the public relations practitioner stated his problem(s) clearly and provided definitions of terms wherever they are called for?
2. What sort of sample was utilized in the study?
3. Is it appropriate for the study objectives?
4. Were the questions asked in the survey proper pertinent to the problem?
5. What sort of "question mix," or combination of direct and indirect questions, was employed in the survey? Was the mix an appropriate one?
6. What questions should have been asked (regardless of whether direct or indirect) that were not included?
7. Were the analyses of the data defensible? What generalizations were not permitted, and what generalizations not made should have been made?
8. What generalizations, if any, were not in keeping with the sampling utilized in the survey?
9. What steps taken by the public relations practitioner in the light of the research data were defensible? Which were not? What steps should have been taken that were not?
10. What other research approach besides (or in place of) survey research should have been taken in the light of the public relations problem situation?
11. Are data which suggest that your public relations efforts are a "success" more difficult to reflect in subsequent public relations planning than those which suggest that you are in trouble?

A consistent format was employed as far as possible throughout Part III. For example, in each case there is an *introductory* section, which briefly describes the wider public relations context into which the specific case falls. Taken together, these seven passages spell out in some detail the variety of situations within the scope of public relations work and something about the more important tools, techniques, media, and so forth, utilized by practitioners today. Next, each case contains *background information* concerning the company or the association; this should help the reader to examine intelligently the specific problem situation presented. Lastly, in each case there is a section which tries to identify the *actions*

[2] Hugh Cabot and Joseph A. Kahl, *Human Relations: Concepts and Cases in Concrete Social Science* (Cambridge, Mass.: Harvard University Press, 1953), vol. II, Preface.

taken by the public relations practitioner in the light of the research findings. These three sections are common to all seven cases. The other sections vary somewhat as a function of the data obtained, the number of surveys actually involved, whether trend results were available, and so forth.

As their titles indicate, the cases are primarily concerned with the use of survey research in helping to solve public relations problems. There is one exception. Case 7, which describes some of the work done by the National Safety Council (NSC), reports upon the *literature search,* as the research tool. (In this connection, the reader is reminded of the discussion in Chapter 4 of survey research in general and its relationship to other methods of obtaining reliable knowledge, and, in Chapter 5, of the nine basic steps in the research process.) The NSC refinement of this too seldom used basic tool for obtaining reliable knowledge represents a rarely achieved standard of performance that in the opinion of the writer, many more public relations practitioners should try to emulate. By the inclusion of this particular case in our group, a small step is taken toward what was to be the original objective of this book: an exposition of the use of social and behavioral science research to help solve public relations problems. Actually, the writer had to settle for survey research (and the one example of library research).

We hope that in the not too distant future there will be a volume that reflects the fact that a wide variety of research techniques are utilized by public relations practitioners. When such a volume is written, it will mean that a wider range of research techniques *are* indeed being used. This, in turn, will mean that attaining the right-hand end of the problem-solving continuum, spelled out as a necessary goal in Chapter 2, will have become a fact of public relations practice rather than an objective to be striven for.

One other case warrants special mention in this introduction; this is Case 6, which describes the efforts of the American Telephone and Telegraph Company to encourage decentralization of community relations by providing a "survey package" for local telephone company management. When it comes to the application of the survey results, the reader should bear in mind that in this case we are examining the work of *nonprofessionals* in the public relations field. That is, the plans for action based on the survey data were developed by various persons in the local office management who were not public relations practitioners. Any criticism by the reader should therefore be tempered by the realization that the public relations programming was proposed by amateurs.

One final point. In this brief introduction to the cases the reader has undoubtedly become aware of a number of prejudices on the part of the writer; for one, that too few of the research techniques or methodologies of the social and behavioral sciences are being used by public relations practitioners; for another, that the dominance of survey research reflects accurately the state of the art as it exists today in public relations. What might not have been apparent is still another prejudice that should be brought out here: at present, the use of research by public relations practitioners is a "borrowed" phenomena. They have essentially adopted a technique used extensively by advertisers, political scientists, and marketing specialists, to name a few, and this borrowing partly accounts for the difficulties so often encountered by public relations practitioners in using the results of survey research. What is needed is a more extensive *tailoring of existing techniques,* such as survey research, for public relations purposes. In the sense that structured disguised tests and "balloon" tests represent tailor-made modifications of clinical psychology projective techniques for advertising and marketing purposes, public relations practitioners need to experiment with survey research so as to evolve tailor-made modifications for their own purposes. In the other direction, we must encourage *development of new techniques* especially designed for public relations-type problems. Thus, just as special devices were developed for other purposes—such as the Semantic Differential for measuring meaning,[3] the Flesch Formula,[4] the Content Response Code,[5] and the Cloze Procedure[6] for measuring different aspects of printed materials—so, too, must we evolve measurement devices or research tools designed for public relations purposes. There is absolutely nothing wrong with borrowing techniques from other disciplines and applying them whenever possible. However, it is in no way a substitute for developing techniques peculiar to public relations. This is a direction in which the field must move in order to accelerate the progress toward the right-hand end of the problem-solving continuum repeatedly cited as the logical and essential goal of the public relations practitioner.

[3] Charles E. Osgood, George J. Suci, and Percy H. Tannenbaum, *The Measurement of Meaning* (Urbana, Ill.: University of Illinois Press, 1957).

[4] Rudolph Flesch, *How To Test Readability* (New York: Harper & Brothers, 1951).

[5] Roy Carter, "The Content Response Code: A Pre-Testing Procedure," *Journalism Quarterly* (Spring 1955), 147–160.

[6] Wilson L. Taylor, " 'Cloze Procedure,' A New Tool for Measuring Readability," *Journalism Quarterly* (Fall 1953), 415–433.

11 | Case 1

Improving the attitudes of U. S. Air Force personnel toward their host country

CASE OUTLINE

1. Introduction
2. Background information
3. 1960 survey: results of research which uncovered symptoms of public relations problems
   a. interpretations made of the survey data
   b. actions taken by the local information officer
   c. changes made in the base orientation program
4. 1962 Survey results
   a. comparison of 1962 replies to identical questions in the 1960 survey
   b. replies to sample questions included in the 1962 survey only
   c. a summary of the data

INTRODUCTION

In the United States Air Force, the equivalent of the public relations practitioner in civilian life is known as an *information officer*. Like civilian practitioners, information officers function at different levels within the Air Force with varying degrees of responsibility and impact upon problems encountered by their commanding officers. If the information officer is at the squadron level, his commanding officer might be a major or a lieutenant colonel; if he is at the Pentagon, he might report to a general or to the secretary of the Air Force.

The information officer shares another situation with his civilian counterpart: there is wide variation in the degree to which his advice and counsel are sought and followed by his commanding officer. In some instances, he functions on the periphery and is not involved in helping to shape policies and procedures with possible public relations implications. In other contexts, his role is a key one, serving both to anticipate and avoid public relations problems and to "put out the fire," so to speak, when emergency situations arise.

In the case we are about to examine the information officer in question enjoyed a relationship with his commanding officer in which his recommendations and plans were sought, welcomed, and usually followed. As we shall learn, these plans and recommendations proved to be rather extensive and were designed to counteract a surprising negative shift in attitudes by base personnel toward the civilians in the country in which the Air Force base was located.

BACKGROUND INFORMATION

The People-to-People Program was initiated in 1956 by President Eisenhower with the express aim of increasing understanding between Americans and the people of other countries throughout the world. To implement this program, 40 different committees were organized to represent the various major areas of American life. Since service personnel and their dependents are the largest group of official U.S. representatives stationed in foreign lands, they are an important source of influence on our relations with other nations. Negative attitudes of military personnel toward people in other countries are likely to be transmitted to the foreign community and contribute to unfavorable impressions of the United States in general and the Armed Forces in particular.

Because the military plays such an important role in fashioning our relationships with other countries, one of the 40 committees formed was the Armed Services People-to-People Committee. Its overall purpose was to "initiate and conduct a program to give the people of other countries a better understanding of the American way of life and our devotion to freedom." A letter from President Eisenhower directed to Armed Forces personnel summed up this objective as follows:

Dear Fellow Citizen:

As a member of our Armed Forces stationed overseas, you and your dependents are representatives of the American people with the essential mission of building good will for our country.

Service men and women are the largest group of official U.S. personnel stationed in foreign countries. As a result, people form their personal attitudes toward our country and our American way of life to a great extent by what they see and hear about American service personnel and their dependents.

As you serve abroad, the respect you show foreign laws and customs, your courteous regard for other ways of life, and your speech and manner help to mold the reputation of our country. Thus, you represent us all in bringing assurance to the people you meet that the United States is a friendly nation and one dedicated to the search for world peace and to the promotion of the well-being and security of the community of nations.

Sincerely,[1]

In keeping with this mandate, and prompted by a desire to make a positive and measurable contribution to better understanding between Americans and peoples of other countries, the U.S. Air Force conducted a series of exploratory opinion-attitude studies during the period 1958 through 1961. Based on a worldwide random sampling which covered all Air Force bases, stations, and other installations, these surveys were designed to determine the attitudes of Air Force personnel toward the peoples and cultures of countries in which they were stationed.

The probability sample was made up of 10% of all officers and 5% of all airmen and was based on the last two digits of service numbers selected from a table of random numbers. The questions sought responses from officers and airmen who had served overseas for a period of 60 days or more since 1951. The current situation in a given country was determined by analyzing the responses of those actually overseas at the time the questionnaire was administered or who had returned within one year. Data from these surveys were used to identify negative attitudes, distorted stereotypes, and potential community relations problems. The information was then relayed to overseas commands to help eliminate these undesirable conditions wherever they were found to exist.

The following material in this case write-up is a review of actions taken at one overseas base to overcome unfavorable attitudes of USAF service personnel toward their host country (as brought out by a 1960 USAF survey).[2] Also included is a summary of the progress made in correcting the negative situation revealed in the study by means of a systematic public relations program.

The name of the particular country must remain anonymous, but this lack of identity will not detract from our understanding of this case. We can say that Country X is a developing nation. (A survey conducted there by a private international research organization revealed remarkably favorable attitudes toward the United States, and this country is considered one of America's staunchest friends and admirers.) As in other developing countries, there had been an upsurge in nationalism in Country X, but violence against Americans was not one of its manifestations. The country is not even moderately wealthy, but politically it is a democracy, and a reasonably strong one. There was a serious pilferage problem on the Air

---

[1] *Yank,* special issue (1960), p. 2.
[2] In line with security requirements, the source of the information in this chapter may not be identified further. It was communicated to the author in a confederated USAF study carrying the annotation, "A 'scientized' version of the questionnaire and original survey data. . . ."

Force base, but it was no worse than at other bases where attitudes toward the local people were far more favorable.

The data based on service personnel's attitudes toward Country X were brought to the attention of the information officer in that country because the unfavorable attitudes revealed in the 1960 survey were so negative. Indeed, the results came as a shock to those in positions of authority. Compared with other bases, the results were the worst in that area of the world—and almost the most unfavorable anywhere in the world. For example, 66% of the airmen stated that they felt "fairly insecure" or "very insecure" regarding encounters with civil authorities. The figure was twice as high as for the next highest country, and forty percentage points higher than for those countries that might be termed roughly comparable. Under the circumstances, such insecurity appeared almost pathological.

In this case we see how the use of an opinion-attitude survey uncovers symptoms that suggest the existence of certain problems to be solved by the public relations practitioner. Without this survey data the information officer would have probably remained ignorant of the fact that he had problems on his hands. We shall also see in this case two of the main uses of the survey technique: (1) the specific answers to questions contained in the survey will serve as a diagnostic tool that will help the public relations practitioner identify his problems; and (2) the survey data will indicate certain approaches to solving the problems that should prove to be more effective than others that might be taken.

The term *symptoms* was used deliberately because the survey data *do not indicate* what the problems are; rather, they reflect the fact that certain problems do exist. Just as headache, fever, and dizziness are important only to the extent that they signal some bodily malfunction(s), so it is that the negative attitudes of Air Force personnel toward people in the host country, revealed by questions asked in a survey, pointed to malfunctions that existed somewhere within the operation of an Air Force base in an overseas setting.

Let us look at the task of the information officer, armed only with the information that extensive negative attitudes existed. Several important implications could be identified:

1. These negative attitudes were certain to be transmitted to the local community—if they hadn't already been—with a corresponding set of reactions from the townspeople, which would probably make matters worse. Hundreds of local civilians were employed at this particular base, and it was quite possible that their own efficiency would be impaired by their awareness of the negative attitudes held by our airmen and officers. Moreover, these attitudes would quickly become known to the employees' families, friends, and neighbors outside the base. This threatened the long-range and mutual interests of both countries.

THE U.S. AIR FORCE

The danger of communist-inspired insurgency in new and developing nations is in evidence throughout the world. It is reasonable to assume that in some of these countries the average American serviceman plays a more important role by virtue of his presence as a representative of a democracy than by his position as a defender against possible attack. Each serviceman is bound to have an impact in his contacts with the local populace; how he acts toward them is a reflection of how he feels toward them. Whether or not his role is positive, whether he promotes support of the United States and its principles of equality of nations and the dignity of the individual, will depend greatly upon the attitudes he displays.

2. Actual economic loss to the United States might also follow. The cost of sending personnel and their families overseas is high; each capable person who voluntarily extends his tour represents considerable saving in tax dollars. It seems likely, however, that unfavorable attitudes toward the local people might well cause a serviceman to return to the United States upon completion of his normal tour instead of extending it for another year or two—a great expense in terms of transportation costs alone.

3. Lastly, a deterioration in "mission accomplishment" might occur. It was apparent that if experienced persons could be kept at their jobs for one or two extra years, organizations would be able to perform their work more efficiently. In addition, keeping inexperienced replacements at a minimum would lessen any disruptions to the overall mission of the base.

With the above background we are now prepared to examine the highlights of the 1960 survey data.

1960 SURVEY: RESULTS OF RESEARCH WHICH UNCOVERED SYMPTOMS OF PUBLIC RELATIONS PROBLEMS

Let us begin by examining some of the data that alerted the local information officer of Country X to problems that required his attention. Table 11-1 contains some of the key questions in the survey conducted in 1960.[3] We shall discuss the interpretations placed upon them afterwards.

Interpretations made of the survey data

First, one might observe that the attitudes of the airmen and officers toward the people of the country in which they are stationed are generally neutral or leaning a little toward the positive side. For example, in Question 1 the largest percentage of replies were in the "neither good nor bad" category (43% and 38% respectively), and quite a few percentage points away from the next nearest category in either the negative or the positive direction. At the same time, however, the positive direction ("good opin-

[3] We are omitting other questions in the survey, such as those dealing with marital status and reactions to the internal communication program.

Table 11-1. Key questions in the 1960 survey

	Officers	Airmen
1. What is your opinion of the people generally, of the country you serve in?		
Am now overseas or served overseas since 1 Jan 59:*		
a. Very good opinion	7%	11%
b. Good opinion	25	20
c. Neither good nor bad	43	38
d. Bad opinion	16	17
e. Very bad opinion	8	10
f. Don't know	1	4
Served overseas prior to 1959:†		
g. Very good opinion	14	17
h. Good opinion	46	45
i. Neither good nor bad	24	30
j. Bad opinion	11	3
k. Very bad opinion	3	3
l. Don't know	2	2
2. Which of the following best describes the extent of your contact with the people (nationals) in the country you are now serving in?		
Am now overseas or served overseas since 1 Jan 59:		
a. Know such nationals only through usual on-base contact	12%	9%
b. Have not talked to such nationals off the base at all	4	6
c. Have not talked to such nationals off the base to any great extent	12	16
d. Have talked to some extent with business people only off the base	9	5
e. Know some nationals fairly well	37	32
f. Actually know some nationals very well	26	32
Served overseas prior to 1959:		
g. Know such nationals only through usual on-base contact	13	16
h. Have not talked to such nationals off the base at all	3	8
i. Have not talked to such nationals off the base to any great extent	10	17
j. Have talked to some extent with business people only off the base	9	9

*Size of this sample, here and throughout the table: 105 officers and 310 airmen.
†Size of this sample, here and throughout the table: 119 officers and 208 airmen.

Table 11-1 (Continued)

	Officers	Airmen
k. Know some nationals fairly well	37	27
l. Actually know some nationals very well	28	23

3. *In general, what is your view of how the people in the country you are serving in feel toward the people of the U.S.?*

Am now overseas or served overseas since 1 Jan 59:

a. Very good opinion	8%	
b. Good opinion	45	
c. Neither good nor bad	28	
d. Bad opinion	9	
e. Very bad opinion	2	
f. Don't know	8	

Served overseas prior to 1959:

g. Very good opinion	21	
h. Good opinion	53	
i. Neither good nor bad	17	
j. Bad opinion	3	
k. Very bad opinion	3	
l. Don't know	3	

Toward our armed forces personnel stationed in their country?

Am now overseas or served overseas since 1 Jan 59:

a. Very good opinion	5%	6%
b. Good opinion	40	22
c. Neither good nor bad	28	34
d. Bad opinion	16	22
e. Very bad opinion	6	8
f. Don't know	5	8

Served overseas prior to 1959:

g. Very good opinion	13	11
h. Good opinion	49	42
i. Neither good nor bad	26	31
j. Bad opinion	6	8
k. Very bad opinion	3	3
l. Don't know	3	5

Table 11-1 (Continued)

	Officers	Airmen
4. *Do you (or your family) feel secure or insecure regarding encounters with the civil authorities in the overseas country you are now serving in?*		
Am now overseas or served overseas since 1 Jan 59:		
a. Feel completely secure	4%	6%
b. Feel fairly secure	12	13
c. Feel neither secure nor insecure	16	15
d. Feel fairly insecure	30	25
e. Feel very insecure	38	41
Served overseas prior to 1959:		
f. Feel completely secure	10	14
g. Feel fairly secure	32	28
h. Feel neither secure nor insecure	24	28
i. Feel fairly insecure	16	16
j. Feel very insecure	18	14
5. *What is the main problem between the Air Force and the people of the country you are now serving in?*		
Am now overseas or served overseas since 1 Jan 59:		
a. None that I know of, or none of significance	10%	11%
On the basis of 100% of the personnel who say there is a problem:		
b. The language barrier	5	3
c. Lack of off-base recreation	3	6
d. The people just don't like us	1	2
e. The people like us only for our money	26	42
f. High prices for goods, services, recreation	2	3
g. Air Force personnel (military and civilian) don't try to understand the people	12	8
h. Air Force personnel behave badly off base	3	7
i. Aircraft problems (accidents, noise, sonic booms)	1	0
j. Automobile accidents	0	*
k. Lack of information on the people and the customs	9	6
l. People envious of our standard of living	24	11
m. Men resent U.S. military dating their women	0	1
n. People resent the amount of money we have to spend	3	2
o. Don't know	11	9

*Less than 1%.

THE U.S. AIR FORCE

Table 11-1 (Continued)

	Officers	Airmen
Served overseas prior to 1959:		
p. None that I know of, or none of significance	15	24
On the basis of 100% of the personnel who say there is a problem:		
q. The language barrier	12	18
r. Lack of off-base recreation	1	6
s. The people just don't like us	1	1
t. The people like us only for our money	18	18
u. High prices for goods, services, recreation	3	3
v. Air Force personnel (military and civilian) don't try to understand the people	18	15
w. Air force personnel behave badly off base	8	7
x. Aircraft problems (accidents, noise, sonic booms)	0	1
y. Automobile accidents	0	1
z. Lack of information on the people and customs	10	7
aa. People envious of our standard of living	19	2
bb. Men resent U.S. military dating their women	1	2
cc. People resent the amount of money we have to spend	3	5
dd. Don't know	6	14

6. *Do you believe there has been any improvement in the relations between U.S. military personnel and the people of the country you are serving in?*

Am now overseas or served overseas since 1 Jan 59:		
a. Yes, a considerable improvement	7%	11%
b. Yes, a little improvement	16	18
c. No, stayed about the same	23	32
d. No, a little worse	33	17
e. No, considerably worse	9	6
f. Don't know	5	11
g. No opinion	7	5
Served overseas prior to 1959:		
h. Yes, a considerable improvement	10	27
i. Yes, a little improvement	19	22
j. No, stayed about the same	33	26
k. No, a little worse	20	10
l. No, considerably worse	6	1
m. Don't know	9	7
n. No opinion	3	7

Table 11-1 (Continued)

	Officers	Airmen
7. What did your orientation program consist of for your overseas tour?		
Am now overseas or served overseas since 1 Jan 59:		
a. Had none	27%	27%
On the basis of 100% of the personnel who received an orientation:		
b. One-time program on arrival overseas only	61	56
c. Continuous program during overseas duty	13	19
d. Comprehensive program prior to departure only	1	1
e. Comprehensive program prior to departure, *and:*		
continuous program while overseas	5	4
one-time program on arrival overseas	1	4
f. One-time program prior to departure only	7	3
g. One-time program prior to departure, *and:*		
continuous program while overseas	4	5
one-time program on arrival overseas	8	8
Served overseas prior to 1959:		
h. Had none	35	14
On the basis of 100% of the personnel who received an orientation:		
i. One-time program on arrival overseas only	35	37
j. Continuous program during overseas duty	21	23
k. Comprehensive program prior to departure only	10	2
l. Comprehensive program prior to departure, *and*		
continuous program while overseas	4	18
one-time program on arrival overseas	9	3
m. One-time program prior to departure only	6	6
n. One-time program prior to departure, *and:*		
continuous program while overseas	7	5
one-time program on arrival overseas	8	6
8. How adequately did the overseas orientation (people-to-people) program prepare you to serve as an ambassador of good will in the country you serve in?		
Am now overseas or served overseas since 1 Jan 59:		
a. No orientation program, or don't remember receiving one	68%	37%

THE U.S. AIR FORCE

Table 11-1 (Continued)

	Officers	Airmen
On the basis of 100% of the personnel who received an orientation and rated it:		
b. It gave me excellent preparation	12	18
c. It prepared me fairly well	29	46
d. It was OK, but left some vital questions unanswered	24	23
e. It was completely ineffective in preparing me	35	13
Served overseas prior to 1959:		
f. No orientation program, or don't remember receiving one	62	28
On the basis of 100% of the personnel who received an orientation and rated it:		
g. It gave me excellent preparation	9	18
h. It prepared me fairly well	43	54
i. It was OK, but left some vital questions unanswered	25	20
j. It was completely ineffective in preparing me	23	8

ion," "very good opinion") outweighs the negative direction. The same can be said of the data in Question 3, in which the respondents felt that the people had a more favorable than negative attitude toward both the people of the U.S. and the Armed Forces stationed in Country X. It is interesting to note that in both Questions 1 and 3 the attitudes of the airmen and officers appear to be a little worse within the past year (the more recent question group, from 1959 until the date of survey in 1960) than they were among those who served overseas prior to 1959, where they were less neutral and more positive about the people in the host country.

This feeling of neutrality, shading toward the positive end, apparently *does not* extend to what one might call "official contacts" or to the leaders of Country X. In Question 4, a total of 68% of the officers and 66% of the airmen replied that they felt "fairly insecure" or "very insecure" regarding encounters with the civil authorities in Country X. Here too, this feeling has increased markedly within the past year, as only 34% and 30% of officers and airmen who served prior to 1959 responded in the same way. This is a distinct shift toward the negative end of the continuum.

Question 6 also points to the fact that some of the respondents feel that their relations are deteriorating. Among the officers there is a definite trend toward the negative end, with the categories "no, a little worse" and "no, considerably worse" adding up to 42% of the responses; while "yes, a little improvement" and "yes, a considerable improvement" totaled only

23% of the responses. With the airman the positive and negative trends are about equal, with the largest single category being the "neutral" one, "no, stayed about the same." If one views these replies in perspective, however, it is clear that the situation has worsened within the past year. For example, for officers who served prior to 1959, the positive categories outweighed the negative categories (29% versus 26%), representing a complete reversal. The pre-1959 Airmen also felt that improvement was much more in evidence (49%) than was deterioration (11%).

Question 5 concerns the main problems in the relationship between the Air Force personnel and the people of their host country. For the officers serving currently or since January of 1959, the two areas that stand out are the somewhat related items "e" and "l." These officers felt that the people liked them only for their money and that they were envious of the American standard of living. These same two problems stand out for the airmen as well, except that the airmen felt much more emphatic about item "e." One could certainly conclude that the respondents who held these derogatory views could be easily swayed in the negative direction on other matters; that is, if an individual feels another is envious and likes him only for his money, it would not be hard to imagine his other attitudes might become negative without too much difficulty.

As in the case of other questions already considered, the earlier period of service reflects the more positive attitudes. The officers and airmen serving prior to 1959 felt less intense about items "e" and "l" ("t" and "aa") but were more likely to stress two-way problems involving questions of mutual understanding (items "q" and "v" for both officers and airmen).

Question 2 tells us something about the extent of contact between Air Force personnel and the people of Country X. The degree of intimate contact (items "e," "f," "k," and "l") had remained just about the same for the officers (contrasting pre- and post-1959 service) and has definitely increased for the airmen. The same generalization holds true for the other categories of contact. Consequently, where the pattern is essentially the same, any differences in attitudes before and after 1959 cannot be readily attributed to changes in the extent and type of contact with individuals of Country X.

Questions 7 and 8 touched upon the orientation programs conducted for overseas personnel. From the replies obtained, it appears that these programs were not consistently held, or that they were of such minor consequence that they were forgotten by the respondent. Question 7 refers to the general orientation for an overseas tour of duty; Question 8 deals with the special orientation program (People-to-People Program) which emphasized the role of the individual serviceman as an ambassador of his country abroad. There was a fair proportion of individuals who had not received either type of orientation. This was particularly true of the People-to-People Program; the respondents in the pre-1959 group, however, undoubtedly include individuals whose tour of duty occurred before the People-to-People Program was instituted. In general, one can conclude that the orientation programs were not extensive, often consisting of a one-time program upon arrival at the overseas base. (Question 7, item "b," and Question 8, item "a"). In the case of the People-to-People Program, its value or impact upon the individual was clearly open to question. For those serving after January 1, 1959, the negative replies (items "d" and "e") totaled 59%; for the pre-1959 individuals, these same questions (items "i" and "j") totaled 48%. Once again, the picture is more flattering for those who served before 1959.

In summary, the data from these eight questions, obtained via the 1960 survey, indicated that the attitudes of the officers and airmen toward their host country, as well as their preparation for their overseas duty, left much to be desired. The way the servicemen feel toward Country X, generally neutral or negative, is continuing to deteriorate, and the prospect for the future, unless something is done, is none too bright.

Actions taken by the local information officer

On the basis of the information collected, it was clear that the base information officer had some reason for concern. Some of the replies to individual questions, the patterns of replies to all the questions as a whole, and the comparisons of pre-1959 respondents with post-1959 respondents suggested that considerable misunderstanding and fear existed among the officers and airmen stationed in Country X.

A reasonable starting point was to generate some hypotheses about the causes of the attitudes that were reflected in the answers. One factor that stood out as curious was that the conditions in Country X were more favorable than in many other locations in the world. For one thing, the base enjoyed an advantage with respect to communication: the people of Country X could speak our language—a great many of them excellently, and most of them well enough to carry on a reasonable conversation. The information officer speculated along the following lines:

Could it be that communication was one of our problems? Did we, unconsciously, feel that since they spoke the same language, they thought the same way, saw things as we saw them? Are we inclined to be more "understanding" of those who speak differently? Were we comparing them—unfairly—with ourselves? Did we just not understand, therefore, why they were different? Did we have a language barrier in reverse?

This introspection led the information officer to seek out "causes" that were close to home. In fact, he decided to examine the orientation program for newly arrived personnel in Country X (the replies to Questions 7 and 8 had already revealed that the program left something to be desired in terms of both completeness and efficacy). First of all, he found that there was no part of the program devoted to community relations—no phase that paid attention to the problems in peoples from differing cultures living together.

Errors in omission were only part of the story. As he began to review the briefings or orientations that were held, the information officer discovered that many of the presentations were stressing negative aspects almost exclusively. The briefers from the Air Police, the surgeon's office, and the legal office, among others, emphasized such topics as health and sanitation conditions off base, black marketing, accidents, crimes, and other similar, uncommon situations. The information officer had reason to believe that newly arrived personnel were leaving the meetings rather frightened; many were heard to remark that they would never go off base.

After discovering these features of the orientation program, the information officer was fairly confident that he had put his finger on one of the factors that was helping to induce negative attitudes on the part of the base personnel.[4]

The orientation program could not be the whole story. However, the information officer decided to focus his efforts upon the total orientation program to see if this would bring about any noticeable change in the attitudes toward the people of Country X. His decision to do this rested on several factors: first, the base orientation program was his responsibility to coordinate, and his position of control made it a relatively easy matter for him to induce changes in the character of the program; second, there seemed to be a logical connection between the negatively oriented briefings and the survey data; consequently, it appeared reasonable to expect that a change in the program should have a noticeable (as measured through subsequent survey data) effect upon the attitudes of the base personnel; finally, the information officer thought it wiser to institute only one course of action to modify these attitudes, so that some reasonable connection could be made between his efforts and their outcome. If modification were made in more than one area, there could be no relating of cause with result.[5]

[4] Obviously, the information officer could not be certain that his conclusions were correct in this instance. For example, it would be reasonable to assume that the negative themes in the orientation programs were probably being duplicated at other bases. In addition, unless one took special pains to place negative topics in a positive or constructive light, it would be natural for a presentation from the surgeon's office or the Air Police to appear worrisome. Why, therefore, did these negatively orientated presentations have a greater impact on the base personnel in Country X than in other countries?

[5] Even with the precaution of instituting only one change, the information officer cannot be certain that any shift in attitudes would be the direct result of his change in the orientation program. He would need a different set of operating conditions to make a more certain cause and effect statement. However, in view of the circumstances, which, incidentally, are typical of the situations that public relations practitioners find themselves in, the information officer's plan is a reasonably good substitute for a more completely controlled experimental situation.

Changes made in the base orientation program

In modifying the orientation program on the base, the starting point was a meeting called by the base commander (briefed, guided, and coordinated, of course, by the information officer), for all persons participating in the briefing of new personnel. At this meeting the assumed relationship between the orientation program and negative attitudes toward Country X was presented and discussed. As a result of the meeting, the base commander ordered a complete revision of briefings. He conceded that it was obviously essential to point out possible problems, but that these problems should be placed in their proper perspective. The commander also informed those attending the meeting that he would personally review each of the briefings to confirm that the changes in orientation were carried out as ordered.

With this general briefing session constituting the impetus for change, a number of other modifications were instituted. First, an effort was made to render the orientation more pleasant by having, for example, the base Air Force band play before the briefings. In the same vein, wives of the airmen and officers were strongly encouraged to attend these briefings, since it was felt that often their only source of information about their host country was their husbands.

Perhaps the most notable change was the addition of a special "community relations" briefing, which stressed that community relations was, in reality, human relations. The presentation examined some of the problems that arise in communicating with others. It analyzed in some detail the concept of "culture shock," a term used to embrace many of the rather frightening and debilitating effects that living in a completely different culture can have upon an individual—such as inducing suspiciousness, withdrawal, and even depression. Among topics touched upon in the presentation was the possibility that fundamental cultural differences existing between the people of Country X and the Americans stationed there might be masked by the very fact that so many people in Country X spoke English. It was pointed out that the same language does not imply the same values and attitudes. The listeners were encouraged to leave the base more often and to extend themselves to make friends in Country X; they were reminded that they were usually welcome to attend many off-base functions—for example, school graduation exercises—and they were urged to avail themselves of these opportunities to mix with people.

Those who attended the briefings were encouraged to read the local newspapers, particularly the feature columns and editorials. They were told that although they might find some of the articles unfairly critical of the United States or the base, it was important to be aware of the local viewpoint in order to recognize the problems that existed between the two cultures. In addition, our people would thereby be in a better position to contribute to the solving of these problems in their many contacts with the local people.

Wives were encouraged to take part in off-base activities through their various school and church organizations and wives' groups; examples were given of the work already being accomplished by some of them.

After the orientation program, lists of recommended books about the country were distributed. In order to emphasize the community relations concept, the base newspaper was employed to further the positive approach sounded in the orientation program. Articles were published about local civilian employees and their contribution to the functioning of the base. The military's radio-television station carried spot announcements about the country in general and of the local area immediately adjacent to the base. Films about the country's culture and history were ordered from the United States Information Service. Tours of the base by local groups were encouraged and expanded considerably. A sign was placed at the exit from the base reminding those leaving to be a good neighbor. Lastly, commanders at all levels of authority were encouraged to discuss community relations at their monthly meetings with their personnel, and various materials were provided for their use to further the success of these meetings.

One last point about the public relations program as a whole; it was not started with a big fanfare and an attempt to make it a let's-everybody-get-together-and-get-behind-this" sort of project. Rather, it represented a fundamental change in the general approach to the whole process of orientation, coupled with a sustained move toward the idea of community relations as a day-to-day process of concern to everyone. Probably very few people were conscious of things being different; it was a quiet, systematic effort to get them thinking positively about their new neighbors, even though the relationship was to be temporary.

1962 SURVEY RESULTS

The revised orientation program was in effect by the summer of 1961. After a year of operation, a follow-up survey was conducted, based on a random sample of 338 individuals (245 airmen and 93 officers) at the same Air Force base. The purpose of the follow-up was to determine whether the attitudes of the base personnel toward the host country had improved, worsened, or remained about the same. It also served to measure the effectiveness of the revised orientation program in modifying the attitudes of the Air Force personnel.

We shall now examine the 1962 replies to the same questions that were asked in the 1960 survey. In each instance a comparison of the two results will give us some feeling for any change in attitudes and an idea of how well the modied orientation program served its purpose. Following

THE U.S. AIR FORCE 127

this analysis, we shall examine a few questions asked only in the 1962 survey; they, too, tell us something about the impact of the revised program. The information officer asked these additional questions because of the opportunity he now had to focus on the reactions of the respondents to his refashioned orientation program.

Comparison of 1962 replies to identical questions in the 1960 survey

The replies to Question 1 in the 1962 survey are as follows:

	Officers	Airmen
1. What is your opinion of the people generally of the country you serve in?		
a. Very good opinion	6%	13%
b. Good opinion	35	32
c. Neither good nor bad	33	37
d. Bad opinion	20	7
e. Very bad opinion	4	4
f. Don't know	2	7

A comparison of the above with the data obtained to Question 1 in 1960 suggests that the general opinion of the Air Force personnel with respect to the people of Country X has improved. The following summary of the extremes and the midpoint of the response categories supports this interpretation:[6]

	1960	1962
"Very good" and "good"	31%	45%
"Very bad" and "bad"	27	11
"Neither good nor bad" and "don't know"	42	44

The positive responses have increased while the negative responses have decreased. In view of the fact that the "neither" and "don't know" category has remained essentially unchanged, it is clear that the shift in opinion has been from bad to good. The reader will recall that the overall

---

[6] These abstracted comparisons are of the airmen only. The same interpretation would be made of the changes in the officers' responses. The 1960 data in this and all subsequent comparisons are taken from the first question group ("Am now overseas or served overseas since 1 Jan. 59").

trend of the data in Question 1 in the 1960 survey was also in the positive direction, with the largest single category "neither good nor bad." The 1962 data reveal that this positive trend is even more marked than before.

What has happened with respect to Question 3? The data are tallied below:

	Officers	Airmen
3. *In general, what is your view of how the people in the country you are serving in feel—*		
Toward the people of the U.S.?		
a. Very good opinion	7%	7%
b. Good opinion	42	33
c. Neither good nor bad	33	34
d. Bad opinion	9	9
e. Very bad opinion	4	4
f. Don't know	5	13
Toward our armed forces personnel stationed in their country?		
a. Very good opinion	7	6
b. Good opinion	36	27
c. Neither good nor bad	38	33
d. Bad opinion	7	16
e. Very bad opinion	3	6
f. Don't know	9	12

Utilizing the same technique as in Question 1, the following summary comparison is obtained:[7]

	1960	1962
Toward the people of the U.S.?		
"Very good" and "good"	53	49
"Very bad" and "bad"	11	13
"Neither good nor bad" and "don't know"	36	38
Toward our armed forces personnel stationed in their country?		
"Very good" and "good"	45	43
"Very bad" and "bad"	22	10
"Neither good nor bad" and "don't know"	33	47

[7] This comparison is between officers, as there were no data obtained from airmen on this question in the 1960 survey.

THE U.S. AIR FORCE

On the basis of these comparisons, the generalizations made in 1960 would appear to still hold for the 1962 survey—the trend is still toward the positive rather than the negative end of the choice categories. In fact, the data from the two surveys are essentially unchanged; that is, the percentages have shifted only two to four percentage points. The only exception to this generalization is in the "very bad" and "bad" category of the "toward our Armed Forces personnel" part of the question. Here the reduction in the negative replies is greater—twelve percentage points.

In our analysis of the 1960 data we distinguished between official contacts and those with the rank and file citizen of Country X. Implicit in this distinction was the fact that Questions 1 and 3 were reflecting the views of American servicemen with respect to the nonofficial citizens. Question 4, however, asked directly about contacts with the civil authorities and the servicemen's views with respect to these contacts. The data obtained from this question in the 1962 survey are as follows:

	Officers	*Airmen*
4. *Do you (or your family) feel secure regarding encounters with the civil authorities in the overseas country you are now serving in?*		
a. Feel completely secure	5%	12%
b. Feel fairly secure	20	19
c. Feel neither secure nor insecure	32	34
d. Feel fairly insecure	21	13
e. Feel very insecure	21	22

The comparisons of the 1960 and 1962 data are summarized in the table below:[8]

	Officers	*Airmen*
"Feel completely secure" and "feel fairly secure"	16%	26%
"Feel fairly insecure" and "feel very insecure"	68	42
"Feel neither secure nor insecure"	16	32

Our comparison table reveals that the official contacts have taken on a considerably more favorable outlook, with a ten percentage points in-

[8] These comparisons are of the officers in the sample surveyed; the generalizations would be equally applicable to the data obtained from the airmen.

crease in that direction and a reduction in the negative category of 26 percentage points; the neutral category ("neither secure nor insecure") has increased 17 percentage points.

In the 1960 survey, we saw in Question 6 a measure of whether the respondents thought their own relationships with the people of Country X were improving or getting worse. Their conclusion was that relations were deteriorating. In addition, when the pre-1959 respondents were compared with the post-1959 group, it appeared that the relationships had apparently worsened within the past year.

What does Question 6 tell us in 1962? The responses are listed below; a comparison of views of both officers and airmen follows:[9]

	Officers	Airmen
6. Do you believe there has been any improvement in the relations between U.S. military personnel and the people of the country you are serving in?		
a. Yes, a considerable improvement	5%	8%
b. Yes, a little improvement	10	21
c. No, stayed about the same	39	29
d. No, a little worse	18	13
e. No, considerably worse	5	2
f. Don't know	11	16
g. No opinion	12	11

	Officers 1960	Officers 1962	Airmen 1960	Airmen 1962
"Considerable improvement" and "little improvement"	23%	15%	29%	29%
"A little worse" and "considerably worse"	42	23	23	15
"About the same"	23	39	32	29

Taking the officers first, the comparison data suggest that an improvement was noted by these respondents; the shift toward the negative direction has apparently been stemmed (reduced from 42% to 23%). The improvement picture is not consistent with this, however, in that the "considerable improvement" and "little improvement" category decreased

[9] The percentages for each year in the comparison table do not total 100%, as the "don't know" and "no opinion" categories were not included.

THE U.S. AIR FORCE 131

rather than increased. The respondents apparently do not think that things are continuing to deteriorate; but, at the same time, they are not saying that the improvement is as marked as it could be. Essentially the same interpretation can be made of the airmen's responses, with the additional observation that a higher proportion of the airmen feel that things are improving (29% versus 15%).

Question 5 asked the respondents what they thought was the main problem existing in the relationships between the Air Force and the people of Country X. The 1962 data on this question follow:

	Officers	Airmen
5. What is the main problem between the Air Force and the people of the country you are now serving in?		
a. None that I know of, or none of significance	14%	10%
On the basis of 100% of the personnel who say there is a problem:		
b. The language barrier	7	8
c. Lack of off-base recreation	*	3
d. The people just don't like us	1	1
e. The people like us only for our money	19	21
f. High prices for goods, services, recreation	1	*
g. Air Force personnel (military and civilian) don't try to understand the people	9	22
h. Air Force personnel behave badly off base	4	7
i. Aircraft problems (accidents, noise, sonic booms)	1	11
j. Automobile accidents	*	*
k. Lack of information on the people and customs	13	12
l. People envious of our standard of living	20	6
m. Men resent U.S. military dating their women	*	*
n. People resent the amount of money we have to spend	7	2
o. Don't know	16	16

*Less than 1%.

If certain combinations of the categories in Question 5 are made, there is a reasonably strong suggestion of a shift away from citing problems that tend to blame the people of Country X and a move toward looking to ourselves as the source of some of the difficulties.

Category 1 stresses the view that the problems are all due to the materialistic orientation of the people and to their envy and resentment of

	Officers		Airmen	
	1960	1962	1960	1962
1. "The people like us only for our money," "They are envious of our standard of living," and "They resent the amount of money we have to spend"	53%	46%	55%	29%
2. "Air Force personnel (military and civilian) don't try to understand the people" and "Lack of information on the people and customs"	21	22	14	34
3. "Lack of off-base recreation" and "High prices for goods, services, recreation"	5	1	9	3

our standard of living and the amount of money at our disposal. In this grouping there is a drop of seven percentage points among the officers and 26 points among the airmen. Category 2, on the other hand, places the blame directly upon ourselves for our problems with the people of Country X. Here the officers remain practically unchanged (21% versus 22%), while the airmen show another marked shift—from 14% to 34%, or 20 percentage points. Category 3 reveals a shift away from blaming the lack of facilities and the general cost of living within the host country. Once again, the airmen change more, but this time the officers are almost equal in terms of overall percentage point shift.

Although the groupings considered above tend to support the contention that base personnel are becoming more introspective in their views about the causes of problems, there is a difference in the degree of shift of the officers and airmen. If we can consider these modifications as reflecting the impact of the revised orientation program, we can logically conclude that the impact has been greater on the airmen than on the officers. This raises some interesting questions.

When we discussed Question 2 of the 1960 survey, which reflected the degree of contact between Air Force personnel and the people of Country X, we concluded that any changes in attitudes from pre-1959 to post-1959 that showed up in the survey were not due to the degree of intimate contact (items "e," "f," "k," and "l") with the local people. Consequently, we concluded that any changes in attitudes noted in Questions 4, 5, and 6 in this period could not be attributed to differences in the extent and type of contact between Air Force personnel and the people of Country X.

What about the period between 1960 and 1962 after the revised orientation program? The 1962 data are listed below, with 1960 figures included to make comparisons easier for the reader.

THE U.S. AIR FORCE

	Officers		Airmen	
	1960	1962	1960	1962
2. Which of the following best describes the extent of your contact with the people (nationals) in the country you are now serving in?				
a. Know such nationals only through the usual on-base contacts	12%	14%	9%	12%
b. Have not talked to such nationals off the base at all	4	1	6	2
c. Have not talked to such nationals off the base to any great extent	12	20	16	10
d. Have talked to some extent with business people only off the base	9	16	5	12
e. Know some nationals fairly well	37	33	32	34
f. Actually know some nationals very well	26	16	32	30

We can see that from 1960 to 1962 some changes have taken place. The most noticeable is the sharp drop that occurred among the officers in categories "e" and "f," which represent the degree of intimate contact between the two groups and the people of Country X. With the two categories combined, the decrease is from 63% to 49%. The airmen, by contrast, remain exactly the same (64% and 64%). The other categories can be interpreted in both a positive and negative light if one views on-base contacts and business contacts as less desirable than those with persons outside of business or routine situations. Examining categories "a" through "d" with this in mind, one would conclude that in the less intimate contacts there is no clear-cut distinction between the officers and airmen. Consequently, the main difference between the two groups lies in the marked downward trend of the intimate contacts made by the officers. One is tempted to speculate and relate these data with the data obtained from Question 5, and come to the conclusion that not only have the officers been "reached" less by the orientation program, as reflected by their less marked "introspective" tendencies, but at the same time they have been less inclined to move out and get to know the people of Country X on a person-to-person basis.

Questions 7 and 8 in the 1960 survey concerned the orientation programs held for Air Force personnel going overseas. Question 7 asked about the predeparture orientation in the United States while Question 8 focuses upon the People-to-People Program held at the various Air Force installations overseas. We will not make comparisons regarding Question 7, as the information officer's revised orientation program had no relevance to the predeparture program in the United States.

With respect to Question 8, the data are reported in a slightly different fashion than was done in the 1960 survey. The reason for this is that care had to be taken to pull out those individuals who had been in Country X less than one year, and from this group use those who had received only one orientation (on arrival overseas). In this way a fair comparison could be made of the two orientation programs.[10] The following data were obtained:

	Before Changes Were Made (1960 Survey)	After Changes Were Made (1962 Survey)
8. How adequately did the overseas orientation (people-to-people) program prepare you to serve as an ambassador of good will in the country you serve in?		
Favorable (items "b" and "c")	47%	75%
Unfavorable (item "e")	22	5
Other (item "d")	31	20

Obviously, on the basis of these data, one must conclude that the officers and airmen modified their attitudes in favor of the orientation program. The number of both favorable and unfavorable replies changed sharply. Likewise, the "other" category ("It was OK, but left some vital questions unanswered.") was reduced substantially.

Replies to sample questions included in the 1962 survey only

The beginning of this section concentrated on a comparison of replies to the same eight questions asked Air Force personnel in the 1960 and 1962 surveys. Some additional questions were asked by the information officer in order to obtain further information about the effectiveness of his revised orientation program. To complete this section we shall examine two of these so that the reader can get a more complete feeling for the sort of data obtained in the 1962 survey.

---

[10] This procedure reduced the size of the sample considerably—from 338, used for the analysis of the other questions in the 1962 survey, to 108 responses in this particular question. For this reason the replies of officers and airmen are combined; the comparison would be less reliable if the two groups were treated separately.

THE U.S. AIR FORCE

	Officers	Airmen
9. Approximately how many times have you visited neighboring cities and communities (other than bars and restaurants) in the past four months (or since you've been here, if less than four months)?		
a. Not at all	4%	9%
b. 1–2 times	24	25
c. 3–8 times	42	27
d. Over 8 times	30	38
10. In reference to helpfulness and friendliness, in general how would you classify most Country X people whom you come in contact with?		
a. Almost all try to be very helpful and friendly	24%	26%
b. Usually helpful and friendly	47	43
c. Not particularly helpful and friendly, but not unfriendly	25	23
d. Cool and somewhat unfriendly	4	6
e. Very unfriendly	*	2

*Less than 1%.

From the responses to these two additional questions, it is clear that great progress was made in the right direction—the direction advocated by the orientation program. In Question 9 there is a fairly strong trend toward an interest in visiting cities and communities. In addition to contributing to a better understanding of the people of Country X, it also increases the probability that more friendships will be made and more opportunities will take place for a mutual exchange of views. This is, of course, consistent with the objectives of the revised orientation program, particularly that portion involving community relations.

Question 10 gets at the attitudes of the base personnel toward the people of Country X in a slightly different manner than did Question 1. Once again, the data are in the desired direction—the greatest proportion of replies are positive (categories "a" and "b"), and the percentage of replies in the negative categories ("d" and "e") is quite small.

A summary of the data

One simple statement can be made about the data obtained from the eight questions repeated in the 1962 survey; the revised orientation program has evidently had the desired impact upon the attitudes of the base personnel toward the people of Country X. This is evidenced by a reduction in their fears concerning contacts with officials of Country X (Question 4), and by an increase in positive attitudes toward the people (Questions 1 and 3). Furthermore, there is some indication that the base personnel are more introspective with respect to identifying the sources of problems between themselves and the people (Question 5).

On the other hand, one cannot say that no more work needs to be done regarding the orientation program. There is some evidence to support the contention that the revised community relations program was more successful with respect to airmen than officers (Questions 2 and 6), and that some of its impact was more a matter of stopping the trend in the direction of negative attitudes than inducing an increase in positive attitudes.

One final point should be repeated—one that was made earlier in this presentation; we cannot be certain that the improvement or changes noted in the replies to the eight comparison questions are due to the revised community relations program alone. It would appear to be a fairly safe assumption, however, as a careful review was made of all other events that occurred during the same period and the conclusion was that most other activities were "normal" or "as usual." That is, no obvious conditions existed that would cause one to attribute the changes to them rather than to the revised community relations program.[11] It should be pointed out that the information officer involved in this whole study was very much aware of the fact that it was possible that events other than the revised program could have brought about the changes. In concluding his own report on this study, he writes:

> Whatever their cause, the previous attitudes had apparently been transmitted from person to person without relation to the actual "community relations" conditions. What seems most significant, the improvement in attitudes came from within. The community hadn't changed; the base had.

[11] An exception to this was the fact that several months prior to the 1960 survey some efforts had been made by commanders to improve their community relations. For example, in the latter part of 1959 the base had held its first open house, and a base-community council had been formed. To what extent these moves had any effect on creating the right type of climate for the improvements noted in the 1962 survey (after the revised community relations package had been in operation for a year), is anybody's guess.

12 | Case 2

Assessing the effectiveness of a speech reprint program upon certain features of the United States Steel Corporation's corporate image

CASE OUTLINE

1. Introduction
2. Background information
3. Results of the survey research conducted
    a. making use of previous research work
    b. stage one
    c. stage two
    d. some highlights of the data obtained in stage two
    e. a summary of the data
4. Public relations program based on research findings

INTRODUCTION

One of the most common portions of the overall public relations programming of most large corporations is the making of speeches at both the corporate and lower levels of the management hierarchy. The impetus for this speech making has two main sources: on the one hand, there is considerable demand for speeches to be given at countless numbers of conventions, meetings, conferences, and social affairs that take place each year in our country and elsewhere (this is particularly true of large corporations, whose leaders are often nationally and internationally known; as a result, company officials are constantly offered ready-made opportunities to express their opinions in public); the second impetus stems from the fact that most public relations practitioners do not sit back and wait for these opportunities to present themselves. The speech making capabilities of the larger companies are usually highly organized. For example, management speakers' bureaus take care of details such as coordinating requests for speakers, making the availability of speakers known, developing standard, or "canned," speeches, as well as assisting or entirely writing specialized presentations, training and coaching the speakers themselves, preparing personal descriptions or vitae, and arranging for the potential follow-up visibility that speech making can offer.

It is the follow-up of a speech that is our main interest in this case. In order to obtain the widest possible audience and greatest impact from a speech—especially one given by a well-known and highly placed officer of a company—many publicity steps are taken prior to the speech itself. Copies of the prepared text are made available to the press; news releases are sent along with a glossy photograph of the speaker, noting the date and time of the speech; coverage of the speech by radio and television is arranged for; in short, every conceivable step is taken to acquaint more people with the speech than were in the audience at the time that it was given.

One of the frequently used means of widening the audience reached is to reprint the speech in comparatively inexpensive pamphlet form and mail it to a selected list of influential people. Most public relations practitioners feel that speech reprints are an important segment of their overall public relations programming. They argue that this is one of the few—if not the only—means of transmitting a communication that permits the speaker to thoroughly and systematically examine a problem area from whatever points of view he chooses. In this way, complex and sensitive issues which are of vital importance to the company (or any other type of organization in question) can be aired and argued from the perspective of the company. A few years ago, Stuart G. Tipton, President of the Air Transport Association, gave a speech entitled, *Shackles on American Air Power—The Air Traffic Control System.* Following this presentation, 12,000 reprints of the speech were sent to such groups as aviation writers, leading magazines, members of the Airport Operators Council, as well as to a large number of government officials involved in establishing policies that affect the many companies engaged in air transport.[1] Of the 12,000, those individuals who read his speech presumably know more about the position of Mr. Tipton and the Air Transport Association with respect to air traffic control systems.[2]

---

[1] Lawrence S. Jeppson, "Speaking Programs," in Howard Stephenson, ed., *Handbook of Public Relations* (New York: McGraw-Hill Book Company, Inc., 1960), pp. 284–285.

[2] An illustration of how widespread a secondary audience can be was the condensation of a talk by Roger Blough, entitled, "Unprofitable Puzzlement," published in the September, 1961, *Reader's Digest.* A few weeks after the condensation was printed, the editors reported that they had received over 400,000 requests for reprints, and the letters had not stopped coming in yet! In fact, 392,250 reprints were distributed in 1966, and 564,000 in 1967. Clearly, the potential "spread of effect" of one talk, under the proper circumstances, can be enormous.

THE U.S. STEEL CORPORATION

BACKGROUND INFORMATION

The practitioner responsible for the public relations programming at the United States Steel Corporation subscribed to the point of view outlined above, particularly with regard to top company officials. The chronology behind the development of their present speech reprint program is as follows: prior to 1950, U.S. Steel officials made occasional speeches, and reprints were prepared to meet the limited demands of the organizations before which the talks were given. Enough extra copies were made to satisfy occasional requests that came to the public relations department and to circulate internally to members of management. As a medium of communication, the speech was at that time a minor aspect of U.S. Steel's public relations program, and it probably had no perceptible effect on attitudes outside the immediate audience to which it was presented.

In 1950 something happened to change the status quo of speech making. A flurry of Congressional investigations had been absorbing the time and energies of corporation officials, and it was apparent that Benjamin F. Fairless, President of U.S. Steel, and other company executives were to be summoned before still other Congressional committees with special axes to grind.

Mr. Fairless was scheduled to speak before the Baltimore Association of Commerce in April, only a week before U.S. Steel officials were to start testifying at hearings conducted by the House Subcommittee on the Study of Monopoly Power, under the chairmanship of Congressman Emanuel Celler. Mr. Fairless knew that the investigation would be a critical test for U.S. Steel and could possibly even force the dissolution of the corporation. Moreover, he felt that American business had been too long on the defensive, engaged in rearguard action that could not prevent the ultimate destruction of the free enterprise system. He decided to come out fighting in his Baltimore talk.

Entitled *Detour Ahead,* the speech was a ringing endorsement of the role of the large corporation in American life. Its effect upon the Baltimore audience was electric, and it was clear that U.S. Steel had in its hands a potentially powerful public relations instrument. Reprints of the full text of *Detour Ahead* were made and sent to a list of nearly 350,000 thought leaders, all members of Congress, and other government officials.

Within days, literally thousands of letters began to pour into the public relations department, overwhelmingly acclaiming Mr. Fairless as a champion of American industrial freedom. Almost without exception, writers asked for additional copies of the speech for friends and associates. When things finally settled down, some 1,276,000 copies had been distributed. Mr. Fairless was deluged with invitations to address other companies, and all the top executives of U.S. Steel shared in meeting this organizational responsibility and opportunity.

With this turn of events, speech making and the subsequent distribution of reprints became a major part of the overall public relations activities at U.S. Steel. Table 12-1 summarizes the number of speech reprints distributed over the past 16 years. From these figures it is obvious that the reprint program became a sizable undertaking at U.S. Steel, one that demanded considerable time, creativity, and effort.[3]

Table 12-1. U.S. Steel Corporation speech reprint distribution program

Year	Number of copies
1950	4,031,000*
1951	9,418,700
1952	2,771,663
1953	2,445,900
1954	2,340,274
1955	653,482
1956	1,856,638
1957	3,659,686
1958	1,767,137
1959	565,446
1960	799,047
1961	2,408,441
1962	474,415
1963	290,297
1964	448,845
1965	415,401
1966	?
1967	?

*Includes distribution of 1,276,000 copies of *Detour Ahead*.

Source: Communications to the author from the public relations staff at U.S. Steel.

[3] The gradual reduction in the total number of reprints distributed (from a high point of 9,418,700 copies in 1951), should not be interpreted as a lessening of emphasis or interest in the speech reprint program at U.S. Steel. Rather, it reflects a change in the method of handling the distribution. An increasing number of letters began to arrive from recipients who pointed out that they didn't have time to read all the reprints; they found themselves setting the speeches aside to be read later, with the result that the reprints accumulated to the point where they finally had to be discarded. Realizing that by overdoing the mailings they risk losing some of their audience, the public relations department took steps to correct the situation. Essentially, this consisted of a careful review of the mailing lists. By aiming reprints at

THE U.S. STEEL CORPORATION

By the late 1950's, it was apparent to many members of management in key U.S. Steel communities that they could use the speaker's rostrum as an effective public relations tool at the local level by accepting the speaking invitations brought on at least partly by the success of the speech reprint program.

There was a stumbling block, however; it was necessary that speaking invitations come far enough in advance to allow sufficient time to prepare a speech and clear it for conformity with corporate policy and legal soundness. Although invitations to top executives usually came in plenty of time, this was not always the case with executives at the plant community level, whose invitations to speak were often extended so belatedly that there was little or no time to prepare adequately for the occasion. As a result, opportunities to speak were sometimes missed.

In 1957, it was proposed that a *Speech Library* be created by collecting major speeches that had been delivered by the corporation's executives, and revising and adapting them for presentation to local audiences in plant cities and other communities where U.S. Steel people were asked to speak. This entailed casting these speeches, already screened for legal and policy considerations, into language better suited to the needs of various community groups, such as service and businessmen's clubs and educational organizations. Upon final clearance, these speeches could be used by any member of management—and on sudden notice (if necessary), as was often the case.

By 1959, there were six basic speeches in the Speech Library, keyed to current interests in such business topics as profits, automation, issues of the 1959 steel strike, taxes, incentives, and, of course, U.S. Steel itself. In that year alone, library speeches were used 50 times; since then they have been delivered as often as 250 times in the course of a year.

Today, U.S. Steel speakers may select from a total of 23 speeches in the library. And in addition to variations on the first six basic themes, talks are available on such subjects as competition, economics, American traditions, and the past and future of the steel industry. Speeches are reviewed annually, revised as necessary, and new themes are added as the demand for them becomes evident.

In 1960, the head of the public relations department and his working associates were confronted by the company's top ranking executive officer with two questions pertaining to the whole topic of speech making and reprinting: "What good are these speeches really doing?" and, "What are we actually getting for the time and money we spend on them?"

It is not surprising that such questions were eventually asked, as Table

---

carefully selected audiences which presumably had a special interest in a particular speech, the total number of reprints distributed in the course of a typical year decreased, but with apparently no reduction in actual readership. Also, a considerable saving in the costs of printing and mailing of reprints was realized.

12-1 certainly reflects a considerable expenditure of time, money, and effort on the part of both the public relations department at U.S. Steel and the officers of the company who gave the speeches. To answer these questions, a well-known commercial research organization was called upon to develop and conduct a rigorous test of the entire speech reprint program at U.S. Steel.

RESULTS OF THE SURVEY RESEARCH CONDUCTED

Making use of previous research work

In their study to arrive at the answers to the two questions concerning the effectiveness of speech reprints, the research organization called upon by U.S. Steel had the advantage of having conducted a corporate image study for the company in 1959. As a starting point in coming up with the information requested, the researchers reanalyzed the data obtained in 1959 to see what light they could throw on the speech reprint program. In this previous study, a probability sample of 2,000 persons had been interviewed and impressions obtained in 50 different categories. The respondents gave their views on a variety of subjects, including U.S. Steel's products, its importance to national defense, and how much interest the company showed in people.

The first step in the reanalysis was to look again at the questions that asked the respondents if they remembered how they had obtained their information about U.S. Steel. The following picture emerged:

Source of information	Respondents citing main source
U.S. Steel's television program	39%
News reports	17
Printed advertisements	12
Speeches, annual reports, and other company literature	2

Source: Phelps H. Adams, Vice President for Public Relations, U.S. Steel, *Do Speeches Pay?* report at the Annual Meeting of Officials of U.S. Steel Corporation, Its Divisions and subsidiary companies, January 10, 1962, p. 5.

With these data as a basis for departure, an analysis was made of the impact of these various sources of information on the respondent. One finding was that the company's television program was doing a rather good job in "reaching the respondent," in that the viewer tended to be more

THE U.S. STEEL CORPORATION 143

positively inclined than the nonviewer. Because of its comparatively strong impact, this source of information was used as a *baseline of comparison* for the speech reprint program.

This constituted the next step taken by the researchers. The impact of the speeches was compared with that of television on eight key topics; the data summarized in Table 12-2 reveals that speech reprints compare very favorably. In fact, there is only one topic ("charges fair prices") on which the regular TV viewer has a higher opinion; on the other seven, the readers of speeches are more favorably disposed, and in some instances substantially so.[4]

Table 12-2. Impact of speeches compared with impact of television on regular viewers

	Readers of speeches (N = 316)	Regular television viewers (N = 250)
High-quality products	61%	47%
Progressive company	45	43
Product leader	55	36
Important to national defense	58	36
Deals fairly with unions	30	25
Forward-looking management	23	22
Shows interest in people	36	21
Charges fair prices	8	20

Source: Adams, *op. cit.*, p. 9.

On the basis of these findings, the researchers decided upon a *two-stage* survey of U.S. Steel's speech reprint program in order to answer the two basic questions (along with others) posed for them. Let us take each stage in some detail.[5]

Stage One

Stage One consisted of interviewing 338 individuals selected from U.S. Steel's speech reprint mailing list. This sample was carefully selected to provide a scientific cross section of the mailing list, reflecting particu-

---

[4] This observation is probably contaminated to some extent—although one can't be certain exactly how—by the fact that those who received the speech reprints were probably very different people from the television audience.

[5] The information in the following discussion is drawn from *An Appraisal of the U.S. Steel Speech Reprint Program: Part I* (Princeton, N.J.: Opinion Research Corporation, May, 1961).

larly seven of the geographical districts of the corporation throughout the United States.

In addition, the researchers were careful to select thought leaders in their respective communities.[6] Each respondent was interviewed by telephone for the purpose of obtaining from present recipients their opinions of the speech reprints.

Ninety-five percent of these respondents were aware that they were receiving speech reprints from U.S. Steel. Of those 95%, 71% reported that they usually read the speech reprints, while another 22% said that they sometimes read them. Two-thirds of those who remembered reading the reprints felt that they learned something from them. The researchers then questioned the respondents specifically on *what* they remembered from the reprints, and they found that the interviewees were able to feed back many of the ideas expressed in the talks they had received. One-third of the respondents made use of the ideas contained in the speeches in their own talks, lectures to classes, and so forth; some 41% passed the reprints along to others after they were finished with them.

Interestingly enough, U.S. Steel was not the only company sending these particular people speech reprints. In fact, 70% of those who received U.S. Steel reprints *also* received reprints from other companies, many of which (nearly 200 in all) were among the largest and most prestigious companies in the United States. Four-fifths of the respondents rated U.S. Steel's speeches as either better than average (57%) or average (23%); only one in a hundred found them less interesting. Ninety percent of the respondents thought that the company was performing a useful service in providing the speech reprints, while only 5% thought that it was not.

To sum up, on the basis of the first stage of the overall survey, it is clear that the reprint program is reaching the intended audience; furthermore, the audience is aware that they are being communicated with, and they are responding to these communication efforts very favorably.

Stage Two

Stage Two of the study was planned to be a more exacting test of the value of the reprints. Specifically, this phase was designed to measure the effect, if any, of the speech reprints on the attitudes of the recipient toward U.S. Steel.

The 1959 study was utilized once again; of the 2,000 persons interviewed at that time, a number of them *had not* received reprints; of these, a cross section of 615 persons was selected and broken down into two groups.

An *exposed group,* comprising 400 of the 615 who had not received

[6] The sample included businessmen, professional people, holders of public office, religious and educational leaders, and others recognized as outstanding citizens.

the speech reprints, were now added to the reprint mailing list. Over a twelve-month period, this experimental group received the following six speeches, listed in the order sent, by title and by U.S. Steel official who gave the speech: *Business Has a Mandate, Too,* by Roger M. Blough; *The Unprofitable Puzzlement,* by Roger M. Blough; *Steel Collective Bargaining in the '60s,* by R. Conrad Cooper; *The Vanishing Incentives,* by Robert C. Tyson; *Soft Policies or Firm,* by R. Conrad Cooper; and, *Dear Mr. President. . . ,* an exchange of correspondence on steel prices between President Kennedy and Roger M. Blough.[7]

A *control group,* comprising the remaining 215 of the total, were *not* added to the mailing list. Because the "did not receive" group of 615 (part of the 2,000 interviewed) had been carefully questioned in 1959 regarding their attitudes toward U.S. Steel, this earlier study constituted the "before" phase of the current study. The researchers already knew what the attitudes of the respondents were toward U.S. Steel and were thus able to measure the effects of the speech reprints sent to the exposed group during the test year. The 215 persons who continued to be unexposed to the reprints, when tested again, served as a control for any change in attitudes toward the company that might have taken place for a variety of other reasons, not attributable to the speech reprints. Lastly, a contrast between the *before* and *after* attitude measures of both the *exposed* and *control* group provided the researchers with what they most wanted to know—the effect, in terms of attitude change, of the speech reprint program at U.S. Steel.

Some highlights of the data obtained in Stage Two

One of the early objectives of the researchers was to establish to what degree the exposed group were conscious of now receiving the test set of six speech reprints. In response to the question, "Here are some booklets that U.S. Steel has been mailing out to people. Do you recall receiving any of these?" the data shown in Table 12-3 were obtained.

When one considers the welter of material that people receive through the mail—particularly those who are sought after for a variety of reasons—the percent who were aware that they received the booklets is quite high. An interesting note to remember is that these speech reprints were unsolicited by the exposed group.

Following this, the investigators then checked the extent to which the reprints were read as a whole; individual speech readership; the use of the reprints; how the respondents felt about the policy of sending out reprints; and what they did with them after they were finished with them.

---

[7] Although *Dear Mr. President* . . . was not a speech, in view of the importance and timeliness of its subject matter, the booklet was distributed as an element of the U.S. Steel speech reprint program and was considered as such in the research work done on the program.

Table 12-3. Awareness of receiving reprints

	Yes, recall	No, did not receive	Don't remember
Total to whom reprints were sent	71%	23%	6%
Men	69	26	5
Women	72	21	7
College graduates	71	19	10
High school graduates	77	21	2
Less than high school	67	27	6

Source: *An Appraisal of the U.S. Steel Speech Reprint Program:* Part II, Princeton, N. J.: Opinion Research Corporation, February, 1962, p. 7.

We shall not go into the details of this portion of the study, but in general, the speech reprints fared quite well.

For the balance of our presentation of the data obtained in Stage Two, we shall concentrate on the changes (or lack of change) in respondents' attitudes as a result of having been exposed to the speech reprints. The data for the exposed group reported in the following tables are based on the replies of persons who received all six of the U.S. Steel reprints and said that they "usually" or "sometimes" read them. The exposed group numbered 192 respondents and the matched control group 197.

One further point; in each group, the column headed "1959" refers to attitude measures taken in the original 1959 study; the column headed

Table 12-4. Familiarity with U.S. Steel

	Exposed group 1959	Exposed group Today	Control group 1959	Control group Today
Know a great deal	21% ⎫	27% ⎫	21% ⎫	24% ⎫
	⎬ 42	⎬ 52 (+10)	⎬ 39	⎬ 43 (+4)
Know a fair amount	21 ⎭	25 ⎭	18 ⎭	19 ⎭
Know just a little	29	25	31	32
Almost nothing; never heard of; no opinion	29	23	30	25

Source: *An Appraisal . . .,* p. 33.

THE U.S. STEEL CORPORATION

"Today" refers to the "after" portion of the study—between November 1961 and January 1962.

To begin with, let us see what effect the speech reprint program had on overall familiarity with U.S. Steel. One of the desirable side effects of any communication program is to bring about an awareness of the communicator, and a speech reprint program is no exception. Table 12-4 provides us with some information in this connection.

On the basis of these figures, one can see that the persons who were exposed to the speeches are definitely more familiar with U.S. Steel than those who were not.

While on the topic of increased familiarity, it is interesting to note that exposure to the speech reprint program had a definite effect upon the respondent's availing himself to other channels of communication from the same company. It so happens that U.S. Steel had a television program, and when the researchers asked the respondents about it, they found the following:

	Exposed group 1959	Today	*Control group* 1959	Today
Say they have watched U.S. Steel TV program at some time	81%	92% (+11)	86%	80% (−6)

Source: *An Appraisal*, . . . , p. 47.

Table 12-5 concerns the image of U.S. Steel. In order to obtain the data, the researchers handed each respondent a set of 50 cards, on each of which was a single statement such as, "Treats its customers fairly," or "Makes high quality products," or "Tries to make too big a profit." The respondent was asked to select from these cards the statements which he particularly associated with U.S. Steel—as many or as few as he wished—and to discard the remainder. More general categories shown in the table represent the average of choices based on three to seven specific items. Thus, we see that in 1959 only 12% of the exposed group selected items that expressed dimensions of good customer treatment; whereas, today, 23% did so—representing an increase of 11 percentage points. By contrast, the control group increased by 5 points. One further explanatory note about the table: the first six categories are positive in nature; the last, "criticism of bigness," is, of course, a negative item.

Looking at the results, we see that in the six positive dimensions of U.S. Steel's image, the "plus" changes of the exposed group were greater

Table 12-5. Image of U.S. Steel

	Exposed group 1959	Today	Control group 1959	Today
Customer treatment (average vote on 5 items)	12%	23%	11%	16%
Corporate leadership (average vote on 7 items)	25	35	28	32
Defense contribution (average vote on 3 items)	17	23	18	21
Employer role (average vote on 7 items)	19	30	20	22
Concern for individuals (average vote on 5 items)	12	19	11	13
Product reputation (average vote on 5 items)	31	42	33	40
Criticism of bigness (average vote on 5 negative items)	10	8	9	9

Source: *An Appraisal . . .*, p. 37.

than in the control group. Also, in 1959 the "product reputation" category was the most positive. This suggests that the company already enjoyed a fairly good reputation. In the one negative category, the control group remained unchanged, while the exposed group dropped slightly.[8]

[8] This is the first time in the analysis of data from Stage Two of the overall study that the question arises of the specific relationship between the six test speech reprints and the changes in attitudes of the respondents. The hypothesis to be tested by the before-after design of this research project was the effect of the test speech reprints upon the attitudes of the respondents toward a variety of questions concerning certain business topics. The data taken as a whole indicates that the general objective of the test was realized, despite the many other communications that these same respondents were being exposed to from other sources.

The circumstances were not ideal. The researchers were forced to make use of questions from the 1959 survey that, in most instances, were generally, not specifically, related to the contents of the reprints sent to the exposed group. The speeches were originally given with certain objectives in mind, to be sure, but these objectives were not necessarily consistent with the survey questions asked in the 1959 study (the "before" portion), and in 1961 (the "after" portion). For a complete test of a speech reprint program, one would have to design the before and after questionnaires to accurately complement the subject matter of the speeches. This was not possible as there was duplication and unequal overlap of topics in the six speeches. Likewise, the content of the speeches should reflect the questions to be asked. For example, uneven exposure to the various topics in the questioning had a definite bearing on the answers given and further hindered the researchers' ability to pinpoint the causes of shifts in the respondents' attitudes. Of the topics under discussion in Table 12-6, all but the last, "political issues," had been treated in one or more of the six reprints; two of the topics, "Government control of prices," and "union negotiations," were discussed in four of the reprints. The perfect test is an unlikely occurrence in applied public relations practice, as the probability of satisfying all the requirements —with regard to the test questions, the speech writing objectives, and the audience— is very low. Inevitably, one or more factors in combination would reduce its effectiveness. In view of all the considerations involved in an ideal test of a speech reprint program, the one reported in this case study is a reasonably close approximation of a perfect sample.

Table 12-6. Affirmative attitude toward U.S. Steel's giving its views on public affairs matters

	Exposed group 1959	Exposed group Today	Control group 1959	Control group Today
Government control of prices	59%	81% (+22)	65%	71% (+6)
Union negotiations	67	87 (+20)	74	80 (+6)
Tax legislation	53	71 (+18)	50	56 (+6)
Problems of inflation	64	77 (+13)	66	70 (+4)
Social legislation	44	57 (+13)	44	49 (+5)
Political issues	35	46 (+11)	38	34 (-4)
Average for six items	54	70 (+16)	56	60 (+4)

Source: *An Appraisal . . .*, p. 27.

Another interesting aspect of the data stems from the following question asked of respondents: "Do you think a company like U.S. Steel should or should not try to make the company's views known on subjects of this kind?" The responses were in terms of "should," "should not," and "no opinion;" and Table 12-6 gives a breakdown of the "should" category.

Although in 1959 a high number of individuals already favored the notion that a company should express its views (compare the low initial percentages in Table 12-5), the improvement seen in the exposed group is quite marked. Apparently the *act* of speaking out (and making others aware of it) causes people to be more likely to support the *right* to speak out. One can't help noting in passing that data such as these are a clear mandate to the public relations practitioner to counsel his company or client to make its views known.

Closely related to the findings and generalizations in Table 12-6 were some further data which represented an extension, or extrapolation, of the impact of the speech reprint program on the attitudes of the respondents. At one point during the interview, they were asked: "Of course, you couldn't be sure without actually knowing the company's views; but on which of these topics would you *probably agree* with U.S. Steel's views, and on which would you *probably disagree?*" Table 12-7 contains the "probably agree" responses. Apparently, speeches are not particularly effective in making the reader more prone to accept the views of the company on future issues; here the overall differences between the exposed group and control group are negligible.

An important question raised by these data is whether all of the topics shown received the same amount of attention in the six reprints, or, indeed, whether some of them were mentioned at all (see again footnote 8).

Table 12-7. Probable agreement with U.S. Steel views

	Exposed group 1959	Today	Control group 1959	Today
Government control of prices	35%	44% (+9)	28%	40% (+12)
Union negotiations	33	47 (+14)	30	42 (+12)
Tax legislation	25	38 (+13)	26	30 (+4)
Problems of inflation	41	48 (+7)	31	35 (+4)
Social legislation	27	33 (+6)	21	29 (+8)
Political issues	14	18 (+4)	10	17 (+7)
Average for six items	29	38 (+9)	24	32 (+8)

Source: *An Appraisal* . . . , p. 29.

The researchers do not provide us with specific statements in response to this. About all we can surmise is that on topics that might be discussed in the future, the people who received the reprints are no more likely to agree or disagree with U.S. Steel than are those who did not receive them. However, this is an exceedingly intriguing topic for public relations practitioners, since one aspect of their communication program is to pave the way for acceptance of their organization on issues that may come up in the future.[9]

So far we have been considering data that showed the value or importance of the reprint program. Although the results in general pointed to an endorsement of the speech program, some of the data produced an *opposite* picture; still other data were mixed in their implications. We shall now consider some of these negative results.

One of the objectives of the speech reprint program of U.S. Steel (or of any company) is to "educate" the reader on various facts about the organization. A sensitive point with U.S. Steel is its desire that people be aware of the company's *actual* share of the production market. Being a large organization, it has suffered in the past (as have many large organizations) from an *overestimation* by the general public with regard to its

---

[9] An area of research that closely parallels our discussion above is the work being done by psychologists on what is called attitudinal "inoculation"—the notion that resistance to efforts of persuasion can be induced within an individual by prior communications. In a "supportive defense" situation, the individual receives arguments ahead of time that will support views that he already has, thereby making him less likely to change them upon receiving subsequent persuasive communications to the contrary. In the case of a "refutational defense," an individual is provided with arguments that defend a certain position, and then with opposing arguments that tear down his defense. In other words, he gets "practice" in being confronted with views that attack his own. Such studies illustrate that under certain conditions one is able to "inoculate" a person against changing his views, sometimes even permanently.

THE U.S. STEEL CORPORATION

share of the market. This overestimation can easily carry over into many undesirable associations, such as the company's becoming too big, or that they can afford almost any demand placed upon them by unions. Consequently, one of the questions in the survey had to do with the respondents' understanding of U.S. Steel's share of the market. Table 12-8 summarizes the findings.

Table 12-8. Knowledge of U.S. Steel's share of production

	Exposed group 1959	Today	Control group 1959	Today
Think U.S. Steel share of the market is larger, compared to twenty or thirty years ago	63%	69% (+6)	68%	71% (+3)
Think U.S. Steel produces more than 50% of all product X in the U.S.	33	42 (+9)	38	33 (−5)

Source: *An Appraisal . . ,* p. 45.

On this topic the data show a reversal with respect to the effect of the speech reprints; in both areas, the exposed group has moved in an undesirable direction. It is difficult to account for this reversal. These data do highlight one generalization that is familiar to public relations practitioners and to others concerned with communication and persuasion: people are resistant to change, and it is therefore exceedingly difficult to modify firmly entrenched attitudes, regardless of the topic. One can speculate in another direction and come up with an undesirable side effect to a speech reprint program. The very fact of mounting and maintaining an effort to communicate your views may reinforce the recipient's idea that your organization is a dynamic, successful, or even powerful concern. This image of success may contribute to an exaggerated conception about the proportion of the market your particular company may have. Regardless of the interpretations, the point here is that not all the communication objectives of a company are achieved by this *one* channel of communication.

Let us look at one more example of data that did not strongly indicate the value of the speech reprint program. The following was put to the respondents: "I'm going to read you some statements that have been made about large companies. On each one, please tell me whether you agree or disagree." Table 12-9 summarizes the responses on this topic.

Table 12-9. Overall attitude toward large companies

	Exposed group 1959	Exposed group Today	Control group 1959	Control group Today
1. Large companies are essential to the nation's growth and expansion (agree)	90%	92%	81%	86%
2. In many of our largest industries, one or two companies have too much control of the industry (disagree)	21	21	19	23
3. The profits of large companies help make things better for everyone who buys their products or services (agree)	62	81	67	70
4. There's too much power concentrated in the hands of a few large companies for the good of the nation (disagree)	28	29	30	25
5. As they grow bigger, companies usually get cold and impersonal in their relations with people (disagree)	28	26	31	23
6. For the good of the country, many of our largest companies ought to be broken up into smaller companies (disagree)	43	44	38	41
Average for six items	45	49	44	45

Source: *An Appraisal . . .*, p. 41.

Assuming that the speech reprints spoke favorably about large companies (because U.S. Steel is one), we would naturally expect the exposed group to select the side of the question that reflected a favorable attitude. The data, however, present a mixed picture. In the first item, on the statement that large companies are essential to the nation's growth, the control group increased in agreement more than the exposed group. Admittedly, the exposed group happened to be at such a high level of agreement in the first place (90%) that there was very little room for improvement. However, on several other items as well, the control group moved more in the direction presumably advocated by U.S. Steel than did the exposed group. The one exception is item 3, which concerns profits, in which there was a considerably greater percentage increase in the exposed group than in the control group. (The researchers point out that this particular topic was touched upon in several of the speech reprints.)

In summary, these data present a mixed picture with respect to the effectiveness of the speech reprint program; there is definitely no clear upswing on the part of the exposed group. On the other hand, it may be that lack of additional data makes these data appear inconclusive. The various topics that are included in Table 12-9 are general enough that one can easily read or hear about them in a variety of situations; other companies for example, support the same themes referred to here. Consequently, if the item on profits happened to be the only one consistently touched upon in this particular series of test reprints, with the other items *not* receiving this same attention, then we might expect to get just the data that we did—with essentially no difference between the exposed and control groups, except on one item.

A summary of the data

It is comparatively rare in public relations work that a practitioner is able to obtain any sort of measure of the effectiveness of a segment of his public relations programming. It is even more rare when he is able to get before and after measures—the nature of his public's attitudes *before* he communicates with them and then additional measures *after* he has put a program into motion for a given period of time. We find just such a circumstance in this case. Via a comparatively rigorous test situation, we have seen that speech reprints do have a definite impact upon their intended audience—that they were remembered, regarded favorably, and, competitively speaking, were better than the usual run of speeches sent to various individuals by different companies. Furthermore, these speech reprints produced results with respect to the people who received them (the exposed group); they increased familiarity with the company, and they favorably influenced opinions about the company in terms of customer treatment, behavior as an employer, product reputation, and corporate leadership. There was also a change in attitude toward the role of profits of large companies and, perhaps most important, a feeling that companies have a right to make their views on a variety of issues known to the public. As these views are made known, there is engendered an increased confidence in the businessman as spokesman for the problems facing our society generally. In short, while there were some areas of communication that showed no improvement (knowledge about certain facts concerning the company's production), the data in general suggest that the speech reprint program is an effective facet of the arsenal of communication tools available to the public relations practitioner.

PUBLIC RELATIONS PROGRAM BASED ON RESEARCH FINDINGS

The obvious conclusion to be derived from the research conducted on the effectiveness of the speech reprint program is that it was a success. In terms of what U.S. Steel planned to do with respect to the program, the decision was to keep it going along the lines now established. The majority of the recipients are aware of receiving and are reading the speech reprints; the majority are learning something new about U.S. Steel and the steel industry—especially viewpoints, responsibilities, and problems—each time they receive one. Secondary readership and distribution of the reprints is considerable, and recipients were found to make rather frequent use of the material in informal conversations and discussions. Despite heavy competition from other companies, most people considered the U.S. Steel reprints more interesting by comparison, and the speech reprint program was thought to be performing a useful service.

With respect to how the research was utilized more specifically, the public relations director reports that the major use of the data has been in guiding decisions with regard to subsequent speeches. Several examples are cited to illustrate this:

1. In the first stage of the study (where thought leaders were interviewed by telephone), respondents indicated that they had learned something new about U.S. Steel and the steel industry—particularly with respect to foreign competition and labor relations. Among the subsequent speeches that have touched upon these topics are *A Path Through the International Trade Jungle* and *Purchasing for Progress,* by R.M. Blough, and *Guidelines and the National Interest,* by R.H. Larry.

2. In Stage Two of the study, respondents expressed the feeling that they learned more about U.S. Steel's viewpoints on a variety of problems facing industry, their leadership responsibilities, and critical problems associated with the ability to stay in business. These points have also been covered in subsequent speeches: *It's Time to Be Awake* and *The Business of America,* by L.B. Worthington; *The Private Impact of Public Spending,* by R.C. Tyson; and *The Art of Being Secure* and *The Brighter Side,* by R.M. Blough.

3. In the second stage of the study, respondents exposed to reprints revealed a marked increase in their confidence in business spokesmen. This, incidentally, was a very important by-product of the speech reprint program, since the same recipients are also being exposed to the views of government and labor spokesmen on a continuing basis. Two areas where the businessman was considered to have the greatest credentials were government control of prices and union negotiations. The speeches that have continued to stress these themes are *Freedom and Enterprise,* by R.C. Tyson, and *Return of the Native,* by R.M. Blough.

4. In addition, Stage Two saw a dramatic change in the attitudes of the exposed group toward the role of profits in the free enterprise system, a shift which encouraged U.S. Steel to continue an examination of the topic. Two pertinent speeches are: *Role of Profits in Economic Growth* and *The Common Denominator,* both by R.C. Tyson.

13 | Case 3

Television and public relations:

The Kennecott Copper Corporation

CASE OUTLINE

1. Introduction
2. Background information
3. Results of the survey research conducted
   a. establishing the viewers of "Kennecott Neighborhood Theater"
   b. some characteristics of the viewing audience
   c. direct evidence of impact of the television program
   d. indirect evidence of impact of the television program
   e. a summary of the data
4. Public relations program based on research findings

INTRODUCTION

The printed word, undoubtedly, is still the predominant medium used by practitioners for public relations purposes. There are a number of reasons for its important position in this field. First, the overwhelming majority of public relations practitioners are still "ex-printed word" people—former newspaper men, magazine writers, and editors from all sorts of media. Second, writing constitutes, in any format, proof of the time and effort they have put in on behalf of their organization or client; in an activity where one is always hard pressed to demonstrate "what good the public relations budget is doing," it is comforting to have clippings to turn to. Third, the print medium is wonderfully adaptable; we can utilize mass media (particularly newspapers and magazines) for some of our purposes, and a four-page, limited-circulation booklet for others; we can pay for the printed space we need or we can obtain it free; we can produce copy that has a "life" of only one day (such as an announcement of an open house), or we can produce copy that will be much more enduring, as in the case of an annual report or company history. Last, there is the inescapable fact that print as a medium works. Public relations problems are solved everyday—or helped considerably—by utilizing the printed word; and there is at the present time no other medium to rival it for overall adaptability to such a wide range of problems and purposes.

All the factors which point to the strength of the printed word in public relations work also account in part for the fact that the *spoken word* and the use of *sight and sound combined* play a secondary role to print. Radio, tapes, films, and television each present unique problems for the public relations practitioner, to say nothing of the fact that these media—particularly television—are comparatively costly. In addition, because the majority of public relations practitioners are ex-print people, most of them do not feel at home with these forms of media. Moreover, the advent of television and the improvements in tapes for radio or for specialized audience purposes are developments that have come *after* many present-day practitioners had become committed to careers in public relations. As with anything that is new, there is a certain amount of cultural lag in the utilization of the electronic and related techniques.

Present practices, however, are not necessarily an accurate reflection of what the future will hold for the spoken word and for sight and sound combined in the field of public relations. As technological developments occur in these areas, along with an inevitable reduction in cost and increase in adaptability, the dominance of the printed word may well become a thing of the past. Because of this possibility, it seemed essential that one of our cases reflect the utilization of a medium other than print. Specifically, we shall examine the use of television in the overall public relations activities of the Kennecott Copper Corporation, Utah Copper Division.

BACKGROUND INFORMATION

The Kennecott Copper Corporation came into existence at the turn of the century, primarily because of the work of a young engineer, Daniel C. Jackling, who demonstrated that producing metal from low-grade ore could be made commercially feasible if mass-production methods were used. Specifically, he showed that low-grade ore containing about 2% copper (previous methods had required deposits that contained from 5% to 35%), could be mined profitably from the surface by using large shovels to remove the surface rock and dig out the ore. He also took advantage of new methods of extracting metals from ore (in particular, a process known as "flotation"), thereby revolutionizing copper mining and making increased amounts of the metal available to meet the accelerated growth of world requirements.

THE KENNECOTT COPPER CORPORATION

Two other events preceded the development of Kennecott Copper Corporation. Another young engineer, Stephen Birch, discovered and laid claim to an exceedingly rich copper deposit near Kennicott Glacier, which was to prove to be some of the richest copper mining property in the world. A third engineer, William Braden, found a large deposit of ore in the Chilean Andes. The management and owners combined these different and widely separated deposits into one entity in 1915, and the corporation was named after Kennicott Glacier in Alaska. The spelling of the company, interestingly enough, became changed because of a clerical error; as a result, the organization is known today as the Kennecott Copper Corporation.

After some fifty years of growth and diversification, Kennecott Copper Corporation now embraces all of the important phases associated with copper—mining, processing, and fabrication. Like other major corporations today, they also have a continuous program of exploration for additional mineral deposits, and research into more efficient recovery techniques and reduction of production costs.

Kennecott Copper Corporation has mines, plants, and subsidiary operations in many parts of the United States and throughout the world. One segment is the Utah Copper Division, part of the western mining divisions (Utah, Nevada, Arizona, and New Mexico), with offices in Salt Lake City. Our case will focus upon the activities of the Utah Copper Division, particularly in connection with its use of television to achieve certain public relations goals.

Those responsible for the public relations activities at the Utah Division have long been firm advocates of opinion-attitude research as a means of assessing and guiding public relations programs. One aspect of their overall activity in this area was a television program entitled "Kennecott Neighborhood Theater."

Launched in July, 1965, it was telecast weekly and consisted of a feature movie interspersed with public relations advertising. By special arrangement, Kennecott had first choice of every motion picture released for television from Paramount, Warner Brothers, 20th Century-Fox, Universal, Republic, Columbia, RKO, United Artists, David O. Selznik and Selznik International.

There are numerous reasons behind the selection of a motion picture as the vehicle with which to reach an audience. The primary goal of the Utah Copper Division is to "maintain uninterrupted, profitable production," and to do this the public relations personnel felt that one aspect of their overall programming should be to "promote a favorable public opinion climate, with all segments of the public, including government." In other words, they wanted to reach the general public and television seemed to be one of the most effective means of achieving this.

The Utah Division decided to use a feature movie as their program for the following reasons:

1. Motion pictures are supposedly the best produced and the highest budgeted of all television programs. For example, the average budget per ninety-minute motion picture is $3,000,000. The average budget for a one-hour program produced specifically for television is $110,000; for a half-hour program, $40,000. Clearly, considerably more money is put into scripts, sets, actors, and actresses for a motion picture; therefore, there is greater likelihood of consistently high-quality material.

2. Motion pictures can cater to the diversity of entertainment tastes in a heterogeneous television audience. The major breakdowns applied to feature films are adventure (western, sea, war), musical (comedy, spectaculars), drama (classic, contemporary), mystery (detective, espionage, psychological), and comedy (slapstick, situational, sophisticated). Consequently, although any one movie may not appeal to everyone in the audience, in the long run, films should be able to garner the best "batting average," so to speak.

Because of the orientation of both the advertising and public relations departments of the Utah Copper Division, research was used from the start to obtain various types of information about "Kennecott Neighborhood Theater." Since the beginning of the series, two research organizations, specialists in media audience studies, have been employed at periodic intervals to establish the size of the audience reached by "Kennecott Theater." One of these, the American Research Bureau, established that, from November 1956 through May 1960, 25.6% of all homes in the broadcast area (all 29 counties of Utah, 4 counties in eastern Wyoming, 6 counties in southern Idaho, and 2 counties in eastern Nevada) had watched "Kennecott Neighborhood Theater" one or more times. This area has 294,600 homes, 86.3% of them equipped with at least one television set. The estimate of this one survey firm was that *on the average* "Kennecott Neighborhood Theater" was reaching approximately 63,835 homes. The other firm, covering the period from November 1958 through April 1960, came up with an independent estimate that 25.0% of the total homes in the broadcast area had tuned in at least once to the program. One of the local television stations in Salt Lake City also provided the company with periodic data about the size of the viewing audience and the general acceptance of "Kennecott Neighborhood Theater." In addition to a sizable audience, the data collected from time to time indicated that the program enjoyed an excellent reputation.

A success from the beginning, "Kennecott Neighborhood Theater" has continued to be widely accepted over the years. In the words of the public relations director, "It has actually become an institution, and when the theme music comes on the air, most children immediately recognize it and announce to all and sundry, 'Kennecott's on.'"

However valuable and encouraging the feedback from the survey com-

THE KENNECOTT COPPER CORPORATION

panies might be, the public relations department established a policy of maintaining their own independent investigations with still another research firm, in order to double check the impact of their television program. While size of audience figures are valuable, they do not reflect the attitudes of the viewers toward the program, nor do they give any indication of what impact, if any, the public relations messages interwoven in the total TV program have upon the audience. A general, independent survey was conducted in April of 1959 to determine the public's attitudes toward the overall media efforts administered by the public relations department. We shall study the results of this survey and focus specifically on the role that "Kennecott Neighborhood Theater" has played in communicating to the viewing audience the information that the public relations department wanted to convey.

This case, unlike some of our others, describes the use of research in two additional ways, 1) as an independent check on data obtained from other sources, and 2) as an amplification of what was already known about the success (or failure) of a given segment of public relations programming. It also illustrates the use of research *even though* all indications pointed to this particular program's being very successful. In the words of the director of public relations, "We have tried not to fall into the trap of continuing successful programs and projects merely because they have been successful."

Before turning to the research data, let us consider in some detail the nature of the public relations advertising that accompanied the feature movie on "Kennecott Neighborhood Theater." In general, these messages were designed to create a "positive personality" for the Utah Division and to "show the role of Kennecott as an industrial citizen of the state." Only rarely did they treat copper as an end product. Instead, they featured such themes as the following: (1) operating procedures and processes; (2) employee activities on and off the job; (3) safety methods; (4) employee support of public service projects; (5) private versus public enterprise; (6) role of Kennecott in the economy of the region; and (7) efforts of Kennecott to be a responsible corporate citizen. The reader may get a better idea of the public relations advertising utilized from the material below, which accompanied the feature film for the week of February 1959.

Commercial 1

1. SHARPENING DRILL BIT (*18 secs.*) This is education in the making. You're looking at an improved method of sharpening drill bits at Kennecott's Utah Refinery. Because it's more efficient than the method it replaced, it helps Kennecott operate successfully. And that's why this is education in the making.

2. CHECK PAYMENT
(*16 secs.*)

You see, like everyone else, Kennecott pays its taxes every year. In Kennecott's case, the money comes from the sale of copper. It is actually the direct result of everything Kennecott does to maintain successful operations.

3. SCHOOL SHOTS
(*21 secs.*)

Last year Kennecott's property tax alone mounted to more than nine million eight hundred thousand dollars . . . and about seven million dollars of that will help educate the young people of Utah. Based on current costs of schooling, that's the equivalent of paying for a full year's education for about twenty-four thousand boys and girls.

4. FIRE, POLICE, ETC.
(*15 secs.*)

Other Kennecott taxes help pay for such government services as police and fire protection and road building. All told, Kennecott paid about twelve and a quarter million dollars in state and local taxes last year.

5. OPERATION SHOTS
(*30 secs.*)

And, as we said, this money was the direct result of producing copper successfully. And when we say producing copper successfully, we mean removing waste material at the mine . . . mining the low grade ore . . . processing it at the mills . . . the smelter and the refinery . . . and finally the most important step of all . . . selling the metal. Kennecott's entire income depends on the sale of the copper it produces in our state. And the metal must be sold profitably.

6. SHARPENING DRILL BIT
(*17 secs.*)

So that takes us back again to the more efficient method of sharpening drill bits. It's typical of many improvements developed in all phases of operations . . . improvements that, by increasing efficiency and lowering costs, help Kennecott operate successfully.

7. SPLIT SCREEN SHOTS
(*27 secs.*)

Kennecott's success in producing copper also produces a wide variety of benefits for our state. Among them are taxes that help provide our children with the education they need. When Kennecott takes action to assure the continued profitable production of copper . . . it results in the continuation of benefits for thousands of Utahns. Now, back to the Kennecott Neighborhood Theater and "Slaughter Trail."

Commercial 2

1. SALVAGING SCRAP
(*32 secs.*)

This is an example of a good business practice. Copper scrap is being salvaged at Kennecott's

THE KENNECOTT COPPER CORPORATION 161

Utah Refinery. Preventing waste of valuable metal helps Kennecott operate successfully. Kennecott follows many good business practices in its Utah operations. They not only help maintain the successful production of copper, but they are also a form of conservation.

2. PRECIPITATION PLANT
(*19 secs.*)

Here's another example. At the precipitation plant near the mouth of Bingham Canyon, copper is recovered from waste material on the dumps. This is a good business because it produces additional copper for sale. At the same time it's good conservation because Kennecott doesn't let the copper go to waste.

3. RESEARCH SHOTS
(*31 secs.*)

The partnership of good business and good conservation can be seen at Kennecott's Research Center on the University of Utah Campus. Here tests are made to develop methods for recovering more copper from the low-grade ore at Kennecott's mines. Success here helps Kennecott operate successfully. And, by increasing the yield of a resource, it is actually good conservation. In the long run, anything that helps increase efficiency in the production of copper plays a part in conservation.

4. PNEUMATIC HAMMER
(*13 secs.*)

Equipment like this pneumatic hammer can help improve efficiency. In the hands of a skilled operator, it does a much better job of driving spikes into railroad ties than the old method of hammering them in.

5. CYCLONE CLASSIFIER
(*18 secs.*)

Some improvements are still in the experimental stage. This cyclone classifier is being tested at the mills to see if it's more efficient than the classifiers now in use. If it proves successful, it can be a factor in reducing costs . . . and that will help Kennecott continue to operate successfully.

6. HOLE PUNCHER, ETC.
(*33 secs.*)

At Kennecott, many improvements have been developed to increase efficiency. Even when they're not directly connected with the copper production cycle, they help Kennecott operate successfully. And in the broadest sense, anything that helps Kennecott produce the greatest possible amount of copper from low-grade ore also helps conserve a great resource. Good business practices result in a good conservation program at Kennecott. Now, back to the Kennecott Neighborhood Theater and "Slaughter Trail."

Commercial 3

1. ORCHESTRA REHEARSING (*24 secs.*)	This is the Utah Symphony Orchestra, rehearsing under the direction of Maurice Abravanel. There's a definite connection between this outstanding musical organization and the successful production of copper in Utah by Kennecott. You see, by operating successfully, Kennecott is able to help support many worthwhile community projects . . . and the symphony orchestra is one of them.
2. JENSEN AT MIKE (*15 secs.*)	In addition, Kennecott sponsors a series of 13 hour-long radio broadcasts on Monday night at 8:30, to bring music by this fine orchestra into the homes of thousands of Utahns throughout our state.
3. RED CROSS SCENES (*20 secs.*)	The American Red Cross is another example of service organizations that Kennecott helps support. Because it operates successfully in Utah, Kennecott is able to participate in community activities. So, to an extent, successful copper production benefits the people who are served in many ways by the Red Cross.
4. CLASSROOM SCENE (*30 secs.*)	These students at East High in Salt Lake City are part of a special study being conducted by the Utah Educational Research Council under a Kennecott grant. The purpose of the study is to develop better methods of teaching mathematics . . . and to increase interest in the subject, so that more students will take mathematics courses. This can be an important project, because training in mathematics is the basis for careers in engineering and science . . . a great need in America today.
5. RADIO FREE EUROPE (*18 secs.*)	Radio Free Europe, which beams the message of freedom through the Iron Curtain, is maintained by the Crusade for Freedom. Kennecott supports this organization . . . and C. D. Michaelson, general manager of Kennecott's Western Minings Division, heads the drive for funds in this area.
6. VAUGHN, EK, PETERSON (*14 secs.*)	These are Kennecott employees . . . George Vaughn on the left, Clayton Ek in the center, and Fred Peterson. They're advisors to high school students participating in a Junior Achievement project.
7. PRODUCTION ACTIVITIES (*38 secs.*)	Kennecott helps support Junior Achievement which trains young people for business careers.

The advisors help the future businessmen and women set up their own company. This one was organized to make and sell copper jewelry, and it operates exactly like a regular business. Junior Achievement provides valuable business training for about 400 boys and girls in this area. These few examples of the many worthwhile projects that Kennecott helps support show how the community shares in the success of a business. Now, back to the Kennecott Neighborhood Theater and "Slaughter Trail."[1]

RESULTS OF THE SURVEY RESEARCH

The data to be discussed in this section are obtained from the survey conducted in April of 1959 in the state of Utah. All of the interviews were conducted in the homes of the respondent.

The survey was carried out according to a technique known as an "area probability sample," which afforded each household in the state an equal or known opportunity to be contacted. The sample consisted of 812 individuals. Seven hundred and twelve of the interviews were taken throughout the state; of these a certain number naturally occurred in agricultural areas. However, the remaining 100 interviews were concentrated in the same areas, in order to augment the size of the "farm" segment and thereby increase the stability of the agricultural portion of the total sample. The sample obtained was made to correspond with census figures for age and sex of the respondent; other factors, such as education, occupation, and income, were automatically controlled by the method of sampling employed.

The survey was first designed to ascertain the size and nature of the audience reached by the television and radio programs sponsored by Kennecott in Utah—specifically, "Kennecott Neighborhood Theater," a radio program entitled, "This Business of Farming," and radio broadcasts of the Utah Symphony Orchestra. In addition, Kennecott wanted to obtain the usual readership indices to its newspaper advertisements throughout the state.

After the audience had been described and established for each of the different media, the investigators then measured the impact that the various communication efforts had upon the individuals within the audiences. As pointed out earlier, we will only consider the data obtained from those respondents identified as viewers of the television program.

[1] Mimeographed script, February 6, 1959, transmitted to the author by the Kennecott public relations staff.

Establishing the viewers of "Kennecott Neighborhood Theater"

The first step was, of course, to establish what proportion of the individuals in the sample were viewers of the television show, and to obtain some measure of the frequency of their viewing. They were asked, "Do you, or members of your family, ever watch Kennecott Neighborhood Theater on television on Friday nights?" and, "How often do you watch Kennecott Neighborhood Theater on TV—regularly, fairly often, or only once in a while?" Table 13-1 gives us this information.[2]

Table 13-1. Total audience and frequency of their viewing "Kennecott Neighborhood Theater"

	Statewide, April 1959	Salt Lake County 1959	Salt Lake County 1957	Outside Salt Lake County April 1959
Total audience	70%	79%	66%	63%
Frequency of viewing:				
Regularly	23	28	24	20
Fairly often	23	26	22	19
Only once in a while	24	25	20	24

Source: *The Advertising Program of Kennecott Copper Corporation, Utah Copper Division: An Audience-Impact Survey,* submitted to the Kennecott Copper Corporation by Clark, Bardsley and Haslacher, April 1959, p. 8.

Kennecott's television program is clearly a success. In fact, the researchers who conducted this study reported that, in more than 10 years of research in that part of the country, they had seldom obtained audiences of such magnitude.

Some characteristics of the viewing audience

Because of the objective of the public relations department to reach the general public with this particular portion of their public relations program, it was important to know something of the composition of the television audience. This information would help to determine whether the viewers were a balanced group, or whether certain segments of the general public were for some reason being reached more successfully than others. Table 13-2 summarizes the data.

[2] In this and Table 13-5, data from a previous year are included. Kennecott's long-standing policy of conducting research has made trend analyses possible.

THE KENNECOTT COPPER CORPORATION

According to the data in the table, the television program is apparently reaching a rather heterogeneous group, thereby supporting the implicit assumption being made to this effect. The variations that show up in the figures are to be expected. For example, the professional, college educated, and upper-income groups watched the program considerably less frequently than persons in other occupational groups, with not as much education, and with less income. Other research tends to bring out this same socioeconomic pattern of viewing. By and large, people in the upper levels watch television *less* and are quite selective in their viewing, devoting more of their time to educational television stations. The Kennecott television program survey appears to support this pattern.

Direct evidence of impact of the television program

Having now found out that the television program is attracting an audience, our next step is to establish what impact it has on them. One measure of prime importance is whether or not the viewers correctly identify the program's sponsor. When asked who sponsors "Neighborhood Theater," the respondents revealed the following:

	Correctly identified sponsor
As a percent of total *viewers*	47%
As a percent of total *public*	37

Source: *The Advertising Program* . . . , p. 14

This is a comparatively high percentage of recognition when compared with other studies. To make this point, the researchers asked for sponsor identification of other programs along with "Neighborhood Theater." This is what they found:

Total public	Correctly identified sponsor
"Neighborhood Theater"	37%
"Wagon Train"	23
"U.S. Marshal"	1

Source: *The Advertising Program* . . . , p. 14.

Table 13-2. Audience characteristics of "Kennecott Neighborhood Theater"

| | | Frequency of Viewing* | | |
Characteristic	Total audience	Regularly	Fairly often	Once in while
Total sample, statewide	70%	33%	32%	35%
Area sample:				
Salt Lake County	79	35	33	32
Outside Salt Lake County	63	31	31	38
Weber, Davis	65	43	23	34
Cache, Boxelder	61	28†	31	41
Iron, Sevier	61†	23†	59	18
Utah, Carbon, Duchesne	61	20	35	45
Type of area:				
urban	72	33	33	34
rural, nonfarm	66	34	30	36
rural, farm	58	30	29	41
Sex:				
men	68	30	31	39
women	71	37	33	30
Age:				
21–39 years	75	32	35	33
40 and over	65	35	29	36
Income level:				
upper	75	27	38	35
middle	70	33	31	36
lower	59	58	18	24
Educational level:				
college	67	23	35	42
high school	74	39	32	29
grade school, or none	62	35	24	41
Occupation:				
professional managerial	71	20	31	49
white-collar workers	77	35	40	25
manual workers	71	37	29	34
farmers, ranchers	57	27	31	42
KCC employees	98†	53†	19	28
Union affiliation:				
union	75	34	31	35
nonunion	67	33	33	34
Opinion leaders‡	70	22	34	44

*These figures will vary from those reported in Table 13-1, because the above are computed as percentages of total viewers of the Kennecott program, while the earlier statistics were based on the total interview sample.

Clearly, the Kennecott program outstrips the other two, in spite of the fact that when this survey was taken (1959) "Wagon Train" and "U.S. Marshal" were extremely popular television programs. The investigators point out that these two shows have multiple sponsors. Only 23% of the respondents were able to identify the Ford Motor Company as one of the sponsors of "Wagon Train," in spite of Ford being a large and well-known organization. It should be made clear that the test question concerning sponsorship asked only for the sponsor of "Neighborhood Theater" and did not include the name of the company in the title. This would have given Kennecott an unfair advantage in terms of the survey question; in general, however, as the investigators emphasize, including the sponsor name in the title of the show has a favorable effect upon viewer recall and sponsor identification—a wise move on the part of Kennecott.

After establishing that viewers and nonviewers alike remember the sponsor of "Neighborhood Theater" quite well, the surveyors then obtained measures of the respondents' reactions to the televised public relations commercials in terms of (1) general interest, (2) truthfulness, and (3) the length and frequency of messages.

These three aspects were measured by means of a ten-point scale that ranged from +5 to a −5. The +5 end of the general interest scale represented "very interesting"; the −5 end represented "very dull." The respondent selected the number within the range that best described how interesting he felt the commercials to be. For truthfulness or believability, the +5 end was described as "truthful," and the −5 end "misleading." With regard to length and frequency of commercials, +5 stood for "just right," and the −5 end meant "too many and too long."

With this explanation of *how* the three components of the television messages were measured, let us see how the Kennecott program fared. Table 13-3 outlines Kennecott's rating by the respondents.

From these data it is apparent that the messages included as part of the television program score high on all three points. Moreover, the KCC commercials were rated quite favorably by the same individuals who held television commercials in general in very low esteem.

Table 13-2 (Continued)

---

†Based on a limited number of cases; therefore, the findings should be considered as directional only.

‡The classification "opinion leader" was based on responses to four questions in the interview. If the respondent took an active part in community affairs or tried to convince others about certain community affairs, if he expressed opinions on state or community affairs in the interview, or if he belonged to a civic group or organization or knew a political office holder in the state personally, he was then considered an "opinion leader."

Source: *The Advertising Program . . .* , pp. 10–11.

Table 13-3. Kennecott rating versus television commercials as a whole on interest, truthfulness, and length and frequency

	Very favorable	Moderately favorable	Unfavorable	Undecided
General interest:				
KCC commercials	68%	23%	3%	6%
TV commercials as a whole	17	55	27	1
KCC advantage	51			
Truthfulness:				
KCC commercials	74	15	4	7
TV commercials as a whole	15	48	36	1
KCC advantage	59			
Length and frequency of commercials:				
KCC commercials	58	23	13	6
TV commercials as a whole	11	23	65	1
KCC advantage	47			

Source: *The Advertising Program . . .*, p. 17.

The next thing to find out was the degree to which the messages were being retained by the viewing audience. For this purpose, the viewers were asked, "Would you mind telling me anything you can remember about the sponsor's commercials on 'Kennecott Neighborhood Theater'?" As a result of their questioning the surveyors were able to make three generalizations:

1. Eighty-one out of every 100 viewers were able to recall some facet of "Neighborhood Theater" commercials.
2. The content recalled of the messages was remarkably similar.
3. A great many of the specific points or details of messages were retained.

Table 13-4 demonstrates the messages in descending order of retention. It is interesting to note that the "institutional" character of the messages, stressing the people, processes, operations, and economic impact of the company, was remembered comparatively well. By contrast, the items reflecting product emphasis (generally avoided in the messages) such as uses of copper in home building and general product promotion, were recalled less well.

To give the reader a feeling for the type of recall that this line of

Table 13-4. Retention of "Neighborhood Theater" commercials

Messages Retained	All Viewers
Mining, processing of copper: blasting; views of pit; mining, milling, smelting operations	27%
Contributions to community and state: effect of operation on economy of state; benefits to state; company's interest in welfare of area; building a better Utah	16
Employee benefits; employee welfare program: safety devices, precautions; advancement; training programs; fringe benefits; good place to work; family benefits	16
Efficiency; improvement program: use of new equipment, machinery, improved techniques; efficiency measures necessary for successful operation; waste prevention	11 ⎱ 14
Problems of rising costs: cost problems faced by company; measures taken to cope with costs	3 ⎰
Job descriptions; plant tours: men performing various jobs; plant views; production processes	10
Employee suggestion system: bonuses for new ideas; encouraging employees to suggest improvements	6
General product promotion: explaining, promoting use of copper; copper products	6 ⎱ 11
Use of copper in home building: advantages of copper for plumbing, heating, wiring	5 ⎰
Contributions to education: scholarships; grants to schools; research projects; support of schools	6
Tax contributions: amount, importance of KCC tax dollars; status of company as taxpayer	5
Large employer; heavy payrolls: size, importance of payrolls; employment for Utahns	5
Low-grade ore problems, production	2
Praise for commercials: announcing; number, quality of commercials	2
Miscellaneous	4
Nothing—no retention	19
Total	143%

Source: *The Advertising Program* . . . , p. 21.

questioning elicited from the respondents, an assortment of verbatim comments are listed below.

The poor mountain gets blown up every Friday. The commercials tell about safety programs out there and show various types of jobs and operations. (Service station operator)

They have just a few commercials which are direct and to the point. They stress the safety program, research projects, and the indirect contributions of the company to the state. (Schoolteacher)

They show how the ore is processed and pictures of manufactured products . . . show the amount of taxes they pay to the state . . . big tunnel they have now, and all phases of their work. (Owner of trucking company)

I like the way they show testing and trying new processes out. I'm always looking for someone that I might know. The refinery is very interesting. I like to watch how they peel off the sheets of copper. They're always safety conscious. (Wife of electrician)

They pay guys money for ideas which help the company to save money.

They show what copper is used for, and what percent is low-grade ore, and how they have to operate efficiently . . . safety for employees . . . taxes they pay to support the economy of Utah. (Manager of cannery)

Oh, they let each person (employee) make suggestions on how to save and encourage better production. They pour the ore and skim the foam . . . shows progress. They showed the clothing workers wore, and what precautions they took to protect them. (Wife of farmer)

They tell about the improvements they're making and how they employ 5,600 men. (Retired white-collar worker)

They talk about costs and maintenance of equipment, and how costs now are much greater in relation to their net income than they used to be . . . donations to welfare. (Carpenter)

They tell how they're finding new ways to produce copper cheaper, and how they teach the men their trade and how to advance in their jobs. (Cost accountant)

They show different employees and what they do, and how the company works for the betterment of the community, like giving scholarships to children. (Wife of salesman)

They show the open pit mine and ore cars, and take you all through the smelter. They show new equipment—I remember some new type of wheels. They go through all levels and workings of the mine and show the transportation of the ore. (Wife of electrician)[3]

Indirect evidence of impact of the television program

The data presented in the previous section reflect the degree to which respondents were consciously aware of "Kennecott Neighborhood Theater" and of the various aspects of public relations advertising that accompanied the programs.

In this section we will consider what might be called "indirect" measures of impact. The researchers define this procedure as follows:

Next, an indirect method is employed to measure the impact of Kennecott promotional activities. This is done by contrasting opinions and attitudes of

---

[3] *The Advertising Program of Kennecott Copper Corporation, Utah Copper Division: An Audience-Impact Survey,* submitted by Clark, Bardsley and Haslacher, April 1959, p. 23.

THE KENNECOTT COPPER CORPORATION

those publics *exposed* and *unexposed* to Kennecott advertising on subjects covered by commercials or newspaper advertisements.[4]

If that public *exposed* to Kennecott promotion has more favorable opinions toward the company, or a more coherent conception of its activities, here is indirect evidence of advertising impact.

For these tests, ten themes were taken from Kennecott advertising of the past year. One theme, for example, has been the role which Kennecott plays as a "good business citizen" of the community, typified by its slogan, "A Good Neighbor Helping to Build a Better Utah." Both slogan and "citizenship" recognition questions were contained in the schedule, so that comparisons could be drawn between those *exposed* and *unexposed* to Kennecott advertising.

A second theme test involved consumer acceptance of copper plumbing pipe, an area which has frequently been covered by KCC commercials. Other test subjects, all of which Kennecott has spoken of in its advertising, are absentee ownership, automation, low-grade ore mining, big business, and labor relations.[5]

In order to make an overall appraisal of the effectiveness of Kennecott advertising or communication efforts, the researchers generated what they called a "public relations success score." "Success" meant that the respondent either correctly identified the KCC slogan, or voluntarily named Kennecott as a leading "business citizen." Naturally, the more successful the respondents, the higher the percentage for their particular group. The average success score below was achieved by combining all sorts of exposure (grouping those persons exposed either to TV, radio, newspaper advertising, or a combination thereof) for all themes. The result:

	Average PR success score
Exposed to KCC advertising	66.1%
Unexposed to KCC advertising	54.1
Differential favoring the exposed group	12.0

Source: *The Advertising Program* . . . , p. 55.

On the whole, the exposed group scored higher than did those not exposed to some form of Kennecott advertising or communication. The details of the overall differential favoring the exposed groups are provided in Table 13-5. Apparently the respondents who have been exposed to

---

[4] The reader will recall that the total study, of which the impact of "Neighborhood Theater" is only one part, embraced the effects of radio, newspaper, and other advertising approaches.

[5] *The Advertising Program of Kennecott,* p. 54.

TABLE 13-5. Public opinion appraisal of Kennecott in specific areas, by groups exposed and unexposed to Kennecott advertising

	Total sample	Exposed to KCC advertising	Unexposed
On "Business citizenship":			
voluntarily named Kennecott as a leading "business citizen"	37%*	39%	25%
Identification of KCC slogan:			
correctly identified KCC slogan, "A Good Neighbor Helping to Build a Better Utah"	42	45	20
Is Kennecott ore high or low-grade?			
high-grade	31	32	25
low-grade	55	56	41
undecided	14	12	34
	100	100	100
Benefits of "bigness"			
agreed that it takes big a company like Kennecott to mine copper successfully	91	92	83
disagreed	5	4	7
undecided	4	4	10
	100	100	100
Absentee ownership:			
agreed that Kennecott owners who live out of state could be called "Utah businessmen"	64	64	59
disagreed	25	25	26
undecided	11	11	15
	100	100	100
Appraisal of Kennecott employee fringe benefit program:			
excellent	20	21	7
good	55	55	61
fair	8	8	1
poor	1	1	1
undecided	16	15	30
	100	100	100
Appraisal of Kennecott as a place to work:			
excellent	20	21	10
good	57	57	60
fair	10	10	7
poor	3	3	3
undecided	10	9	20
	100	100	100

THE KENNECOTT COPPER CORPORATION

Table 13-5 (Continued)

	Total sample	Exposed to KCC advertising	Unexposed
Automation:			
agreed that copper industry must use more and more modern machines and methods to stay in business, *even* if it means fewer jobs	78%	78%	72%
disagreed	14	15	10
undecided or qualified	8	7	18
	100	100	100
Type of water pipe preferred if moving into a new home:			
copper	72	73	67
iron	18	18	15
other	3	3	2
undecided	7	6	16
	100	100	100
Which of these companies does the most to promote the economy and prosperity of the state?			
Kennecott	57	60	37
Geneva Steel	15	14	20
Union Pacific Railroad	14	13	28
Utoco	4	4	3
undecided	10	9	12
	100	100	100

*The corresponding recognition figure in 1953 was 13%.
Source: *The Advertising Program . . .* , pp. 57-59.

KCC advertising interpret the themes or attach meaning to them along the lines desired by the public relations personnel of the Utah Division.

The researchers noted in their report that the results for the last item of Table 13-5 were particularly significant, as they represented one of the central themes of Kennecott public relations advertising; namely, that Kennecott was quite active in contributing to the economic well-being of the state. However, the results also confirmed a point that has already been demonstrated by other research: all things being equal, respondents tend to respond favorably to that which is most familiar to them. In other words, a well-known company has an advantage over a company that is not well-known in any sort of comparison test. Consequently, the researchers wanted to make an analysis of the data along the lines of what they call *par for familiarity*. What does this term mean?

Therefore [that is because of this advantage of familiarity], it is customary procedure to set up this "par for familiarity" to determine if a company is doing better or worse *than what actually might be expected of it on the basis of public familiarity*.

"Pars" for familiarity were established for each company by results to this question: "Which *one* of these four companies do you feel you are most familiar with—the one you know the most about?"

Each company's familiarity par is now compared with recognition score as a contributor to the prosperity and economy of the state.[6]

According to the procedure described above, the following data were obtained:

	Par for familiarity	Recognition score	Differential
Kennecott	40%	57%	+17%
Union Pacific Railroad	22	14	− 8
Geneva Steel	17	15	− 2
Utoco	17	4	−13

Source: *The Advertising Program . . . ,* p. 60.

One must conclude from these figures that the KCC communication program is achieving a penetration that extends beyond the fact that it is a well-known company. There is more than just familiarity involved; the respondents are apparently responding to the messages themselves.

We have been discussing the indirect impact of the communication program of KCC in general which includes all the various media the company employs. Because we are more interested in focusing on television in particular, let us look at the effectiveness of each of the various media with respect to its impact upon the respondents. Table 13-6 shows the degree of audience duplication that occurred.

Under the entry "one program or medium," we see that 18% of the respondents were reported as being aware of KCC advertising through TV alone; the figures for the other media are much smaller. These persons represent an "unduplicated" audience, to the extent that their memory can be relied upon with respect to being "reached" by only one of the media. The researchers took this group and assessed their "Public Relations Suc-

[6] *Ibid.,* p. 60.

Table 13-6. Audience duplication between and among media used by Kennecott in advertising and PR programs

	Public reached		
Programs or media	Statewide	Salt Lake County	Outside Salt Lake County
All four media:			
TV shows, farm program, newspaper advertising, symphony program	3.3%	4.2%	2.5%
Three programs or media:	15.7	16.8	14.8
TV, newspaper, and farm program	6.9	7.9	6.0
TV, newspaper, and symphony program	4.9	6.2	3.9
newspaper, farm program, and symphony program	2.8	1.7	3.7
TV, farm program, and symphony program	1.1	1.0	1.2
Two programs or media:	41.6	43.8	40.0
newspaper and TV	28.8	31.4	26.7
TV and farm program	4.2	5.0	3.7
newspaper and farm program	3.9	2.7	4.9
TV and symphony program	2.5	2.5	2.5
newspaper and symphony program	1.3	2.0	.8
farm program and symphony program	.9	.2	1.4
One program or medium:	30.6	29.3	31.6
TV only	18.0	20.6	16.0
newspaper only	9.3	6.7	11.3
farm program only	2.2	1.2	2.9
symphony program only	1.1	.8	1.4
No program or medium	8.8	5.9	11.1
Totals	100.0	100.0	100.0

Source: *The Advertising Program of Kennecott,* op. cit., p. 62.

cess Scores," using the same themes shown in Table 13-5. The results obtained are as follows:

Although we must interpret the above data with greater caution (because of the smaller sample sizes involved in the various single-medium groups), there seems to be a superiority of the effectiveness of TV over both newspapers and, particularly, radio. These data are certainly consistent with the indications from other studies in this area of advertising, that TV has taken over first place as a means of reaching an audience.[7] The

[7] Apropos of this generalization are the data contained in a memo dated August 16, 1965, from Roy Danish, Director of the Television Information Office, National Association of Broadcasters, to all U.S. television stations.

researchers suggest a factor that may account for these differences. The "newspaper only" and "radio only" respondents lived mainly outside the Salt Lake County area, with the "TV only" group residing primarily within the area and therefore closer to the plant site. In addition to providing the "TV only" group with an avenue of information not available to others, seeing the plant on occasion might have served to reinforce their

Reached by KCC	Average PR success score on advertising test themes
TV only	64%
Newspaper only	59
Radio only	53

Source: *The Advertising Program . . .*, p. 65.

To: U.S. Television Stations
From: Roy Danish, Director

A survey taken after President Johnson's July 28 speech on Vietnam substantiates earlier surveys made by Elmo Roper and Associates for the Television Information Office, showing that the public gets most of its news from television. The President spoke on July 28 between 12:33 and 1:14 p.m., EDT. The Sindlinger study was made between 3 and 9 p.m. Telephone respondents were asked their opinion of the President's policy and where they had learned of the speech. More persons cited television as their source than any other medium.

The earlier studies by Elmo Roper included the question, Where do you get most of the news about what's going on in the world? The results in the 1964 Roper poll showed television listed most frequently as the major source of news. Although Roper was dealing with news sources in general and Sindlinger dealing with the source of a specific news story, the polls are closely aligned:

	Sindlinger Source of knowledge of President's speech of July 28, 1965	Roper Source of most news about what's going on in the world (1964)
Television	54.77%	58%
Newspapers	54.12	56
Radio	40.71	26
Friend/people	10.44	5
Magazines	(Not applicable)	8

The Sindlinger poll was based on 993 telephone interviews. The Roper poll was based on over 3,500 personal interviews. Both polls were national projections of the population aged 18 and over.

In the hourly Sindlinger poll, most respondents indicated that they had received

THE KENNECOTT COPPER CORPORATION

general interest in KCC and make them more receptive to the TV messages.

Another important assumption involved in these data is also worthy of mention. In making these media comparisons, it is implicitly assumed that the frequency, type, and extent of advertising on the various media are comparable. If, on the other hand, the radio or newspaper advertising is, in fact, *not* so extensive as that on TV, then the media are not really comparable in terms of amount or frequency, and we are left with a confounding variable. We can't tell whether the TV is better because it is basically a better medium through which to reach an audience with public relations advertising, or whether it is better because it is used for this purpose more extensively.[8]

A summary of the data

The results of this research work are comparatively easy to summarize, since, in general, the impact of "Kennecott Neighborhood Theater" has

---

the news from radio and television. Up to 4 p.m., EDT, radio had a slight edge—38.17% vs. 37.56%—while only 20.53% mentioned newspapers and 17.87% cited a friend.

In the hour from 4 to 5 p.m., most mentions were of television: 47.82% compared with 40.58% for radio, 32.17% for newspapers and 6.38% for friends. Beginning at 6 p.m., newspapers began to edge ahead in the hourly computations. However, the number of multiple mentions—from persons getting their news of the conference from several sources increased.

Significantly, from 5 p.m. to the conclusion of the survey at 9 p.m., the cumulative totals showed television consistently ahead of all other media. The cumulative figures follow:

Source of knowledge of President Johnson's press conference

Cumulative to	4 p.m.	5 p.m.	6 p.m.	7 p.m.	8 p.m.	9 p.m.
Over radio	38.17	39.53	39.48	39.71	40.30	40.71
On television	37.56	43.31	44.50	47.67	52.10	54.77
Read in newspapers	20.53	27.69	34.93	43.89	50.10	54.12
From friend	17.87	11.50	12.13	11.30	10.87	10.44

The final figures at 9 p.m. showed television slightly ahead of newspapers, 54.77% vs. 54.12%, with 40.71% for radio and 10.44% for friends; the percentages total more than 100% because of multiple mentions.

[8] It is only fair to point out that the researchers themselves recognized this point. Their hypothesis was that the themes in the newspaper would be more comparable with those on TV than themes heard on the radio. Obviously, to obtain a more detailed measurement of the comparability of the three media would necessitate a study that would include, among other things, a tabulation of themes presented in the various media.

been substantial and in keeping with the objectives of the public relations department. The following generalizations, taken from the final research report, sum up the highlights of the program's impact:

1. It is delivering a sizeable audience.
2. "Neighborhood Theater" commercials are classified by viewers as definitely superior to those of TV as a whole.
3. There is an unusually high retention of commercial messages, especially of *specifics*.
4. More televiewers accurately identified the sponsor of "Neighborhood Theater" than those of "Wagon Train" and "U.S. Marshal" combined (37%–24%).
5. Kennecott's "PR Success Score" was higher among viewers of its TV show than among those exposed to any other medium or program employed by the company.
6. In Salt Lake County, where a similar study was conducted in 1957, the show has expanded both its total and regular audience, as well as improved its sponsor identification quotient.
7. "Neighborhood Theater" has the largest *unduplicated* audience of any program or advertising medium used by the company.[9]

PUBLIC RELATIONS PROGRAM BASED ON RESEARCH FINDINGS

The use of research to guide both overall and specific public relations programming and planning is firmly entrenched at Kennecott Copper. In this connection, the director of public relations points out that they budget "for both our long- and short-range programs and projects each six-month semester." One healthy item in the budgeting is research—a policy that extends to all aspects of public relations programming, regardless of how successful. Hence the statement, made earlier, "We have tried not to fall into the trap of continuing successful programs and projects merely because they have been successful."

Because of Kennecott's attitude toward a continuing research program (independent surveys have been conducted every two years since the inception of "Kennecott Neighborhood Theater"), their public relations activities can be guided not only by individual research projects, but also by *trend data*. When studies are repeated over the years—as has been the case with "Neighborhood Theater"—gradual changes in such things as attitudes and knowledge about and toward the company can be traced over a long period of time. In this section we shall illustrate how the Kennecott public relations practitioners made use of research data with guidance obtained both from the single 1959 study and from trend data; we shall examine examples of usage from each category separately.

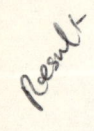

[9] *The Advertising Program of Kennecott*, p. 3.

1959 data only. As was mentioned earlier, the general objective of the public relations personnel at Kennecott, with respect to the utilization of television, was "to create a 'positive personality' for the division (Utah Copper Division), and show the role of Kennecott as an industrial citizen of the state." They wished to achieve this "positive personality" by means of a program that would encourage family participation and exposure to the public relations messages that accompanied the program. In addition, they wanted to select a program whose format and medium would be consistent with population changes—the shrinking of the so-called farm audience and the shift in both residential density and socio-politico-industrial leadership from rural to urban areas. Lastly, they wanted to communicate with this largely urban population by means of a program and via public relations messages[10] that would 1) appeal to a wide spectrum of the viewing audience, 2) be accepted as being in good taste by a large percentage of viewers, 3) be remembered with respect to both general themes and to specifics, 4) be correctly associated with Kennecott Copper as the sponsor in a reasonably high percentage of cases, 5) compete successfully with other programs available for viewing at the same time, and 6) contribute to the overall desired attitude change or maintenance with respect to the corporation.

For the attainment of each of these objectives, the 1959 research data provided solid evidence in favor of continuing to use this particular medium with confidence. In addition, the findings provided Kennecott with explicit justification for its programming and a sound basis for maintaining its budget for this type of endeavor.

Trend analysis only. It was stated earlier that the impact and audience reception of "Kennecott Neighborhood Theater" has been studied every two years since its beginning. The latest survey, comparable in scope to the one we have studied in this case, was completed late in the summer of 1965. An examination of Figure 13-1 illustrates that the continued use of "Neighborhood Theater" is justified. In terms of recognition of Kennecott as a key contributor to the economy, knowledge about the corporation, the favorable attitudes toward it, and the "image" of Kennecott as a place to work, the improvement over the years has been remarkable.

Figure 13-2, which illustrates the increase in total audience and in the three categories of viewing also reveals the remarkable pulling power of "Neighborhood Theater."

---

[10] Over the years these messages have tended to depict the company's operating methods and processes, employee activities (both on the job and off), safety programs and methods, employee involvement in public service projects, and so on. These messages have most often taken the form of "on location" films with narration and participants who are not company spokesmen, with the result that they do not seem to be "propagandists." In addition, they are instructive, interesting, and educational enough that viewers have often expressed as much, or even more, interest in the commercials as in the movie features themselves.

[Figure: Awareness-acceptance trends chart with curves labeled 1953, 1957-59, and 1965, plotted across four categories: "Spontaneously recognize Kennecott as a key contributor to economy", "Feel they know at least something about Kennecott", "Hold 'very favorable' attitudes toward Kennecott", "Rate Kennecott as an 'excellent' or 'good' place to work"]

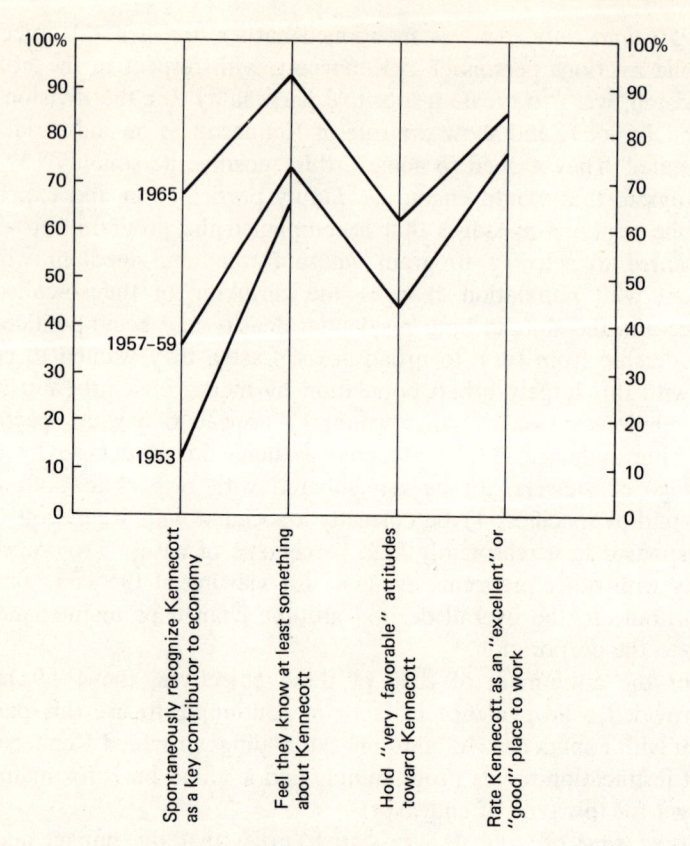

Figure 13-1. Awareness-acceptance trends

Source: *Kennecott Trends in Utah: A Public Opinion Survey,* submitted to the Kennecott Copper Corporation by Clark, Bardsley and Haslacher (Summer 1965), p. 2.

Both of these trend analyses contribute to the general conclusion that the TV program is highly successful and should be continued. We noted this in the 1959 survey alone, but our specific changes were aided by using some of the trend data.

During 1960 and 1961, the following theme was stressed quite strongly. In the open-pit copper mining operation in Utah, a tremendous volume of earth has to be processed to obtain the copper ore. The ore in this part of the country happens to be low grade, with an average copper content of about .0075, or about 15.2 pounds of copper for each ton of ore. In order to mine *one* ton of ore, first it is necessary to remove more than *two* tons of "overburden," or waste material. To put it another way, more than 7,000 pounds of material have to be handled and processed in order to extract a mere 14 pounds of copper.

THE KENNECOTT COPPER CORPORATION

	Total cumulative audience = 92%*			
Regular audience 36%	Frequent 31%	Infrequent 25%	8%	1965

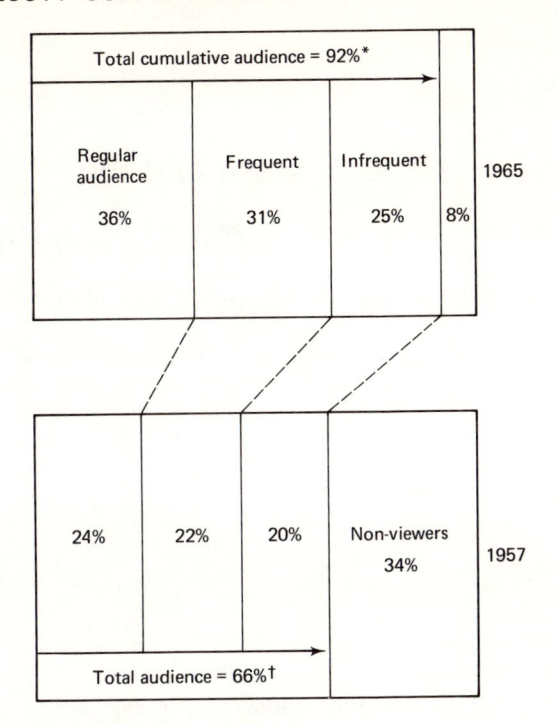

24%	22%	20%	Non-viewers 34%	1957
	Total audience = 66%†			

Figure 13-2. "Neighborhood Theater" trends

* Based on state-wide sample of residents.
† Based on Salt Lake County sample of respondents.
Source: *Kennecott Trends in Utah* . . . , p. 4.

The 1961 survey revealed that people did not appreciate hearing about the company's troubles. In fact, there were sufficient quips on the part of the respondents, referring to "Kennecott Theater" as "Poverty Theater," to suggest that immediate change was necessary. These 1961 data were used by the public relations practitioner as a basis for dropping the operating problems approach. Although an appreciation of the difficulty (and cost) of obtaining copper might make certain respondents more receptive to the prospect of a price increase and more favorably inclined toward tax legislation with respect to corporations, the data weighed against such an argument.[11]

[11] In this connection, one is reminded of the problem that oil companies have in educating people about the costs of discovering and pumping oil. The typical misconception is that one erects a rigging and digs down into the ground, and out comes the oil. Forgotten is the fact that dozens of holes, in an equal number of different locations, must be dug before the one successful oil well is found. Also forgotten is that some of these "holes" are several miles deep and require extensive and costly equipment. As in the case of mining copper, the operations that fail to produce the desired raw material have to be figured into the costs of the successful ventures.

14 | Case 4

The cholesterol scare and the diet-heart disease problem: what the American Dairy Association did about it

CASE OUTLINE

1. Introduction
2. Background information
3. Results of the survey research conducted (findings versus assumptions)
   a. awareness of the diet-heart disease issue
   b. "dimensions" of the awareness
   c. views on the relationship between certain foods and heart disease
   d. where do people get their information?
   e. what sort of professional information do they receive?
   f. a summary of the data
4. Public relations program based on research findings
   a. dairy industry or "internal" efforts
   b. external efforts—concentration on target audiences

1. INTRODUCTION

Few people would deny the old adage that in numbers there is strength; that many people banded together working for common causes or goals are superior to individuals attempting to reach these goals on their own. Likewise, we are all increasingly aware of the numerous pressures or forces, stemming from many quarters, that affect our lives and businesses—public opinion, local, state, and federal regulation, and foreign competition, to name a few. To help cope with these pressures and maximize the resources and efforts of as many people as possible, numerous trade and professional associations have sprung up during the past 50 to 100 years. Trade associations are usually defined as being made up of "competing or related

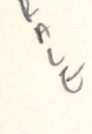

THE AMERICAN DAIRY ASSOCIATION

business units" that have joined together, voluntarily, to pool their resources and form a nonprofit organization that will champion their causes and further their interests on a broad front. Professional associations, by contrast, are usually made up of individuals who have banded together for the same reasons, also forming a nonprofit organization. The following quote attests to the growth of trade associations—the type of organization upon which we will focus in this case:

> In the United States there are some 12,200 trade organizations—2,000 representing manufacturing industries, 5,100 covering distribution services, and 5,100 covering other businesses and services. The number has risen 50 percent since 1940 and is fifteen times what it was fifty years ago.
>
> Some 1,700 associations are national, the rest are regional or local.
>
> According to a study by the United States Chamber of Commerce, this is how 299 diverse trade associations operate to help their members in the area of selling:
>
> 178 collect and distribute inquiries for members' products or services.
> 90 conduct research among consumers for buying and selling data.
> 75 conduct research among outlets for products to determine buying and selling influences.
> 120 forecast trends and other business possibilities.
> 110 study or provide information on merchandising.
> 37 perform other marketing services.
>
> The Chamber of Commerce survey also showed that of 634 associations:
>
> 362 place advertising or furnish members with advertising aids.
> 530 publicize their industry.
> 178 operate exhibits or trade shows.
> 383 compile and distribute statistics on production inventories, labor, operating costs, and other market and organizational data.
> 83 associations utilize public relations and publicity consultants.[1]

Clearly, the growth of trade associations has been phenomenal, particularly since 1940; this is not the only noteworthy observation that can be made about them, however. Although trade associations are far from realizing their full potential, either as social forces in our society or as spokesmen for their particular segments of industry, nevertheless some very creative and interesting public relations work is being done by them. Our case list would be incomplete without at least one case drawn from the activities of a trade association. We have selected the American Dairy Association (ADA).

The American Dairy Association, organized in 1940, is financed and controlled entirely by dairy farmers and, as a trade association, does not

---

[1] Kalman B. Druck, "Trade and Professional Associations," Howard Stephenson, ed., in *Handbook of Public Relations* (New York: McGraw-Hill Book Company, Inc., 1960), pp. 100–101.

represent the dairy companies. Farmers invest two cents in the association —on a voluntary basis—for each 100 pounds of milk they market off their farms. Approximately one-half of all the milk sold each year in the United States is represented by the ADA. Its program is a national one, and the budget for 1965 was eight million dollars. These millions of dollars are spent on a wide spectrum of activities involving market research, product development, nutrition research, public relations, nonbrand advertising, and merchandising.

The ADA is distinct in its activities from the National Dairy Council, a separate organization which is twice as old as the ADA and which was formed to generate nutrition research and nutrition education. The ADA, however, provides one-half of the budget of the Council, the other half being supplied by the dairy processors and equipment suppliers.

The NDC prepares a wide variety of excellent age-graded materials for school use in teaching nutrition, and it also produces materials aimed at physicians, dietitians, and other categories of health educators. In addition, the NDC has developed a network of locally organized Dairy Council units which conduct their educational efforts at the local level. In a sense, the National Dairy Council focuses its communication efforts more on specialized audiences than on the general public, with an emphasis on furthering the educational process; the American Dairy Association, on the other hand, utilizes various forms of the mass media and is less concerned with making an impact on formal health education programs throughout the country.

In the case to follow, we shall see how the ADA handled a problem that confronted the entire dairy industry; this will provide an illustration of public relations functioning by an association, as distinct from the public relations arm of a company or some other type of organization.

2. BACKGROUND INFORMATION

The word *cholesterol* has been frightening the dairy industry for a long time. In the late 1950's and early 1960's, questions about the relationship between diet (specifically, the role of animal fats in the diet) and atherosclerosis[2] began to appear more and more frequently in both scientific and general public literature. By 1960, many people in the dairy industry were greatly alarmed by this increasing linkage between animal fats in one's daily diet and the incidence of heart disease. Information on the relationship ap-

[2] Atherosclerosis is a form of arteriosclerosis, or hardening of the arteries, which occurs when fatty substances form or are deposited in the walls of the arteries, tending to clog the vessels and restrict the flow of blood. When this occurs in arteries which supply blood to the heart muscles, this is coronary atherosclerosis. (*Public Relations Tips for Dairymen*, Chicago: American Dairy Association, Vol. 1, No. 2, February, 1961, p. 6).

peared in the popular press, and a good many of these same dairy people were convinced that this was causing the leveling off in the per capita consumption of certain dairy products.

In early 1960 there was discussion in the industry about the possibility of conducting a massive program of research and public information to combat the threat of the diet-heart disease assertions. The proposal was based primarily upon the *assumption* that the American public was generally aware of and concerned about the possibility that milk-fat ingestion might cause atherosclerosis.

However, those responsible for public relations within the American Dairy Association had serious reservations about the wisdom of a special program for this purpose. Their hesitation was based on several key factors:

1. There was no scientific (though much intuitive) evidence that the idea of a relationship between fats in the diet and heart disease was being accepted by the general public. More to the point, there was also no evidence that this diet-heart disease linkage was actually hurting sales of milk and other dairy products to any serious degree.

2. The American Dairy Association, the National Dairy Council, and other dairy groups had, for a period of years, been providing financial support to scientists investigating the general problem of heart disease. It had also been generally agreed that additional funds should be provided to encourage more research. In short, the long-standing position of the dairy industry was one of generous aid to research in the field of nutrition—to answer questions about the role of milk in human nutrition and to add to the industry's store of information that might be used to promote both the drinking of milk and the value of dairy products generally.

Because of this active identification with research in nutrition, the public relations personnel associated with the ADA realized that the diet-heart disease question was, in a sense, a *controversy among scientists*. The fact that there were equally competent scientists on both sides of the issue indicated that any public information campaign designed to combat the presumed negative aspects of the controversy would have to be based on trying to confuse the public. No one had definitive information; whatever data existed was inconclusive, open to question, or downright wrong, depending upon who was doing the interpreting. Consequently, an information program would have to consist of counterclaims and hypotheses and would serve to cloud, not to clarify, the issue.

3. The ADA's public relations department argued that the policy of answering every charge brought against the use of milk or dairy products did more harm than good, inasmuch as it tended to pit a commercial interest (the ADA representing the dairy farmers) against scientists whose integrity was virtually impossible to challenge. This point, incidentally, was used to answer certain people in the dairy industry who felt that the ADA

should pattern its public relations program at least in part along the lines of the Tobacco Institute, which seemingly followed the practice of trying to refute, or at least answer directly, every charge made against the use of tobacco.

Out of this discussion came the conclusion that a more scientific basis was needed for coming to a decision about what should be done. Accordingly, a commercial research organization was employed to do a nationwide study on consumer attitudes toward milk and dairy products.[3]

RESULTS OF THE SURVEY RESEARCH CONDUCTED[4]

In the late spring of 1961, the research organization interviewed 3,067 individuals of 15 years of age and over and comprising both sexes. On the basis of this national probability sample, the researchers were able to generalize to all Americans 15 years of age and over. We shall limit ourselves to the highlights of the findings of this comprehensive study.

FINDINGS VERSUS ASSUMPTIONS

Awareness of the diet-heart disease issue

Our first major concern with the data obtained is how they compare with the assumptions held by the public relations personnel of the American Dairy Association and by others in the dairy industry prior to the survey. Particularly, how do they relate to the *reservations* of the public relations practitioners with regard to launching a massive information program to counteract information being circulated about the relationship of diet to heart disease? First, let us consider the data that have implications for just how *aware* the general public were about the diet-heart disease controversy. One question asked in the study was, "Some people have been concerned that diet and the kinds of foods people eat may be associated with heart disease. Have you heard anything about this?" The findings were as shown in Table 14-1.[5]

From these data it is clear that more and more people are aware of the possible relationship between diet and heart disease; since the 1956

---

[3] It should be added that this was the eleventh in a series of nationwide studies that the American Dairy Association had commissioned for various reasons. This indicated that it was a well-established tradition at ADA to make use of research as a guide in its public relations, marketing, and other decisions.

[4] The data in this section are taken from a report entitled *Highlights from a Study of Public Attitudes Toward and Uses of Dairy Products,* submitted to the American Dairy Association by Universal Marketing Research, an affiliate of Alfred Politz Research, Inc., 1961.

[5] The reader is reminded that this study was one of a long series which took place over a period of years; consequently, trend data were available with which to compare the 1961 results.

Table 14-1. Awareness of the diet-heart disease controversy (base: all people interviewed)

Time	Percent
Fall 1956	26%
Spring 1957	36
Spring 1959	34
Fall 1959	36
Spring 1961	50

Source: *Highlights from a Study of Public Attitudes Toward and Uses of Dairy Products,* submitted to the American Dairy Association by Universal Marketing Research, an affiliate of Alfred Politz Research, Inc., 1961, p. 6.

study, the percentage has nearly doubled. Although there appears to be some basis for concern, the findings should be examined in some sort of perspective. For instance, it would be useful to know how awareness of this issue compares with awareness of the cigarette-cancer relationship, an issue which—in some people's minds at least—is similar to the diet-heart disease controversy. Accordingly, in the spring of 1961, the investigators asked, "Some people have been concerned that cigarette smoking may be associated with cancer. Have you heard anything about this?"

Table 14-2. Comparative awareness of similar health issues (base: all people interviewed)

Issue	Percent
Diet-heart disease relationship	50%
Cigarette-cancer relationship	88

Source: *Highlights . . . ,* p. 7.

Although it might be better to have a number of issues to compare with, it is useful to have data on even this one other commonly publicized health topic. On the basis of the comparison, it would appear that a 50% awareness of the diet-heart disease issue is not unusually high.

"Dimensions" of the awareness

Mere awareness of the topic does not, of course, tell us anything about the proportions of negative and positive views; the data cannot be interpreted without more information. For this reason, a number of additional questions were asked of those who said they were aware of the diet-heart disease issue; for example, Tables 14-3 and 14-4 show the *sort* of people that constituted the "aware" group.[6]

Table 14-3. Groups most aware (base: the 50% of the total population who said they were aware = 100%)

Classification	Percent
Professionally employed	72%
At least some college education	70
Employed as managers or officials or were proprietors of their own business	67
Belonged in the upper socioeconomic levels	64

Table 14-4. Groups least aware (base: the 50% of the total population who said they were aware = 100%)

Classification	Percent
People 15-19 years of age	39%
Operatives (factory workers) and laborers	38
Some grade school education	37
Belonged to lower socioeconomic levels	36

Source: *Highlights...*, p. 8.

People were also asked questions that threw some light on how well informed they were about the diet-heart disease question; for example, "Here are some statements about heart disease. Will you tell me whether you believe or don't believe each one?"

Another closely related question was put to the respondents, in this case to all of those who had been interviewed. They were asked, "Here

[6] The headings "most aware" and "least aware" stem from interpreting answers to other questions on certain details of the awareness. If an individual was misinformed on some feature of the diet-heart disease relationship, he was scored as "least aware"; if he was correctly informed, he was classified as "most aware" (see Tables 14-5 and 14-6 on "information and misinformation").

THE AMERICAN DAIRY ASSOCIATION

Table 14-5. Information and misinformation about heart disease (base: the 50% of the population which claimed awareness of the diet-heart disease relationship = 100%)

Statement	Believe	Do not believe	Don't know
Diet is the only factor causing heart disease	5%	85%	10%
A person's blood should contain *no* cholesterol	11	52	37
Medical doctors know the cause of heart disease	31	47	22
The human body manufactures some of its own supply of cholesterol	57	4	39
People with low cholesterol in the blood never have heart disease	10	42	48

Source: *Highlights* . . . , p. 9.

is a list of items which may or may not cause heart disease. Would you indicate for each one whether you believe or don't believe that the item causes heart disease?"

At this point, let us stop and consider the data presented in the pre-

Table 14-6. Information and misinformation on causes of heart disease (base: all people interviewed)

Possible causes of heart disease	Believe	Do not believe	Don't know
Overweight	86%	4%	10%
Underweight	16	56	28
High blood pressure	79	5	16
Low blood pressure	24	38	38
Cholesterol in the blood	41	7	52
Diabetes	30	25	45
Cigarette smoking	39	32	29
Daily exercise	9	72	19
Aging (getting older)	52	30	18
Worry and frustration	74	11	15
Heredity (or family background)	40	32	28

Source: *Highlights* . . . , p. 10.

vious four tables. First, with respect to our question about what sort of people are most aware of the diet-heart disease issue, the responses suggest that they are those with greater amounts of formal education; they are higher on the socioeconomic scale; they are more likely to be professional and managerial people or self-employed. This is certainly consistent with what might be expected, since the controversy is a comparatively complicated one that requires better-than-average ability to grasp the issues involved. Also, these data are confirmed by many other studies that point out that the better educated, managerial, professional, and self-employed individuals with higher incomes tend to read more and are better acquainted with current events and issues than those at lower levels; hence, they are more likely to interpret what they read carefully and accurately. This last point brings us to the question of how well-informed people are about the diet-heart disease issue.

The previous two tables, which dealt with information and misinformation, indicate that people are intelligently aware about the diet-heart disease issue and, in addition, that they are quite discriminating about the manner in which they interpret what they read and hear.

Views on the relationship between certain foods and heart disease

To understand more clearly the dimensions of awareness, the investigators next asked a series of questions that went into more detail about the "diet" in the diet-heart disease relationship. They asked, "What kinds of foods have you heard might be associated with heart disease?"

Fats are obviously the most salient in people's minds among the categories of foods associated with heart disease. This opinion increased sharply from 1957 to 1961, which suggests a direct relationship with the

Table 14-7. Trends in association of foods with heart disease (free response) (base: all who heard = 100%)

Foods mentioned	Spring 1957	Spring 1959	Spring 1961
Milk	3%	4%	4%
Other dairy products	3	10	13
Coffee	2	2	2
Fattening foods	9	8	6
Fats	47	54	73
Starches	6	6	6
Fried foods	2	6	7
Rich foods	8	5	7

Source: *Highlights...*, p. 11.

THE AMERICAN DAIRY ASSOCIATION

increasing volume of literature about the diet-heart disease issue. However, it would appear from the data in Table 14-8 that (1) people do not think exclusively of milk and dairy products when they use the word "fats," and (2) more pertinent, their eating behavior does not seem to be affected very much. To those who answered "fats" or "fatty foods" in response to the previous question, the investigators asked, "Could you name some specific foods?"

Table 14-8. Trends in association of dairy foods with heart disease (base: all who replied "fats" or "fatty foods" = 100%)

Foods mentioned	Spring 1959	Spring 1961
Milk	2%	5%
Ice cream	1	1
Butter	6	17
Other dairy products	3	4

Source: *Highlights...*, p. 12.

We see that there is an upward trend in the milk and butter categories but not for other dairy products. Apparently, people are more selective in their interpretation of how the term "fats" applies to dairy products in general. Incidentally, the researchers who conducted the study suggested that recent efforts promoting "low-fat" or skim milk could very well be contributing as much to this interpretation concerning milk as a "fat" (and butter as a derivative of milk) as do the articles dealing with the relationship between diet and heart disease.

The picture is clarified even more when we consider what this knowledge is doing to the eating habits of the people interviewed. A series of three related groups of data will be considered here. The following question was asked of those who were aware of the diet-heart disease issue: "Will

Table 14-9. Consumption of dairy products (base: those who are aware of diet-heart disease issue = 100%)

Food	Eating less dairy products	Eating more dairy products
Skim milk	4%	5%
Whole milk	9	8
Butter	14	4
Dairy products	8	9

you please tell whether you think you are eating more or less _____[7] than you were a year or two ago?"

When this same question is asked of the 13.5% of those aware of the issue *who had changed their eating habits as a result,* we get the responses in Table 14-10.

Table 14-10. Consumption of dairy products (base: the 13.5% of all people interviewed who have changed their eating habits = 100%)

Food	Eating less dairy products	Eating more dairy products
Skim milk	4%	10%
Whole milk	13	7
Butter	28	4
Dairy products	12	8

Source: *Highlights . . . ,* p. 15.

Table 14-11. Consumption of dairy foods (base: the 34% of all people who have heard of diet-heart issue but who have *not* changed their eating habits = 100%)

Food	Eating less dairy products	Eating more dairy products
Skim milk	4%	3%
Whole milk	8	8
Butter	10	4
Dairy products	7	9

Source: *Highlights . . . ,* p. 16.

Lastly, what do the results look like for the 34% of those aware of the issue *who had not changed their eating habits as a result?*

On the basis of the previous three tables we can see more clearly the relationship between awareness and the effects of this awareness on the eating habits of the respondents. In general, their habits have changed very little; the one exception has been with respect to the consumption of butter. As a result, not all dairy products are equally affected, which raises a very important question: What has brought about this change?

Although there are no final answers in this study on the causes of these

---

[7] Various foods were inserted at this point in the question. *Highlights, op. cit.,* p. 14.

changes in eating habits, one important insight was brought out; the question of diet for controlling one's weight is probably as important as awareness of the diet-heart disease issue in modifying the behavior of those persons who have changed their eating habits. For example, the study showed that 17.3% of all adults were on a diet of some kind, an increase from the 13.8% noted in the survey conducted in the spring of 1959. Also, 22% of the people *who are aware* of the diet-heart disease issue are on a diet of some type. Furthermore, the better educated, higher socioeconomic groups often lead sedentary lives and are twice as likely to be on diets as those at the lower levels. But dieting has not increased nearly so much as awareness of the diet-heart disease issue during the past six years.

What is apparent is that more people think that dairy foods are fattening. The number of people who list dairy products as foods to be avoided for weight-watching purposes increased nine percentage points between 1959 and 1961, but the total is still much smaller than for those who name such items as bread or potatoes (see Table 14-12).

Table 14-12. Image of dairy products (base: percent who say they would not have eaten the item had they been interested in keeping their weight down or reducing on a diet)

Food	All adults, Spring 1959	All adults, Spring 1961
Bread	68%	64%
Butter	29	28
Soft drinks	15	19
Plain milk	5	12
Cheese	7	10
Fruit	2	3

Source: *Highlights . . .*, p. 30.

As was noted earlier, the researchers suggest that perhaps much of the growing conviction that milk is fattening is a result of the promotion of skim milk and low-fat milk. If public attention is called to the higher fat and calorie levels in whole milk *as compared with* skim or low-fat milk, it is possible that many people may be assuming that whole milk is, simply, heavy in fat and calories.

Where do people get their information?

Public relations practitioners, as communicators, are always interested in where people get their information on a given topic, as well as the nature of the information itself. Some of the survey data are pertinent with regard to sources of information. The question, "Could you tell me where or from whom you learned about diet and heart disease being associated?" elicited the answers shown in Table 14-13.

Table 14-13. Source of information for learning that diet and heart disease may be associated (base: all people who have heard that diet and heart disease may be associated = 100%)

Source	Percent*
Newspapers, magazines	47.0
Friends or relatives	25.0
Doctors	18.0
Radio, television	14.0
Courses in school	6.0
Advertisements	2.0
Doctor via articles, TV, radio	1.0
Cookbooks, leaflets	.4

*Multiple replies permitted; total therefore exceeds 100%.
Source: *Highlights...*, p. 22.

In view of the role that dieting in general plays, the investigators also asked the same group, "Have you ever obtained information about diets in general from any of these places? Which ones?" The replies are shown in Table 14-14.

The mass media, in the form of newspapers and magazines, are the

Table 14-14. Sources of information on diets (base: all persons interviewed = 100%)

Source	Spring 1959	Spring 1961
Newspapers, magazines	17%	45%
Radio, television	13	33
Friends or relatives	6	29
Cookbooks, leaflets	15	16
Courses in school	15	12
Food packages, labels	7	12
None; don't know	5	43

Source: *Highlights...*, p. 32

THE AMERICAN DAIRY ASSOCIATION 195

dominant source of information both about the diet-heart disease issue and about diets in general. In fact, a sort of "box score" can be made summarizing a portion of both tables.

Table 14-15. Where do people get their information?

Source	Dieting in general	Diet-heart disease
Newspapers, magazines	45%	47%
Radio, television	33	14
Friends or relatives	29	25
Doctors	13	18

What sort of professional information do they receive?

One quite important source of information about the diet-heart disease issue and the question of dieting in general is the family physician or the related health specialist. What these professional people tell their patients is of particular concern to the public relations practitioners representing the American Dairy Association. The following questions asked have particular relevance here: "Have you ever received advice about your diet from a doctor or dentist or dietician?" "What was the particular condition that led the (doctor, dentist or dietician) to give you the advice?" "Do you remember what particular advice was given?" "Anything else?"

Table 14-16. Professional advice received about diet for heart condition (base: all people reporting professional advice on diet for heart condition = 100%)

Advice	Spring 1959	Spring 1961
Diet to lose weight; eat less	21%	38%
Avoid or cut down on fats or fatty foods	25	38
Proper diet; special diet (no indication of weight problem)	26	30
Drink milk or drink more milk	3	0
Avoid or cut down on dairy products (other than milk)	1	7
Answers which could not relate to dairy products	54	61
Don't know; don't remember	2	1

Source: *Highlights...*, p. 23.

Table 14-17. Professional advice received about diet for weight control (base: all people reporting professional advice on diet for overweight = 100%)

Advice	Spring 1959	Spring 1961
Diet to lose weight; eat less	47%	74%
Avoid or cut down on fats or fatty foods	17	20
Proper diet; special diet (no indication of weight problem)	14	4
Drink milk or drink more milk	2	0
Avoid or cut down on milk	1	0
Avoid or cut down on dairy products (other than milk)	2	1
Eat or eat more dairy products (other than milk and fat-reduced products)	1	1
Eat fat-reduced dairy products	2	1

Source: *Highlights...*, p. 34. Note that whereas the 1961 column adds to more than 100% because of multiple answers from respondents, the 1959 column adds to less because the entries do not include all the answers, only those that offered a basis for comparison to show trends.

The data from Tables 14-16 and 14-17 suggest two important interpretations: (1) so far as the heart patient perceives the situation, professionals have not suggested any sharp cutting-down on dairy products; (2) Professionals are not making any special effort to recommend reduced consumption of dairy products for their weight-conscious patients.

A summary of the data

Although we were unable to present all of the data obtained from this survey, the reader should have a reasonably good grasp of what the public relations personnel of the ADA found out via the research that was done for them. Before going on to an examination of the public relations program that was developed in the light of these findings, let us summarize the highlights of the study with a few generalizations. This should permit us to see the relationship between the research and the programming more easily.[8]

[8] The five headings below, as well as the discussions paraphrased in the first person, are taken from a booklet entitled *The Public Speaks* (Chicago, n.d.), which was put out by the ADA for "everyone in the dairy industry." This booklet was a report from the ADA concerning the research that had recently been conducted for them and the implications of this research for both the ADA and the dairy industry in general.

1. *"We must remember that it pays to keep our shirts on."* Changing consumer attitudes and eating habits is exceedingly difficult and a slow process at best. There are times when we in the dairy industry are upset because we seemingly cannot persuade the general public to do what we think is best for health—to drink at least three glasses of milk every day, for instance. On the other hand, the public's resistance to change can work in our favor, and there is evidence that this is just what is happening amid the increasing attention being paid to the diet-heart disease relationship. Although we cannot stop trying to educate the public to the importance of dairy products in daily life, there is no reason for us to panic; the assumption some have made that the general public has been unduly affected by all the talk about diet and heart disease *is not supported by data.*

2. *"We must use the facts already available more often and more effectively."* The questions concerning the precise relationships between diet and heart disease are a long way from being answered as yet. However, there is no shortage of solid information on the value of dairy products in daily diet. Consequently, we should continue to avoid getting into a controversy with scientists and likewise avoid doing anything to confuse the issue by exerting claims and counterclaims. Instead of promoting theories, we should stress the sound ideas that presently exist about the use of dairy products for daily good eating to promote health.

3. *"We must give scientists support to find the answers."* The only way that the diet-heart disease controversy will be settled is through research. We must continue to support scientific research in the spirit that we have maintained all along—the attitude that the dairy industry is interested in improving the knowledge scientists have about human health in general and about the relationship of diet to health in particular, regardless of the ultimate nature of these findings.

4. *"We must avoid 'knocking' milk fat in promoting other products."* Two of the more important findings to emerge from the research we have supported are that (1) the American public—particularly the more educated and affluent, who are at the same time more aware of the diet-heart disease controversy—continues to be and is increasingly preoccupied with weight control (in fact, the diet-weight control question would appear to be far more important to it than the diet-heart disease controversy); and (2) the food which people most often feel should be avoided for dieting is "fats" or "fatty foods." On the basis of these data, it would appear safe to conclude that trying to promote the sale of skim milk through approaches which emphasize the fat in whole milk and, by implication, the fact that milk is a high-calorie food will produce only short-term gains. The more immediate effect is to depress the sale of other dairy products in the process of boosting the sale of skim milk. The longer-range effect could be to cause people increasingly to equate fats and fatty foods with dairy products in general, not with milk alone.

5. *"We must emphasize more often and more effectively the positive values of dairy products in adult diets."* All the above generalizations lead to one important conclusion: we must encourage adults to use milk by communicating the idea frequently and in new ways. This positive approach is aided by the fact that every reputable weight-control plan or diet calls for the inclusion of milk and other dairy products. With all sorts of authorities behind us, we cannot help but benefit from a program of communication that highlights the essential and enjoyable aspects of milk and milk products in the adult human diet.

PUBLIC RELATIONS PROGRAM BASED ON RESEARCH FINDINGS

A discussion of the public relations program that was developed in the light of the research findings most logically reflects the generalizations introduced in the previous section, as the program itself follows this same pattern.

To begin with, the findings were compared with the assumptions that were held before the research was conducted. In summary, the public relations personnel of the ADA felt that (1) the research served to support their earlier position, "that the dairy industry should not engage in a public brawl with scientists over the diet-heart disease issue," (2) the research supported the assumption that the public was *not* being unduly affected by the cholesterol scare, (3) the attitudes of the adult American public about the values of drinking milk were still very positive and constituted a frame of reference that could be capitalized upon, and (4) lastly, the long-standing program of supporting scientific research in the general area of nutrition was more than vindicated and clearly should be continued. In the light of this assessment, the public relations program that emerged following the research took the following lines.

Dairy industry or "internal" efforts

Internally, the ADA people felt that they had a job to do to restore a degree of calmness among people in the dairy industry and to mobilize efforts toward a positive course of action (as opposed to contesting adverse statements about milk or dairy products in daily adult diets). One effort was to enable the many dairymen to be more effective spokesmen for the industry. In a special monthly publication entitled *Public Relations Tips for Dairymen,* a steady flow of articles was generated that expounded on variations of the basic information in the study and, in addition, on related principles of communication or social and behavioral science information that were pertinent to the topic under discussion. Let us examine briefly one of the issues of the newsletter to illustrate how this was done. The lead headline was "Accentuating the Positive Will Help Eliminate or Devalue the Negative." To support the contention of this headline, several subpoints were developed in this issue that restated some of the findings of the study and at the same time related them to social and behavioral science principles.

One of the findings was that people were not unduly affected by the diet-heart disease controversy. In other words, beliefs and attitudes are resistant to change. The following is a quote which states this in a slightly different context:

Too frequently in our daily efforts to earn our bread and butter, as well as in some of our off-the-job community activities, we forget that *people are bundles of attitudes,* and we overlook, too, the point that *attitudes ordinarily do not change quickly or easily.* Men cling to their attitudes because to do otherwise would bring a certain amount of discomfort.

This is an extremely important point to keep in mind. People do not let their attitudes be shaken easily because the set of attitudes which any of us might have is our adjustment to our culture, our way of reacting to our environment and to other people. Few of us have the stamina, mentally or morally, that is required to make frequent changes in attitudes. Instead *we seek more support for the attitudes we already hold.*

A little farther on a psychologist is quoted in order to relate the point made above to a current psychological theory:

Dr. Leon Festinger, professor of psychology at Stanford University, and his associates are responsible for what is known as *the theory of cognitive dissonance.* Stated very simply, *this theory suggests that when any of us are exposed to conflicting points of view, the usual procedure is to try to fit them together to reduce the conflict—or dissonance—that has arisen.*

Dr. Festinger says that, once we have resolved the conflict in favor of one point of view or the other, we tend to think more about the favorable points in the alternative we accepted and more about the unfavorable points in the rejected choice. He also believes *that the more a person is subjected to dissonance, or conflict, the greater will be the effort to reduce it—that is, to eliminate the conflict by accepting or rejecting or combining the conflicting points of view.*[9]

At this point, the article has brought about a combination of the research data and the thinking of a psychologist who has done considerable research in the area of persuasion. With this achieved, it then continues by pointing out what the implications for action are:

The cognitive dissonance theory has some very practical meaning for communicators and for dairymen in particular at the present time. Let's see how the theory applies in the case of milk.

Studies of public attitudes toward milk show very clearly that part of grow-

[9] *Public Relations Tips for Dairymen,* Vol. 3, No. 3 (March 1963), 1.

ing up in America, for most of us, is acquiring a very highly favorable attitude toward milk as a basic and important, as well as a very good tasting food. Even those who profess to dislike the taste of milk usually agree that milk is a wonderful food that everyone should have.

With this generally very favorable attitude existing toward milk, any attack against milk creates a certain amount of conflict—or dissonance—for some people. We would be mistaken to assume that all people are affected by attacks on milk, for we must remember our old friend *selective perception* (along with *selective exposure* and *selective retention*) which has been mentioned in these pages before. *For many people, in fact, perhaps for most people, no dissonance will occur when milk is attacked because the attack will not be noted or will be ignored if noted.* Dairymen, because of the economic and emotional attachment to milk, will surely note the attacks. Beyond this, how many people note and remember the attack will usually depend upon the basis of the attack or the unfavorable mention of milk.[10]

Following this presentation of the relationship between dissonance and the adverse publicity about the diet-heart disease controversy, the newsletter article then points out that *awareness* (of the controversy) and *concern* are not the same thing—that the former does not necessarily imply the existence of the latter. It goes on to suggest that one of the most effective steps dairymen can take is to reduce the conflict that people might feel about the issue, by avoiding controversy and putting forth positive information about dairy products. In this connection the newsletter states:

In a situation where there are no clear-cut answers, it is far better to avoid public controversy whenever possible. A conflict will always attract more attention simply because it is given greater coverage in the mass media. Also, the people who do not note the issue . . . look at the sources of information. A commercial interest attempting to defend its products which have been suggested as culprits in a major health problem is obviously at a serious disadvantage in a dispute with a scientist or health agency.

If the mass media engage in editorializing and cartooning the farm subsidy programs, it is the feeling of some people that farmers should attempt to justify the costs of farm programs by pointing the finger of subsidy at other groups. Many people interpret this to mean that farmers think that, just because someone else is "getting his," taxpayers have an obligation to provide farm program subsidies. This does not really win many friends for government farm programs.

Most efforts to "fight back" in such problem areas are quite worthless and probably do much more harm than good. In most cases, "fighting back" simply adds fuel to the fire and may help to break through the screen which selective perception has raised to keep these issues out of most people's thinking.[11]

With this background of theory and practice combined to argue for a given point of view, the newsletter article then turns to what can be done:

[10] *Ibid.*, pp. 1–2.
[11] *Ibid.*, pp. 2–3.

There is very little that dairymen can do at the present time to eliminate some of the major problems that tend to influence dairy foods consumption adversely. Dairymen are helping to finance research to find some answers to the diet-heart disease questions, but it is likely that this problem may be quite a few years away from solution. Whether we have radioactive fallout in our food and water supply depends to a great extent upon efforts to get an agreement that would end the testing of atomic weapons. Whether the farm program problem will be reduced in scope is going to depend upon a good many different groups, including the Congress, the President, and many others.

It would certainly appear to be almost fruitless to engage in efforts to "fight back" when there really are no very strong points to be made about these problems at this time. Instead the most sensible direction to travel at the moment would appear to be to *concentrate far more effort in reconfirming the favorable attitudes that most people now hold about dairy foods and the dairy industry.* As far as the public generally is concerned, it may very well be that attitudes about farm programs may be influenced not by the knowledge of how efficient farmers have become but rather by reaction to the farm products themselves. Most people simply do not take time to be concerned, either favorably or unfavorably, about the efficiency of agriculture or of the automobile factory. Judgments are based, ordinarily, on the values which the consumer sees in the end product. Most of us confine our attitudes to a rather tiny share of the world in which we live.

Several public attitude studies in the past year or so have indicated that there may be some weakening in the generally favorable attitudes toward milk as nature's most nearly perfect food or as the food that is essential to all ages. At least part of this is a result of increased knowledge of nutrition which leads many women to the realization that such dairy products as ice cream and cheese are nutritionally adequate substitutes for fluid milk.

On the other hand, and of much more concern (regarding what it portends for the future if the situation is not corrected), there appears to be a very small, but surely growing, number of people who have reached a state of dissonance about milk's role in the good health of our people. They have heard the questions being asked about milk, but we dairymen, apparently, have not been doing enough to reinforce the favorable attitudes which most people have toward our products. The result is that a few more people do doubt the importance of milk in the diet.

To counteract this situation it behooves all of us to work much more diligently toward better public understanding of the kind of role that milk can play in giving us healthful, balanced diets.[12]

By now the reader should have a fairly good grasp of the type of internal education effort that emerged following the research study via *Public Relations Tips for Dairymen.* Here are some of the succeeding themes that were expressed in lead headlines and followed up in more detail in the copy:

"When the Chips are Down, a Good Many People Turn to the Facts for Guidance"

[12] *Ibid.,* p. 3.

"Ignorance About Causes of Heart Disease Will Continue To Pose Problems for Food Industries"

"Positive Approaches May Help 'Immunize' Against Unfavorable Changes in Attitudes"

"Heart Disease Developments Require Careful Interpretation To Avoid Misunderstanding"[13]

Throughout the issues of the periodical, the basic approach is the same. The fundamental goal: to educate the rank and file dairyman to what he faces and to what he should do and why, with a strong reliance upon principles derived from the social and behavioral sciences.

External efforts—concentration on target audiences

As in the case of the internal public relations program, we can only touch briefly on the external programming. Perhaps the best example is the special public relations advertising series that combined a number of insights provided by the research findings. Specifically, the series achieved a synthesis of the following points:

1. The ads were directed to the more highly educated, professional, managerial, and self-employed individuals that the research had indicated were a) more aware of the diet-heart disease controversy, and b) more likely to read about this topic—especially if the copy were informative and contained *ideas* worthy of their time.[14] To pinpoint this audience more closely, these ads were run in publications such as the *Atlantic Monthly, Harper's, Editor & Publisher,* the *Quill,* the *American Press, National Publisher, Publishers' Auxiliary,* and *Broadcasting.*

2. The theme of the copy contained in the advertising stressed the ideas that a) no one knows all of the answers about the diet-heart disease relationship, and b) those interested in the production of food have no business setting themselves up as experts in this area. The only expert an individual should rely upon is his own family physician; whatever he suggests with respect to eliminating certain foods (particularly dairy products)

---

[13] See *Public Relations Tips for Dairymen,* Vol. 2, No. 11 (November, 1962); Vol. 4, No. 7 (July, 1964); 5, No. 4 (April, 1965); and Vol. 2, No. 2 (July, 1962), respectively.

[14] In an issue of *Saturday Review* (February 13, 1965, p. 74) Elmo Roper stated that he believed more and more businesses will be doing the sort of advertising the ADA has been carrying on for many years. This remark was made in the context of a discussion of advertising in the 1970's. Mr. Roper went on to say, "The first change I expect to take place is that there will be more advertising devoted to the transmission of ideas rather than simply to the selling of products. There will, in other words, be more corporate advertising, more advertising concerned with improving public relations. We exist in a society where public relations—human relations—are increasingly important, and there will be increasing awareness that the ideas and feelings and attitudes that form the substance of these relations are as crucial to the well-being of many corporations as the movement of products."

FEEL LIKE A PING PONG BALL?

Don't eat this. Don't eat that. Calories. Cholesterol. Polyunsaturates. Heart disease.

The current rash of do-it-yourself diets and food fads is enough to make you feel like a ping pong ball. Bouncing from claim to claim.

Should you change your diet or not? Are these dangers real or not? Are they *proved* or not? Is there *someone* you can trust in all this?

There is. Your physician.

And the first thing he'll probably tell you is: don't change your diet unless you're sick.

And if you are sick, trust *him* to get you back on the right diet—not unproved food claims.

Even if he asks you to cut down on some of the products we represent, that's all right with us.

Because no one knows your individual health problems like your physician. We don't. (And other food people don't, either.) There's no such thing as a universal diet.

For good nutrition, the American Medical Association (October 12, 1962) recommends a well-balanced diet chosen from these four basic food groups: (a) The Milk group (milk, cheese, ice cream), (b) The Meat group, (c) The Vegetable-Fruit group, and (d) The Bread-Cereal group.

That's why we urge you not to endanger your health with do-it-yourself food plans or to change your diet because of widely publicized food fears—like cholesterol.

Your physician will tell you this himself. Trust him. We do.

We're people, too.

american dairy association
Voice of the Dairy Farmers in the Market Places of America

Figure 14-1. An American Dairy Association advertisement

* Full text of the American Medical Association statement of Oct. 12, 1962, available by writing: Heart Diet, American Dairy Association, 20 N. Wacker Drive, Dept. D, Chicago 6, Ill. Source: Transmitted to the author by the Public Relations Division, American Dairy Association. This ad appeared in newspapers which are members of the Suburban Press Foundation in late October and early November 1962.

is perfectly all right with the dairy industry. After all, no one knows an individual's health needs better than his physician.

This theme did a number of things; it wisely avoided the controversy; it was consistent with the ADA's long-time policy of supporting research in nutrition by reinforcing the stand that what the scientists find out about nutrition would be the guide for action by the dairy industry; lastly, it was consistent with the findings of the survey research, which found physicians and other health specialists to be essentially neutral about the role of dairy foods in the daily diet.

3. The copy took advantage of still another of the research findings—that people's concern about foods was more in terms of diet and weight control than in terms of health hazards. Also, of all the people interviewed, the better educated, higher-income groups were the most conscious of their weight.

Figure 14-1 reproduces one of a long series of ads that brings together all the points listed above. It is a good example of the ADA's public relations advertising effort. Here are a few lead headlines, with accompanying subthemes, for some of the other ads in the series:

"Are Food Fads Unbalancing Your Diet?" Subthemes: false health information is being spead; there is no such thing as a perfect food for man; there is a strong case for milk for people of all ages.

"Overeating Has Become a Major Health Menace." Subthemes: weight control is a matter of eating habits; many of us must change our eating habits; whatever the specific diet we settle upon (under the advice of our physician), a balanced diet is the important point; evidence cited for the inclusion of dairy foods in a well-balanced diet.

"Food Men Should Not Try To Be Medicine Men." Subthemes: dietary treatment of an illness is a decision which should always be made by your physician; milk's contribution is big; "cholesterol confusion" reigns; dairymen again pledge cooperation.

15 | Case 5

Petroil Development and Research Corporation[1]: how one company assessed its reputation as a research organization within the scientific community

CASE OUTLINE

1. Introduction
2. Background information
3. Results of the survey research conducted
    a. The 1960 survey: before implementing a program
    b. The 1960 survey: some highlights
        —where the most significant research is being done today
        —Petroil Development and Research Corporation's standing in the oil industry
        —Petroil Development and Research Corporation's standing outside the oil industry
        —evaluation of media that reach the scientific community
    c. The 1960 survey: a summary of the data
4. Public relations program based on research findings
    a. internal portions of the public relations program
    b. external portions of the public relations program
    c. the 1963 survey: some highlights
        —where Petroil remained about the same or worsened
        —where Petroil improved
    d. The 1963 survey: a summary of the data

[1] The name of the actual company involved in this case must remain anonymous. However, the details are real and are described as they occurred within the organization. The fact that its identity must be withheld should in no way detract from the reader's (or the instructor's) ability to use this case as a teaching aid.

INTRODUCTION

There are a number of organizations in existence, both in this country and abroad, that are in a very peculiar situation from the standpoint of public relations planning and programming. This is particularly true of two categories of companies; one is the organization that does not deal directly with the general public in any "retail" sense; the other is the research and development company.

Companies in the first category do not sell directly to the consumer, but act in a supplier capacity with respect to others that *do* deal directly with the general public. There are hundreds of organizations that fall into this particular group, and their communication decisions are complicated by their lack of contact with the consumer.

Within this general category there are two subcategories that we must consider, (1) the company that does not sell directly to the consumer public —and *they* (the public) *couldn't care less,* and (2) the company that does not sell directly to the consumer public—and under some circumstances *they* (the public) *could care* and *might care.*

Let's take a couple of examples that illustrate the first situation. An organization produces industrial temperature control devices, such as the device that goes into an automatic breadwrapping machine. The consumer —that is, the housewife who buys the bread—couldn't care less about the machinery that was used to wrap her bread, not to mention any component parts of the machine—such as a temperature control device. Another example, the temperature control device that goes into the refrigeration unit that enables a truck to haul frozen foods. Once again, the housewife who buys the frozen foods hasn't the faintest interest in the temperature control unit used in the equipment that kept her foods frozen while they were being delivered by truck.

The second situation (or subcategory) can be illustrated as follows; the same company that manufactures temperature control devices can find itself in a position in which, under some circumstances, the consumer *could care* and *might care.* For example, there are temperature controls and temperature sensing devices to avoid fires and explosions, for instance, that go into airplanes. It may well be that a passenger flying to Europe would be quite interested in knowing that his plane was protected by such devices. Now the question comes up, should the manufacturer try to educate people who fly about the existence of these safety measures and about the role of supplying them to the airplane companies? Or perhaps this same organization makes devices that protect refrigerator motors from unnecessary damage as they start and stop, thereby prolonging the life of the motor, and, hence, the overall unit. As in the case of the airlines passenger, a consumer might be interested in this information. Should the manufacturer try to communicate with the consumer so that, as he goes to purchase a refrigerator, he will ask the salesman whether or not it is protected by such and such a motor protector unit manufactured by such and such a company?

We could go on and on with different examples of both subcategories of organizations that do not have direct contact with the consumer. The point we are trying to make, however, is that these particular situations do pose difficult decisions with regard to setting up a fruitful communication program—both from the public relations and the advertising point of view.

Organizations that fall into the second general category are, in some ways, in even more of a communication dilemma. The "products" of a company that does basic and applied research[2] are not "products" in the usual sense of the word. They are very often new ideas about products or technologies, or new ways of looking at old problems; this sort of "product" is very difficult to communicate about. In addition, there may be the confounding situation in which the research and development company is part of a larger industrial complex, with the result that its services are not for sale to the general public or to other organizations, but, rather, are reserved for the parent and/or affiliate companies.

In spite of the fact that these companies do not produce material objects and, like those in the first category, are not in touch with the general public, they need to be well known for a number of reasons. For one, when the research and development organization is part of a larger corporate complex, the other companies in the affiliation generally *do* sell to the general public, and under conditions of intense competition. Consequently, the better known the research and development arm happens to be for its research efforts, the greater the advantage of the overall company in the general marketplace. In addition, because such organizations need to attract talented scientists and engineers from a wide variety of fields, they need to be well known, particularly in the "scientific community." Finally, there is the wisdom of being well known among investment specialists, investment funds, and general stock purchasers, whose numbers are growing by leaps and bounds every year.

To sum up, we have tried to set the stage for our next case by making the reader aware that there are many organizations that do not have direct

---

[2] While there has not been an entirely satisfactory distinction made between the two terms *basic* and *applied*, their connotations are as follows: *basic*, or *fundamental research*, embraces those efforts in which the scientist is interested in obtaining information essentially for its own sake—even though he may have no idea how the findings of his research will be used, if at all; *applied research*, on the other hand, is directed toward solving some particular problem, very often one that may have sales or competitive implications, if solved by the scientist, for the company. As with many distinctions, the extremes of the two terms are comparatively easy to identify—it is not difficult to give examples of "pure" basic research and "pure" applied research. There are, of course, in-between efforts that are a little of both, making classification not so simple.

or easily identifiable relationships with the consumer public. The public relations planning and programming required for such companies is a complex matter and differs greatly from programs in companies that *do* have direct consumer contact.

The case that we are about to consider falls into the second major category—that of research and development organizations. Petroil Development and Research Corporation, a research and development company in the petroleum industry, recently underwent extensive reexamination of its public relations efforts to reach the scientific community. This case serves to illustrate the communication dilemmas that confront research and development companies of its type.

BACKGROUND INFORMATION

Petroil Development and Research Corporation is one of the world's largest research firms. Established in the early 1930's, it is among the nation's oldest research organizations.

The work engaged in by Petroil Development and Research encompasses a variety of projects and programs, ranging from advanced research of an exploratory nature to applied research and engineering. Approximately 25% of the company's work is long-range in nature.

In its early years, Petroil was mainly concerned with development work or applied research. That is, it did comparatively little fundamental research. In recent years, however, it has shifted its research efforts so that more fundamental and chemicals research is conducted.

The public relations people are acutely aware that a considerable lag exists between doing research, especially fundamental research, and being able to inform the scientific community about it. For example, it is not unusual for two years to elapse between completing a research project and having the results of this research published in a scientific journal. In addition, the public relations people are very conscious of the relationship between a company's research reputation and its ability to attract top research people who are essential if an organization is to continue to make contributions to fundamental knowledge in the area of the physical sciences.

For these and other reasons, the corporation's public relations manager concluded that it was essential for a comprehensive assessment of the reputation of his company among members of the scientific community to be made so that an intelligent public relations program could be developed.

RESULTS OF THE SURVEY RESEARCH CONDUCTED

The 1960 survey: before implementing a program

Before attempting to implement specific public relations programs, the company hired an outside organization to do a survey of attitudes toward

PETROIL DEVELOPMENT AND RESEARCH CORPORATION

its standing and reputation in the scientific community. The overall objectives of the survey were as follows:

1. To obtain a scientific evaluation of the status and reputation of the Petroil Development and Research Corporation in the scientific community.
2. To acquire guidance on how best to allocate money and manpower for the scientific community phase of the company's public relations program.
3. To provide baselines of opinion against which the effectiveness of the company's public relations program can be measured at regular intervals in the future.

The specific information sought by the public relations division was, how is the company regarded, and how does it compare with other research organizations? In addition, how does the petroleum industry compare with other industries, such as the chemicals, electronic, aircraft, and automotive industries? The points used as a basis for comparison are as follows:

1. Basic research.
2. Technical achievements.
3. Engineering skills.
4. Number and quality of technical papers.
5. Quality of individual scientists and engineers.
6. Participation in scientific societies.
7. General support of science education and research.
8. Opportunity for professional advancement.
9. Opportunity for advancement by technical people to positions in management.
10. Quality of technical management.
11. Salaries for technical people.
12. Quality of laboratories, equipment, and supporting laboratory personnel.

Additional information that the public relations division wanted can be summarized as follows:

1. How important is the reputation of the president of a technical company in relation to the company's reputation?
2. How do people in the scientific community rate Petroil's products in comparison with (*a*) other oil companies, and (*b*) products of major companies in other industries?
3. How do scientific people form opinions about a technical company?
4. Which media are most effective in reaching scientific people?

The term scientific community was defined as consisting of the following components:

1. Professors of scientific and engineering subjects.
2. Undergraduates in the scientific fields.

3. Graduate students in the scientific fields.
4. Industrial research personnel.
5. Government research personnel.
6. Technical editors.

With these objectives in mind and with the target audiences defined, a survey was conducted which consisted of interviewing the respondents on a variety of open- and closed-end questions.[3] In all, a probability sample was taken of 668 scientists in 19 colleges and universities, and in 10 additional geographical areas.[4]

The sample was distributed as follows:

College seniors   124
Graduate students   123
Faculty members   134
Industrial employees   182
Government employees   105

The scientific disciplines represented among those interviewed were as follows:

Chemical engineers   178
Organic chemists   126
All other branches of chemistry   208
Other scientific disciplines   156

Deliberate emphasis was placed on those disciplines of greatest interest to the petroleum/chemical industries.

The 1960 survey: some highlights

Although we cannot here examine all of the data that were obtained in the 1960 survey, we shall look at some of the more important findings under the following headings: (1) where the most significant research is being done today; (2) Petroil's standing in the oil industry; (3) Petroil's standing outside the oil industry; and (4) evaluation of the media that reach the scientific community.

Where the most significant research is being done today. One of the questions asked of the respondents was, "As far as your particular field of

---

[3] The terminology *open end* and *closed end* refers to the manner in which replies were elicited from the respondent (see again Chapter 8, pp. 77–95). In an open-end situation the respondent is asked a question to which he is free to reply as he wishes; the interviewer may probe from time to time—attempt to clarify points he does not understand or ask for more details or greater information; but essentially it consists in allowing the respondent to say what he *wants* to say in answer to a given question. The closed-end question requires the respondent to pick from a number of choices supplied him by the interviewer—for example, "very favorable," "favorable," "undecided," "unfavorable," or "very unfavorable."

[4] The term *scientists* refers here to persons in the physical sciences—physics and chemistry, for example.

science is concerned, where do you feel the most significant research is being done today—in government, in industry, or at colleges and universities?" The responses to this question are summarized in Table 15-1. The total scientific community clearly points to the colleges and universities as being the most active. Although industrial research organizations come off a rather poor second (34% versus 54%), they are still decidedly above the government in the eyes of the interviewees (12%).

Table 15-1. Where the most significant research is being done today

	Colleges and universities	Industry	Government
Total scientific community	54%	34%	12%
Senior	51	42	7
Graduate student	73	19	8
Faculty	74	17	9
Government	42	36	22
Industry	35	54	11

As might be expected, those in industry rate industrial research over academic-based research, but all groups are agreed that government research is in the last place. Graduate students and college and university faculty members, by the same token, even more strongly give university research as their first choice.

The leadership of the university based research is nicely summarized by the following quote from one of the respondents:

There can be no question where the most significant research is being done today. Unless it is in the area of direct product development, even the main research being done in industry and in the government was originally started in the university laboratory.

Petroil Development and Research Corporation's standing in the petroleum industry. Another important phase of the interview consisted of a series of questions designed to assess the standing of the company with other leading oil companies (We shall refer to these as Companies A, B, and C). The questions dealing with four dimensions of comparison: (1) reputation for basic research; (2) reputation for applied research (technical and engineering achievement); (3) role played by the company in encouraging activities of professional societies, publication of research results by company scientists, and so forth; and (4) opportunity for growth (both financial and professional) for scientists within the company.

In the first question, on basic research, the respondents were asked to

Table 15-2. Closed-end rating
in the area of basic research

Petroil	29%
Company A	27
Company B	10
Company C	12

rank Petroil against the three other petroleum organizations. Table 15-2 summarizes the results. Table 15-3 includes data on the second phase, the open-end questioning on the same subject.[5]

On the basis of the closed-end responses, Petroil has a slight lead over Company A with respect to reputation for doing basic research. Taken

Table 15-3. Open-end rating of the four oil companies in the area of basic research

	Petroil	Company A	Company B	Company C
Positive	27%	33%	20%	5%
Are involved in basic research, do basic research	14	21	17	1
Do diversified research, not limited	9	6	1	2
Give scientists a free hand, permit undirected research	4	6	2	2
Negative	18%	9%	15%	8%
Research is too limited, slanted, narrow	11	5	—	—
Don't do enough basic research	7	4	15	8

[5] This feature of the interviewing technique should be explained here. In each question area the respondent was first asked to rate the companies on a closed-end scale that ranged from a score of one (most positive) to a score of four (most negative). Following this, he was asked to "describe fully and freely all of his positive and negative ideas." In this way, the interviewer obtained "first impressions" as well as more "thoughtful and profound evaluation" on each point. At times this produced results that were inconsistent—a person might rate a company in one way on the closed end, but in subsequent discussion contradict himself. This did not happen very frequently, but when it did, the researchers felt they had achieved a greater depth of understanding of the respondents' attitudes.

together, these two companies are in an entirely different league from Companies B and C. However, when the interviewers probed more fully into the basis of the classification—that is, into such words as "largest," "biggest" and "best known"—the two top companies sometimes changed places. In Table 15-3, the open-end data imply that "Company A does more basic research. Equally interesting is the fact that Petroil received the highest percentage of negative replies, particularly on the narrowness of its research efforts. The opinion researchers themselves sum up this mixed picture with the following:

> It is [Petroil's] greatest assets which seem to stand most in the way of its reputation *for* basic research. It is precisely because [Petroil] is considered to be one of the giants of the petroleum industry that the scientific community expects the most of [Petroil] in the field of basic research—including a broadening out from oil and chemical research.

The second dimension of the standing of Petroil in the oil industry has to do with applied research—the respondents' views about the company's level of technical achievement. The interviewees were asked to rank the four companies with respect to their applied research programs and their facilities, particularly laboratories and personnel assisting the scientists. The closed- and open-end replies to this questioning are summarized in Tables 15-4 and 15-5.

Table 15-4. Closed-end rating in the area of applied research (technical and engineering achievement)

	Petroil	Company A	Company B	Company C
Quality of laboratories, equipment, and supporting personnel	42%	31%	16%	24%
Level of technical and engineering achievement	33	26	11	16
Quality of individual scientists and engineers	25	24	10	14

From the standpoint of technical and engineering achievement, it is clear that Petroil fares much better here than in the area of basic research. On practically every item in the two tables, it is rated higher than the other oil companies. The category that caused the public relations people at Petroil some concern was Company A's higher rating on "knew scientists or head of research organization." This was an important factor in the company's subsequent public relations program, and, as we shall see later, survey results of this sort received special attention.

The third dimension, the degree to which the company supports and participates in furthering scientific knowledge, is reflected in Table 15-6.

Table 15-5. Open-end rating in the area of applied research (technical and engineering achievement)

	Petroil	Company A	Company B	Company C
Good laboratory equipment and facilities	22%	15%	8%	6%
Excellent scientists, opportunity to work under the best men	14	10	5	7
Knew scientists or head of research organization	11	15	10	11
Do good applied research	10	13	7	2

The picture is somewhat mixed. Although Petroil ranks high in its reputation for supporting science education and research, it only ties in the next category and falls considerably behind in the last.

Table 15-6. Closed-end rating of fulfillment of role and responsibility in the scientific community

	Petroil	Company A	Company B	Company C
Participation in scientific societies	23%	23%	11%	14%
General support of science education and research	23	13	6	12
Number and quality of technical papers	11	17	4	4

The final dimension of the general questioning was a comparison of the four companies with respect to the opportunities they offered for growth, professional development, job advancement, and so forth. The responses in these areas are seen in Tables 15-7 and 15-8. In both the closed- and open-end responses, Petroil does rather well in comparison with the other companies. The only disquieting portion of the data is the "double-edged" quality of its reputation for bigness. Most of the negative comments (22%) in Table 15-8 are related in some way to the disadvantages of the company's large size.

PETROIL DEVELOPMENT AND RESEARCH CORPORATION

Table 15-7. Closed-end rating in the area of growth and opportunity

	Petroil	Company A	Company B	Company C
Is dynamic, has prospects for growth	27%	22%	12%	18%
Salaries for technical people	27	19	12	18
Opportunity for professional development	24	20	10	16
Opportunity for advancement by technical people to positions of management	23	20	11	16
Has reputation as a "human" company	14	12	7	7

Table 15-8. Open-end rating in the area of growth and opportunity

	Petroil	Company A	Company B	Company C
Positive	31%	23%	25%	17%
Large, prestige company, best reputation in its field	11	7	8	2
Pay good salaries	9	2	8	5
Progressive	6	7	2	3
Chance to advance	3	2	5	3
Good place to work for scientists	2	5	2	4
Negative	22%	4%	7%	8%
Too large, the individual gets lost	10	—	2	5
Poor personnel policies	5	—	1	—
No chance to develop and advance	3	1	3	2
No security, too competitive	2	2	—	—
Don't encourage individual initiative	2	—	1	—
Poor salaries	—	1	—	1

To summarize this second general area of questioning, these data seem to support the interpretation that, when compared with three other major oil companies, Petroil is somewhat weak on basic research, strong on technical achievement, good on facilities and staff, and somewhat mixed with respect to fulfillment of social responsibilities and on its reputation as a good place for scientists to work.

Petroil Development and Research Corporation's standing outside the oil industry. A petrochemical company's competitive position with regard to personnel, prestige, and reputation is not limited to other oil companies. Another phase of the interview was devoted to obtaining a comparison of Petroil with other major companies known for their outstanding research activities in other fields. We shall call these Companies L, M, N, O, P, and Q. The same four dimensions were used in this comparison as in the previous one concerning companies within the oil industry. Because of space limitations, we shall examine only one of these dimensions in detail—the area of basic research. The results of the questioning are summarized in Tables 15-9 and 15-10.

Table 15-9. Closed-end rating in the area of basic research

Company	Percent
Petroil	29
Company L	77
Company M	70
Company N	60
Company O	45
Company P	41
Company Q	29

It is immediately obvious from the data on the closed-end questioning that Petroil is out of the running with respect to five of the six companies; it is tied with Company Q for last place. In the open-end table Petroil fares even worse, claiming both the smallest percentage of positive remarks and the largest percentage of negative comments received.

On the other three dimensions of questioning, Petroil's relative position is equally poor, ranging anywhere from the bottom position to the middle of the scale.

To conclude our examination of how Petroil compares with the six other companies, let us look at Table 15-11, which represents a summary of the ratio of positive statements to negative statements obtained for *all* of the open-end questions.

Table 15-10. Open-end rating in the area of basic research

	Petroil	Company L	Company M	Company N	Company O	Company P	Company Q
Positive	27%	64%	78%	50%	38%	56%	39%
Are involved in basic research, do good basic research	14	34	36	21	27	24	14
Do diversified research, not limited	9	11	37	22	7	28	19
Give scientists a free hand, permit undirected research	4	19	5	7	4	4	6
Negative	18%	7%	8%	6%	7%	10%	15%
Research is too limited, slanted, narrow	11	6	2	*	1	6	8
Don't do enough basic research	7	1	6	6	6	4	7

*Less than 1%.

We see that Petroil is last in line, with two and one-half positive comments for every negative one volunteered by the respondents. These data are a source of particular concern, as the public relations personnel at Petroil properly point out. It is one thing to cope with *lack* of information about a company—to communicate more accurately or more fully exactly

Table 15-11. Ratio of positive to negative statements

Company	Ratio
Company L	5:1
Company M	5:1
Company Q	5:1
Company N	4½:1
Company O	4:1
Company P	4:1
Petroil	2½:1

what the firm is doing in the area of basic research—but it is another problem entirely to be faced with combating negative attitudes that have already been formulated. Substituting positive attitudes for negative ones requires creative and time consuming efforts.

Evaluation of Media That Reach the Scientific Community. Our last category of data collected by the researchers concerns some guidelines on the best way to reach the scientific community more effectively.

One question was, "Do you think industrial research organizations are doing a good job of telling you about their research activities and goals?" A summary of the responses revealed approximately a three-to-two no-confidence vote of the public relations job being done by industry. Among the reasons cited for this are the following: companies want to keep their competitors in the dark—15%; failure to publish a significant number of high-quality papers—6%; advertising is too consumer oriented and does not stress research—7%; publications are insincere, research talk just a gimmick—4%.

The respondents were asked to indicate what companies, inside or outside the petroleum industry, they thought did the best job of keeping them informed of their research activities. Table 15-12 summarizes the replies to this question.

For each company mentioned, the respondents were then asked *why* they thought that particular company was doing the best job. Table 15-13 summarizes the reasons given by some of the respondents.

PETROIL DEVELOPMENT AND RESEARCH CORPORATION

Table 15-12. Companies doing the best job of telling about their research activities

Company	Percent
Company M	30%
Company N	19
Company L	18
Petroil	7
Company P	5
Company Q	5
Company O	4
Company A	4
Company C	1

Table 15-13. Why five companies do the best job of telling about their research activities

	Petroil	Company L	Company M	Company N	Company A
Do more advertising in mass mass media, i.e., newspapers, magazines, television	37%	37%	52%	59%	12%
Publish their own technical journal or newspaper, issue material	28	39	27	24	48
Advertise in technical and engineering journals and magazines	18	16	13	12	4
Are most active, most heard about	11	3	5	5	15
Have the best recruiters	7	6	6	4	4
Scientists and engineers participate more and give lectures on campus	4	4	10	9	8
Have the best recruiting literature	2	2	—*	—	—
Advertise in school magazines	—	2	—	4	4
All other	2	2	1	2	4

*Less than 1%.

Table 15-14. Advertising recall

	Petroil	Company L	Company M	Company N	Company O	Company P	Company Q	Company A	Company B	Company C
Remembered advertising	57%	53%	74%	73%	54%	52%	45%	23%	32%	18%
Product information, slogans, company makes the best product, outstanding in its own field	39	8	61	51	38	19	37	30	12	11
Remembered place where ad was seen or heard	12	15	10	11	5	23	18	5	9	4
Recruiting literature	6	15	4	10	13	9	8	2	1	1
Basic research, contribution to public good through research, research achievement	—*	34	15	8	2	5	4	3	—	—
Institutional ads stressing progressive nature of the company	—	—	9	9	4	8	6	—	—	7

*Less than 1%.

PETROIL DEVELOPMENT AND RESEARCH CORPORATION   221

From these data one may interpret that the comparatively low position accorded Petroil in Table 15-12 is more a function of the *content* than of the *form* or frequency of communication activities, because in Table 15-13 we see that:

1. Petroil recruiters are given the best rating;
2. Petroil advertising in technical journals is in first place;
3. Petroil is rated second as the most active research organization;
4. Petroil's consumer advertising is tied for third place.

This interpretation of the need for revising content rather than changing some other feature of the mass communication program is reinforced by data obtained from questioning the respondents about what advertising they recalled of the various companies (Table 15-14).

Table 15-15. Scientific community exposure to mass media and technical journals (closed-end)

	Total	Senior	Graduate student	Faculty	Government	Industry
New York Times	28%	17%	24%	37%	26%	31%
New York Herald Tribune	2	—*	—	2	1	7
Wall Street Journal	11	7	5	14	13	15
Large metropolitan newspapers	81	82	84	73	87	77
General college alumni publications	63	67	38	35	97	88
Time	40	50	51	42	—	36
Newsweek	13	11	16	19	14	9
Life	37	50	33	31	37	37
Look	6	14	7	2	6	3
Saturday Evening Post	23	33	15	25	18	21
Scientific American	17	25	22	19	16	9
Chemical & Engineering News	40	40	42	39	23	50
Chemical Engineering Progress	17	10	12	15	6	33
Industrial & Engineering Chemistry	13	4	4	14	8	26
Journal of the American Chemical Society	24	7	36	45	20	16
Chemical Week	11	1	3	4	8	28
Science	7	6	7	8	11	3
Don't ready any journals	7	22	10	1	3	1
Watch TV	81	73	72	71	92	91
Watch TV for 7 or more hours	34	29	22	23	55	41

*Less than 1%.

Clearly, the major impact of the Petroil communication program is in the products area. Although product information ranks comparatively high among all the companies, it is for Petroil by far the single largest recall category. By contrast, there is no recall of literature advertising Petroil's basic research work, whereas it is the area of highest recall for the labs of Company L, for example. In the words of the researchers, who interpreted this and the previous two tables together, "The basic appeal is to the scientific community as consumers, *not scientists. This kind of advertising will sell Petroil gasoline but not Petroil research*" (italics added).

The last aspect of exposure to media had to do with which various mass media and technical journals were viewed and read regularly. Table 15-15 summarizes the habits of the respondents along these lines.

Concerning these data the researchers summarize as follows:

We have already seen the missing dimension in Petroil's message to the scientific community—the spirit of true dedication and participation in scientific advancement and the future.

The ways to convey this image are many and already have been used. Grants and scholarships can enhance the reputation but cannot make it. There is no doubt that the mass media such as TV, magazines, radio and newspaper are read and listened to by the scientific community; that in general terms these media can convey the message and create the atmosphere. *But the scientist must also be reached in his own world and in his own language.* The technical journals offer the greatest opportunity to do this job . . . for they are read by 97 percent of the scientists interested in new information and new enlightment.

Chemical and Engineering News reaches the broadest audience of scientists, 40%; *The Journal of the American Chemical Soc*iety, 24%; *Chemical Engineering Progress,* 17%; *Chemical Week,* 11%; *The Journal of Analytical Chemistry,* 8%; *The Journal of Organic Chemistry,* 7%. In the petroleum field, *Petroleum Refiner* is read by 4%; *Oil and Gas Journal* by 3%.

These magazines and professional journals offer the most active marketplace for displaying Petroil's talent and creativity in reseach.

The 1960 survey: a summary of the data

From our examination of the highlights of the 1960 survey, it is obvious that the public relations department of Petroil is faced with a substantial job if it wishes to rectify some of the incorrect (to them) perceptions held by the scientific community in such areas as their basic research work and their personnel policies. Petroil's position as a leader in the petroleum industry is unbalanced where applied research versus basic research is concerned; by the same token, some of the advantages of bigness are also perceived as disadvantages— particularly by the scientist who would like to choose his area of research and who, at the same time would prefer not to get lost in the shuffle of a large organization.

In addition, as one of the major spokesmen for the industry of which it is a part, Petroil has a sizable job to do if it wishes to garner a larger share of the positive attitudes of the scientific community toward the petroleum industry as compared with other industries.

We have seen that the survey data provide a basis for the development of a public relations program more likely to reach its target audience than one developed without such data. A number of the findings have explicit implications for the public relations practitioner should he decide to "take the long road back" in correcting the image of Petroil Development and Research Corporation.

PUBLIC RELATIONS PROGRAM BASED ON RESEARCH FINDINGS

A public relations program was launched consisting of seven major subsections, geared both to Petroil employees and to the scientific community as a whole. Let us begin with the internal efforts—apprising the employees of Petroil, whom they realized were members of the scientific community, of the research going on within their own company.

Internal portions of the public relations program

One means by which the public relations practitioners could reach their own employees was through their own company publication, *The Live Wire*. They decided to institute a program of articles designed to stress consciously and deliberately the research activities going on within the company, and they launched the series with articles by the top Petroil research people. These articles gave a frank presentation of the company's public relations objectives; they also explained why it was important that its work in basic and applied research become better known within the scientific community. Also, the articles encouraged the research personnel to publish their research in their respective professional journals, attend and give talks at professional meetings, and take a more active role in their own professional societies.

To help spur on this interest in research and publishing, two additional steps were taken:

1. A letter was sent by the president of Petroil Development and Research to all technical personnel, spelling out his personal interest in having technical people publish their research, and reiterating that publication would be important in furthering one's career within the company.

2. A formal technical publications policy was prepared and distributed. It clearly defined responsibility of technical people and management with regard to publications.

The next aspect of the internal program might be considered as a coordinating effort—"harnessing" the technical people in order to make an impact on the science community outside the company. One step was the development of a technical speakers' bureau which was made available to colleges and universities across the country and which utilized the services of top-level senior technical men as well as younger scientists at Petroil. An attractive booklet was developed containing a listing of all technical talks available, together with a brief abstract of each talk. To give the reader an idea of the range of the speeches, the following topics are included in the table of contents: (1) "New Sources of Energy"; (2) "The Origin of Petroleum"; (3) "Fundamental Chemicals Research"; and (4) "Petroleum Products: Their Manufacture and Properties."

Another effort to encourage penetration into the scientific community was a coordinated plan to bring top company management representatives before important meetings of such organizations as the American Association for the Advancement of Science and the National Association of Science Writers.

Lastly, a biennial company-campus symposium series was initiated to bring together scientists of the company with outstanding authorities from college and university campuses. Among the activities of this symposium series were the presentation of scientific papers by the visitors as well as by company scientists, and tours of the laboratory facilities so that outsiders could get first-hand knowledge of the company's physical plant.

The foregoing are some of the highlights of the internal portion of the overall public relations program. These activities, incidentally, were designed in the light of survey data which suggested that the company's attempts to make its work better known were *not inadequate* but, rather, *not particularly appropriate* for the scientific community. The reader will note that all these new efforts—those designed for the scientists within the company, as well as those intended to reach the scientific community—were developed with an eye toward conveying the serious, scientific nature of the research work, both basic and applied. Emphasis was put on basic research, however, since this was the area of weakness noted in the survey findings.

External portions of the public relations program

At the same time that the internal steps were taken, a series of major efforts was launched to reach the scientific community by means of the mass media and through specialized publications with small circulations. The point of departure for the external effort was the development of an exceedingly sophisticated science community advertising program, which was based on a theme that stressed basic research activities at Petroil. Basically, the approach consisted of a series of advertisements placed in *Chemical & Engineering News*. (The reader will recall that this was the most widely read publication according to the survey data on the reading habits of the scientific community studied.) These advertisements covered a full page, of which one-half was an attractive, abstract color photograph of some aspect of a scientist's work, and the other half a frankly technical description of the work.

Closely related to this advertising series was the inauguration of a publication consisting of descriptions of research work being done by Petroil scientists. All the articles were reprints of publications from the most significant technical journals. This special publication was widely distributed to the scientific community, and people were invited to write for additional copies or for further information about the research work.

It should be noted that the external portion of the public relations program also reflected the survey data obtained. First of all, as we saw earlier, the selection of *Chemical & Engineering News* for the advertising series was based on readership habits as brought out in the survey—the publication was the single best place to spend the advertising dollar. Second, the advertising series was designed solely for the scientific community. It was intended to present the research activities of Petroil personnel in a manner that would 1) convey the high quality of the research work being conducted, 2) reestablish a proper balance in the eyes of the science community with respect to basic research versus applied research (it was hoped that the series would show basic research to be more prevalent than applied research rather than the other way around), 3) communicate to the readers that Petroil was not trying to "hide" its research activities from scientists in other settings, particularly in colleges and universities, and 4) highlight the fact that a scientist at Petroil could do basic research that interested him and that he was not always required to do applied research that might interest him less and contribute little to the general store of scientific knowledge.

The 1963 survey: some highlights

We have found in our other cases that there is not always data available to tell us something about the effectiveness of our public relations program *after* it has been in existence for a period of time. This case, however, does provide us with such information. The public relations division of

Petroil used the same researchers to repeat essentially the identical survey[6] some three years later, after the public relations program had been in effect for about two and a half years. We shall examine some of the data from the second survey for the purpose of illustrating (1) where Petroil remained about the same or worsened with respect to its standing within the scientific community, and (2) where Petroil improved with respect to its standing within the scientific community.

Before comparing the 1960 and 1963 survey data, it is important to consider what the researchers spell out in some detail in their 1963 report concerning the changed climate of world opinion (including the scientific community, of course) that had taken place in the three-year period between the first and second studies. In 1961 the Russians had successfully orbited their first cosmonaut, Yuri Gagarin, thereby ushering in the manned space age. The United States performed a similar feat approximately a year later. The net effect of these events, the researchers suggest, was to produce a definite change in the attitudes of the scientific community. They write in this connection:

With the advent of the space age, a new elan appeared in the ranks of the scientific community, earmarked by increased determination, greater personal involvement and responsibility; sharper, more rigid standards for judging sincerity, performance, outlook and membership privileges in the scientific community.

Naturally, the sentiments expressed above cannot be precisely pinpointed, as the survey was not designed to find out how the entry of the United States and Russia into the space age had affected the attitudes of scientists; but it does point up the fact that some truly momentous changes had taken place between the first and second studies—changes which were bound to affect the data obtained in the second study. Unfortunately, we can only speculate about the exact nature of these effects on our survey data.

[6] The same technical sampling methods were employed in the second study as were utilized in the 1960 survey. In 1963 a probability sample of 600 individuals were interviewed from the same 19 colleges and universities and the same ten geographic areas as before. The interviewees were distributed as follows:

	1960	1963
Total sample	668	600
College seniors	124	126
Graduate students	123	110
Faculty members	134	120
Industrial scientists	182	144
Government research scientists	105	100

Table 15-16. Where the most significant research is being done today

	Colleges and Universities			Industry			Government		
	1963	1960	Net change	1963	1960	Net change	1963	1960	Net change
Total	47%/48	54%/51	−7/−3	35%/40	34%/42	+1/−2	18%/12	12%/7	+6/+5
Senior									
Graduate student	65	73	−6	23	19	+4	12	8	+4
Faculty	70	74	−4	21	17	+4	9	9	—
Government	33	42	−9	36	36	—	31	22	+9
Industry	30	35	−5	47	54	−7	23	11	+12

*Previous figures shown have been repercentaged on base 100% to provide more accurate comparison.

227

Where Petroil remained about the same or worsened. Table 15-16 compares the data obtained when respondents were asked where the most significant research was being done today.

These findings suggest that the importance of government research has increased (here is a place where one could reasonably argue that the attention garnered by the space flights has resulted in a greater awareness of and respect for government research efforts). By the same token, university research has slipped, with industrial research remaining essentially the same.

Interestingly enough, the reputation of industrial research has increased among graduate students and among college and university faculties. This is more than offset, however, by a drop in the industrial scientist's enthusiasm about his own work. One leading scientist expressed this feeling in the following remark:

There is nothing wrong with what we do—in fact, we're doing great. But how can you compare new products with new worlds?

Our next comparison shows the relationship of Petroil to the same three leading petroleum companies in the area of basic research—one of the themes that the public relations program tried to stress. Tables 15-17 and 15-18 summarize the results.

Table 15-17. Closed-end rating in the area of basic research

Company	1963	1960	Net change
Petroil	29%	29%	—
Company A	27	27	—
Company C	15	12	+3
Company B	11	10	+1

Although one must conclude from these data that Petroil's supposedly narrow research orientation and their emphasis on applied results have increased during the period between the 1960 and 1963 studies, their overall reputation for basic research has remained relatively the same. The researchers acknowledge that the results are discouraging, yet believe that had the public relations program *not* been in effect, Petroil's position would be even weaker than in 1960.

Another situation in which Petroil remained essentially unchanged or worsened is its rating, along with the six other major companies (outside the oil industry) with respect to conducting basic research. The closed-end data are summarized in Table 15-19.

Interestingly enough, Company L increased its standing, pulling even farther away from the others. This leadership is accentuated by a drop in the position of Company M. Petroil remained unchanged—although because

PETROIL DEVELOPMENT AND RESEARCH CORPORATION

Table 15-18. Open-end rating in the area of basic research

	Petroil 1963	Petroil 1960	Company A 1963	Company A 1960	Company B 1963	Company B 1960	Company C 1963	Company C 1960
Positive	29%	27%	35%	33%	20%	20%	13%	5%
Are involved in basic research, do basic research	15	14	20	21	17	17	7	1
Do diversified research, not limited	9	9	10	6	1	1	4	2
Give scientists a free hand, permit undirected research	5	4	5	6	2	2	2	2
Negative	22%	18%	12%	9%	15%	15%	9%	8%
Research is too limited, slanted, narrow	14	11	8	5	4	—*	2	—
Don't do enough basic research	8	7	4	4	11	15	7	8

*Less than 1%.

of the drop in Company Q's position, it no longer tied for last place with Company Q, as in 1960. The researchers suggest that the ability of Petroil to maintain its 1960 position is of some value, particularly in view of the more stringent standards expected of research companies as a result of events between 1960 and 1963.

Table 15-19. Closed-end rating in the area of basic research

Company	1963	1960	Net change
Company L	82%	77%	+5
Company M	65	70	−5
Company N	51	60	−9
Company O	50	45	+5
Company P	35	41	−6
Petroil	29	29	—
Company Q	25	29	−4

The open-end remarks in the same question area are found in Table 15-20. These results illustrate the worsened position of Petroil with regard to basic research. Note that the negative remarks have increased, especially with respect to the comment about the limitation and the slant of Petroil's research.

Table 15-20. Open-end rating in the area of basic research

	Petroil 1963	Petroil 1960	Company L 1963	Company L 1960	Company M 1963	Company M 1960	Company N 1963	Company N 1960	Company O 1963	Company O 1960	Company P 1963	Company P 1960	Company Q 1963	Company Q 1960
Positive:														
Involved in basic research, do good basic research	29%	27%	67%	64%	74%	78%	42%	50%	42%	38%	52%	56%	35%	39%
	15	14	42	34	30	36	18	21	31	27	26	24	12	14
Do diversified research, not limited	9	9	9	11	34	37	20	22	9	7	26	28	20	19
Give scientists a free hand, permit undirected research	5	4	16	19	10	5	4	7	2	4	—*	4	3	6
Negative:	22%	18%	4%	7%	8%	8%	10%	6%	8%	7%	10%	10%	11%	15%
Research is too limited, slanted, narrow	14	11	3	6	2	2	2	—	3	1	6	6	5	8
Don't do enough basic research	8	7	1	1	6	6	8	6	5	6	4	4	6	7

*Less than 1%.

230

PETROIL DEVELOPMENT AND RESEARCH CORPORATION

Where Petroil improved. As one might expect, the picture is not totally disheartening. There were a number of instances in the 1963 survey that showed the public relations programming to have been worthwhile. For example, we see in Table 15-21 that Petroil has increased its standing in the oil industry as an employer, so far as being a place with opportunity and challenge and a desirable place for a scientist to work. These dimensions are obviously important to Petroil, in addition to its research reputation, in attracting competent scientific personnel.

Table 15-21. Comparison rating in the area of growth and opportunity

	Petroil 1963	Petroil 1960	Company A 1963	Company A 1960	Company B 1963	Company B 1960	Company C 1963	Company C 1960
Is dynamic, has prospects for growth	26%	27%	18%	22%	14%	12%	22%	18%
Salaries for technical people	24	27	17	19	11	12	15	18
Opportunity for professional development	24	24	19	20	10	10	15	16
Opportunity for advancement by technical people to positions of management	28	23	18	20	12	11	15	16
Has reputation as a "human" company	18	14	15	12	7	7	7	7
Good place for a young scientist to work*	45	—	47	—	36	—	37	—
Good place for a young engineer to work*	49	—	47	—	29	—	35	—
Opportunities for international activities	38	—	32	—	20	—	7	—

*Not asked previously.

One analysis that was made of the 1960 survey was to combine all the positive and negative remarks from the open-end questions and express them as a ratio (see Table 15-11). The same sort of analysis was done in the 1963 study, with the results shown in Table 15-22.

From the table one can see that of the seven companies (including Petroil) three had fewer positive to negative remarks in the 1963 study;

one, Company P, remained unchanged; Petroil increased, as did Companies L and O. In view of the concern shown over the results of the 1960 survey, these data point to a step in the right direction.

Table 15-22. Ratio of positive to negative remarks

Company	1963	1960
Company L	6:1	5:1
Company O	4½:1	4:1
Company Q	4:1	5:1
Company P	4:1	4:1
Company M	3½:1	5:1
Petroil	3½:1	2½:1
Company N	3:1	4½:1

In the 1960 survey, interviewees were asked to indicate which companies they thought were doing the best job of decribing their research activities and why. Their answers were summarized in Tables 15-12 and 15-13, and are compared to the 1963 findings in with Tables 15-23 and 15-24.

Table 15-23. Companies doing the best job of telling about their research activities

Company	1963	1960	Net change
Company M	30%	30%	—
Company L	29	18	+11
Company N	21	19	+ 2
Petroil	13	7	+ 6
Company O	8	4	+ 4
Company P	4	5	− 1
Company Q	3	5	− 2
Company A	3	4	− 1
Company C	1	1	—

The results are encouraging. Petroil is one of the two companies that evidenced the largest improvement with respect to publicizing its research activities—an increase of eleven percentage points for Company L, and six points for Petroil. In addition, during the same period three companies decreased their standing and two remained the same.

Table 15-24. Why five companies do the best job of telling about their research activities

	Petroil 1963	Petroil 1960	Company L 1963	Company L 1960	Company M 1963	Company M 1960	Company N 1963	Company N 1960	Company A 1963	Company A 1960
Do more advertising in mass media	45%	37%	37%	37%	44%	52%	43%	59%	20%	12%
Publish their own technical journal or newspaper, issue material	28	28	35	39	25	27	25	24	34	48
Advertise in technical and engineering journals and magazines	16	18	13	16	10	13	10	12	8	4
Are more active, more heard about	14	11	12	3	3	5	7	5	14	15
Have the best recruiters	12	7	7	6	8	6	8	4	8	4
Scientists and engineers participate more and give lectures on campus	2	4	2	4	8	10	5	9	3	8
Have the best recruiting literature	6	2	4	2	3	*	4	*	4	*
Give information about basic research	7	†	12	†	14	†	11	†	8	†
All other	4	2	2	2	2	1	2	2	2	4

*Less than 1%.
†Not asked in 1960.

233

Table 15-25. Advertising recall

	Petroil 1963	Petroil 1960	Company L 1963	Company L 1960	Company M 1963	Company M 1960
Remembered advertising	62%	57%	65%	53%	77%	74%
Product information, slogans, company makes the best product, outstanding in its own field	39	39	8	8	54	61
Remembered place where ad was seen or heard	11	12	16	15	9	10
Recruiting literature	9	6	20	15	9	4
Basic research, contribution to public good through research, research achievement	14	—*	60	34	22	15
Institutional ads stressing progressive nature of the company	7	—	5	—	2	9

*Less than 1%.

Also encouraging is the analysis of why the respondents thought a certain company was doing the best job (Table 15-24). Out of the nine categories, six reveal increases, one remained the same, and two of them decreased. While all the categories *should* have increased—that is, from the standpoint that they all represented areas of effort on the part of the Petroil public relations people to be more "visible"—perhaps the most gratifying are categories 1 and 8. The first category shows that the respondent was more conscious of Petroil's increased efforts in the mass media area, and category 8 reflects the fact that this advertising now contains information about basic research. Certainly this last category summarizes much of what the public relations program was trying to achieve. One line of questioning that produced results inconsistent with the overall favorable picture shows up in category 3, where there is a decrease in perceived advertising in technical engineering journals and magazines. In view of the campaign—for example, in *Chemical & Engineering News*—one might have expected this category to have increased. On the other hand, it is possible that some respondents did not consider *Chemical & Engineering News* as technical or as much an engineering journal as the *Journal of the American Chemical Society* or the *Journal of Analytical Chemistry*. Another negative picture emerged in category 6, which indicates that the respondents do not yet think that Petroil scientists are participating more in lecturing on the campus. One possible interpretation is that this portion of the public relations program has not existed long enough for it to have had the desired impact.

Table 15-25 (Continued)

Company N		Company O		Company Q		Company A		Company B		Company C	
1963	1960	1963	1960	1963	1960	1963	1960	1963	1960	1963	1960
<u>62%</u>	<u>73%</u>	<u>54%</u>	<u>54%</u>	<u>40%</u>	<u>45%</u>	<u>25%</u>	<u>23%</u>	<u>32%</u>	<u>31%</u>	<u>15%</u>	<u>18%</u>
44	51	29	38	30	37	25	30	25	12	11	11
11	11	3	5	10	18	5	5	8	9	4	4
11	10	13	12	6	8	3	2	2	1	3	1
15	8	10	2	3	4	7	3	2	—	1	—
3	9	6	4	5	6	6	—	—	—	4	7

Table 15-25, the last comparison table, gives a more encouraging picture of the impact of the overall public relations program. An examination of this table reveals that the mass media advertising portion of the public relations program is having the desired effect. In four out of the six categories, Petroil has registered a gain in percentage points, especially in the last two, where the increases are fourteen and seven percentage points respectively. The only reversal was in the third category.

The 1963 survey: a summary of the data

The researchers who conducted both of the surveys for Petroil Development and Research Corporation summarized the 1963 study as follows:

The three-year story of Petroil's progress in improving its position in the scientific community can be briefly and succinctly described.

The gains achieved: concrete results in reputation as an employer of scientists; a breakthrough in the efforts of a stronger message of basic research resulting from the general advertising program.

The immediate needs: more emphasis on basic research; more effective communications with the scientific community—through advertising in technical and scientific journals; disseminating of scientific and technical literature; publication of more technical and scientific papers; more effective use of displays; more active participation in scientific meetings.

Petroil has won an invitation into the scientific marketplace. Now the time has come to move in as actively as possible, accepting its full role and responsibility, enhancing its reputation through deeds and well-directed words.

The reaction of the public relations division to these results was one of optimism, with the overall feeling that the program devised in the light of the 1960 survey was on the right track. Essentially, the program that they recommended following the 1963 study was the same as the earlier one, but with increased emphasis on distribution of materials to the science community; placing more Petroil scientists on college campuses; greater output of articles by top management reflecting the company's shift in emphasis toward basic research; and development of opportunities for top management to speak to leading members of the scientific community.

16 | Case 6
American Telephone and Telegraph Company: a research-based effort to decentralize community relations planning and programming

CASE OUTLINE

1. Introduction
2. Background information
3. Exploratory research
4. A more precise field test
5. The survey package
6. Comparison of data obtained by professional and local telephone company interviewers
    a. ratings
    b. unfavorable experiences reported
    c. unusual favorable experiences reported
    d. data obtained by special probing
7. Hammond, Indiana, local team reaction
8. Conclusions of the Business Research Division
9. The survey package in operation
10. The Burbank, California, findings
11. The plans for corrective action
    a. Concerning our telephone bills
    b. Concerning our prices charged for service and equipment
    c. Concerning the way we sell services and equipment
    d. Concerning the benefits and working conditions for our employees
    e. Concerning the participation of the company and our employees in civic and community affairs

INTRODUCTION

Public relations activities, by their very nature, must be decentralized; they do not lend themselves easily to being farmed out, even though there are certain aspects of an overall program—for instance, the company newspaper or the annual report—that can be purchased from a public relations consulting firm or handled by a given public relations department. In addition, administration of certain company functions, such as a speakers' bureau, plant tours, or the writing of speeches, can be handled by a consultant or department. By the same token, many important aspects of an overall public relations program must be handled locally by local people. However, when a company operates on a large scale, as does the company in our present case, there are going to be definite problems in the areas of local control, implementation, and planning of certain public relations programs. It becomes prohibitive, both in terms of time and cost, to duplicate the public relations facilities of the home office in all the various locations that a large company typically operates.

The need to be able to decentralize the public relations activities of a large corporation is pressing. This is perhaps best seen in that portion of overall public relations planning known as *community relations*. By this term we mean all of the contacts, both planned and unplanned, that occur between a company's employees (and administrative personnel) and persons in the local community. The term also embraces the impersonal contacts, via different types of communication media, that have implication for the relationship between the company and the local community. It follows that "good" community relations refers to those personal and impersonal contacts which result ultimately in a better understanding and acceptance on the part of both parties toward each other. The main objective of a company's community relations program is to deserve and then gain the community's acceptance and support of the organization.

Sixty or 70 years ago, the concept of a community relations program was unnecessary; business activity was essentially locally made products sold to residents by local merchants who were usually life-long residents of the community. As a rule this meant that the businessman was an integral part of the community, that he knew most of the residents personally, and that he was as concerned as the next man about the future of the town and its general welfare. This state of affairs gradually gave way to larger towns and larger businesses to go along with them. Inevitably, there followed increasing barriers to understanding and to communication between business and community. These barriers required calculated efforts to overcome them, and as a result there developed a recognition of the need to concern oneself about community relations.

Obviously, there is no such thing as a general, or basic, community relations program, since what is required in one community is not needed in another. The goals of one program differ greatly from those of another; so do the methods by which these goals are attained. A number of common objectives, however, do apply rather well to most community relations programs. Canfield has developed a list which summarizes these objectives:

AMERICAN TELEPHONE AND TELEGRAPH COMPANY

to inform the community about a company's policies, operations, and problems and to tell the story of what it makes, how many people it employs, the amount of its payroll, what it pays in taxes, what it spends locally, how it regards its community responsibilities, and what it contributes to the social and economic life of the locality;

to inform all people connected with a company about its operations and to stimulate them to tell the corporate story to their friends and neighbors in the community;

to correct misunderstandings, answer criticisms, and repel attacks on a company and its policies by local pressure groups who are misinformed about the company and industry;

to establish a company as an important factor in community life through contibutions to local institutions and participation in neighborhood affairs;

to find out what the local public is thinking and saying about a company and its policies and operations;

to promote the welfare of a community by advertising its advantages and attractions to tourists, and by promoting its resources and industrial potential to attract new industry;

to win the support of a community during labor contoversies through a candid discussion of the issues involved and the company's position;

to get acquainted with a community by inviting local groups and opinion leaders to meet corporate executives and see how a concern operates;

to aid community education through cooperation with schools and colleges in providing educational materials and furnishing facilities and equipment for training youths and adults;

to provide cultural leadership by encouraging a greater appreciation of art, music, and drama, and an enrichment of community life;

to aid cattle raising or agriculture in areas where community welfare is dependent on the prosperity of the surrounding farms or ranches;

to promote community health by supporting local health progams and by aiding the local Red Cross and hospitals;

to support local sports and recreation activities by providing facilities and equipment and sponsoring events for neighborhood and community groups;

to support local youth programs to combat juvenile delinquency and gain the good will of future citizens of the town;

to promote a better understanding of national and local affairs through the organization of community forums and discussion groups for youth and adults of the locality;

to aid local government in the improvement of public services and facilities;

to cooperate with other companies in a community in promoting a better understanding of business and in advancing community welfare.[1]

[1] Bertrand R. Canfield, *Public Relations Principles, Cases and Problems*, 4th ed. (Homewood, Ill.: Richard D. Irwin, Inc., 1964), pp. 190–191.

240   SEVEN CASES

As this list of objectives is examined, it becomes readily apparent that most of them cannot be attained unless the individual responsible for their achievement has certain information. He needs to know what misunderstandings exist, what criticisms are being voiced, what gaps there are in community knowledge about his company, what needs of the community should be attended to, and so on. Almost all of the items above require feedback of information from the local community before action can be taken. How can a large company, operating in many different locations, encourage the development of sound community relations programs on the local level—programs that are based on reliable information? Our present case provides us with one company's answer to this perplexing problem of decentralization in community relations programming as a part of overall public relations activities.

BACKGROUND INFORMATION

The American Telephone and Telegraph Company is the parent company of the Bell System. The Bell System can be visualized by means of the chart depicted in Figure 16-1.

The Bell System provides about 85% of all telephone services in the United States. By any standard, whether it be physical assets, total number of employees, customers served, or dollars invested, the Bell System is big

---

American Telephone and Telegraph Company

Provides advice and assistance to associated operating companies. Also handles the operation of long distance services.

Western Electric Company

Responsible for the manufacturing, purchasing, and distributing of equipment and supplies for the Bell System. In addition, it maintains specialized personnel to install equipment in the Bell System's telephone central offices.

Bell Telephone Laboratories

Conducts all of the research and development work for the Bell System, including the Western Electric Company.

Associated Operating Telephone Companies

A group of 23 regional telephone companies operating in every state in the United States, with the exception of Alaska and Hawaii. These regional telephone companies provide complete services for their respective customers through their efforts and with the aid of services received from the American Telephone and Telegraph Company.

Figure 16-1. The Bell System

Source: American Telephone and Telegraph Company, "The Telephone in America" (New York, n. d.), p. 6.

AMERICAN TELEPHONE AND TELEGRAPH COMPANY

business indeed. Approximately 775,000 men and women are employed, requiring an annual payroll of over $4.75 billion.

One of the major functions of the American Telephone and Telegraph Company is to advise and assist all the associated companies in their common problems. It acts as a catalyst in accelerating the flow of new ideas and methods developed anywhere within the Bell System. For example, the business research group, a member of the comptroller's department of A.T.&T., services other departments within the parent company and throughout the entire Bell System by doing general economic research, various business conditions studies, and market and public relations research. As we shall see in this case, the business research group was requested by the public relations division to work with them in developing a tool that would enhance their own community relations efforts, as well as those of Bell System companies across the country.

Because the Bell System operates in such a high proportion of all the cities and towns of the United States, it is not surprising that they have placed great emphasis on the community relations phase of their overall public relations programming. Nor is it surprising that those responsible for community relations were acutely aware of the importance of feedback from the local community in planning a sound community relations program. They knew, for example, that other companies turn to the development of information programs if their local people are unable to determine the specific needs of the community. Such programs might consist of showing films, conducting company tours, increasing the activity of the company speakers' bureau, or relying more on kits containing community relations material. These kits generally include tips on how to reach specialized publics within the community—such as professional people, women, or clergy—as well as blueprints on how to hold plant tours, dedications, press parties, and so forth. Because the home office (or material supplied by the home office) in this case plays the larger role in stimulating community relations activities, these stopgap programs which stress general information represent a retreat from decentralization of the community relations function.

One of the most frequent reasons for a breakdown of decentralization in community efforts is that information gathering at the local level is not possible. In order to develop a sound community relations program, one needs reliable information about the community itself—information that is solicited at the local level by means of survey research. A breakdown occurs when there is a lack of professionally trained personnel capable of conducting this research.

Faced with this problem, the public relations division of A.T.&T. wondered whether it was possible to develop a reasonably standardized survey package that could be utilized by local personnel in order to obtain pertinent and accurate information from a representative cross section of specified publics in the community. To answer this question, they called upon the business research group of the company to undertake a pilot study on the feasibility of such a package. The telephone company believes that its community relations program begins with its customers; therefore, it was decided that the pilot study would be conducted with a given segment of its own customer public.[2]

EXPLORATORY RESEARCH

The approach taken by the business research group consisted of a period of preliminary research, followed by a more complete field test of the survey package in a sample community. In the preliminary pilot study the town of Newburgh, New York, was selected as the locale to test out (1) the establishment of certain information goals, (2) the development of the appropriate interview schedule and procedures, and (3) a comparison of the information obtained with the information desired. On the basis of this preliminary work, the researchers were convinced that the request of the public relations division could be met. Specifically, they found that:

1. The questionnaires were basically sound and workable.
2. The instructions were easy to follow and the interview comparatively simple to conduct.
3. The procedure itself was capable of developing a large variety of information leads with a minimum amount of time and effort.

A MORE PRECISE FIELD TEST

The town of Hammond, Indiana, was selected as the test town. It was chosen primarily because the management of the local telephone company showed an interest in the study and expressed willingness to try out whatever procedures the business research group developed. It might be added, however, that Hammond happened to be typical of the many small communities in which A.T.&T. and its associated companies operate across the country.

In February, 1963, a two-part study design was implemented. Two teams consisting of (1) five professional interviewers, and (2) twelve members of the local telephone management,[3] carried out duplicate surveys

[2] Although this exploratory work was performed on telephone company customers, the information derived from this research might well be applicable to any segment of the community. For example, the preparation of sampling plans, interview instructions, or the questionnaire itself, would need only comparatively minor modifications to enable the user to obtain information suitable for his community relations program with respect to some other public (other than customer public) or publics in the community.
[3] The local team included a dial service chief, chief operator, supervising engineer, traffic supervisor, district installation superintendent, district construction supervisor, wire chief, exchange repair foreman, business office manager, business office supervisor, sales manager, and engineer.

AMERICAN TELEPHONE AND TELEGRAPH COMPANY

on two separate but similar samples of telephone customers. Some of the more important objectives of this study were as follows:

1. To determine whether the local telephone company management would be able to use effectively the survey package provided them.[4]
2. To ascertain the reactions of the local management team to the survey package.
3. To determine whether the local management team would be able to use the survey package without biasing the results.
4. To ascertain how quickly and effectively the local team could summarize and analyze the data; and, most important, how long it takes them to prepare, *on their own,* a community public relations planning and action program.

Each of the two sets of interviews was conducted among a cross-section sample of Hammond telephone customers. Twenty key addresses for each team were selected at random by the Indiana company's statistical people.[5] A total of 290 interviews were completed—134 by the local team, and 156 by the professional interviewers. The two samples were comparable in terms of age and economic status. Because the professional group did more interviewing in the evening, they obtained a somewhat larger proportion of men (46%) than women (36%) in their sample. Key interviews were successfully accomplished by both groups in about two out of every five attempts; "not at home" was the principal reason for failure. The interviews each lasted about half an hour for both the professional and local management teams.

THE SURVEY PACKAGE

Before going into the comparison of the two independent surveys, let us examine in a little more detail the survey package provided for the local telephone management, beginning with the questionnaire itself. Essentially, the interview was built around how the respondents rated a series of 19 items that concerned some aspect of the company's relationship with its customers (see Figure 16-2 for the list of items).

For each of the first 17 items that had been checked "poor" or "fair," the respondent was asked whether his rating was based on an unsatisfactory personal experience of some sort, and, if so, if it has happened locally

---

[4] The survey package refers to all the material supplied by the business research group: (1) the questionnaire, (2) instructions for interviewers, including such details as where to interview, whom to interview, and when to interview, and (3) guidelines for analysis of the data.

[5] This procedure is known as "cluster sampling." The particular "clusters," or comparatively homogeneous groupings of people, were selected randomly. Each key address was the starting point in a given cluster of homes. According to strict procedure, the person at a key address was interviewed first. Seven or eight additional interviews were then made in telephone homes along a prescribed route in the vicinity of that key address. In this way a random sample was obtained which was representative of the total population of telephone subscribers in the town.

On the basis of your feelings and experiences, please rate the Telephone Company on each of the following items. Simply place a check after each item in the one box that you feel best describes your opinion.

Items	Poor	Fair	Good	Excellent	No opinion
1. The quality of their local service	☐	☐	☐	☐	☐
2. The quality of their long distance service	☐	☐	☐	☐	☐
3. The quality of their repair service	☐	☐	☐	☐	☐
4. The quality of their information service	☐	☐	☐	☐	☐
5. The quality of their telephone directories	☐	☐	☐	☐	☐
6. The quality of their public telephone (pay station) service	☐	☐	☐	☐	☐
7. The quality of the job they do in installing or moving telephones	☐	☐	☐	☐	☐
8. The condition of the telephone equipment in my home	☐	☐	☐	☐	☐
9. Providing equipment that enables me to hear or be heard easily	☐	☐	☐	☐	☐
10. Their treatment of party line customers	☐	☐	☐	☐	☐
11. The way they handle their customers' requests	☐	☐	☐	☐	☐
12. The location of the company's business office here	☐	☐	☐	☐	☐
13. The way they bill their customers	☐	☐	☐	☐	☐
14. The prices they charge for their services and equipment	☐	☐	☐	☐	☐
15. The way they sell their services and equipment	☐	☐	☐	☐	☐
16. The type of employees they have	☐	☐	☐	☐	☐
17. The benefits and working conditions they provide for their employees	☐	☐	☐	☐	☐
18. Their efforts to keep customers informed about the telephone business	☐	☐	☐	☐	☐
19. The participation of the company and their employees in civic and community affairs here	☐	☐	☐	☐	☐

Figure 16-2. Telephone Company questionnaire

Source: American Telephone and Telegraph Company, "Community Relations Fact-Finding Interviews" (New York, n. d.), Exhibit 2. This in-house report was transmitted to the author along with the Burbank materials discussed later in this chapter (pp. 000 ff.).

Experience Report Form

Field Report Card No. _____   Line No. _____

Rating List Item No. _____   Rating Given _____

1. What happened? How long ago? Where? What did you do? What did you say?
   What did they say? What did they do? What happened next? What finally happened?

2. At the time, how did you feel about what had happened?

3. What do you feel the company should have done in this case? Are there any suggestions you'd like to make about this?

Experience relates to:

- ☐ Plant
- ☐ Traffic
- ☐ Commercial
- ☐ Public relations
- ☐ Personnel relations
- ☐ Accounting
- ☐ Other _____

- ☐ Interviewer has taken immediate action*

  No action taken, but experience suggests the need for:
- ☐ Immediate action
- ☐ Study for possible future action
- ☐ No action

Interviewer: Note date and nature of action taken: _____

Figure 16-3. Report form following up "poor" and "fair" responses

Source: American Telephone and Telegraph Company, "Community Relations Fact-Finding Interviews," Exhibit 3.

within the past year or two. If these conditions were met, the nature of the experience was probed in detail, and each item and accompanying experience recorded on a separate Experience Report Form (see Figure 16-3).

Incidentally, the interviewer was specifically instructed to find out how irritated the customer had been at the time of the experience, and to note whether this information was volunteered or had to be elicited by probing.

The next step in the interview was to discover if any unfavorable experiences had been encountered by those who rated these same 17 items either "good" or "excellent." Such experiences, no matter how slight, were also recorded on a separate Experience Report Form. Following this, the respondent was asked to describe any instances in which he had been especially pleased by something telephone people had done—when, for example, he felt they had really gone out of their way to give him good service. These experiences were recorded on a form that was essentially the same as the one shown in Figure 16-3. As a final step in the interview, the respondents were questioned on items 18 and 19; this special probing was done with all the interviewees, regardless of how they had rated the company on these two items.

The data, obtained by means of the interviewing just described, were later analyzed, interpreted, and integrated into a community relations program. Before getting into these subsequent stages, however, we want to consider another element of the survey package—the one which provided the local telephone company management with information on how to conduct an effective interview.

These instructions to interviewers were ten typewritten pages long and included the following subheadings:

>Materials you will need
>Where to interview
>Number to interview in each neighborhood
>*Whom to interview*
>*Field route to be followed*
>When to interview
>Introducing the interview
>Administering the rating list
>Probing for unfavorable experiences
>Recording unfavorable experiences
>*Probing for unusual favorable experiences*
>Probing on items 18 and 19
>Concluding the interview
>Some interviewing suggestions[6]
>Some suggestions for recording interviews

Although we cannot reproduce all ten pages here, the reader can get a better appreciation of these instructions by reading the following few excerpts:

[6] The local management received training from the business research division on how to interview. Part of their instruction required the trainees to play the role of an interviewer conducting an interview. Naturally, the amount of time that could be devoted to this phase of the overall survey package was somewhat limited.

AMERICAN TELEPHONE AND TELEGRAPH COMPANY

Whom to interview

You are to interview only responsible adult members of families having telephone service. Do *not* interview in places of business, in nontelephone homes, or in homes where someone living in the household is a Telephone Company employee.

Interview both men and women (one per home), preferably in about equal numbers. In order to reach an adequate number of men, it may be necessary in some homes, at least, to ask first to see the man of the house, and to interview a woman only if the man is not available. Some evening or Saturday interviews may also be desirable in order to obtain the proper proportion of men.

Field route to be followed

Make your first attempt at the key address indicated on the Field Report Card, and proceed from there as follows:

As you leave the key address and reach the sidewalk—with your back to the door—turn left and make your second attempt at the next house. Work only on one side of the street, turning left at each street corner. Follow this procedure until you have completed 7 or 8 interviews, going completely around the block if necessary. Do not skip any homes on the side of the street you are working. Do not, however, conduct more than two interviews in any one multifamily building.

If after going around the key address block, you have not obtained 7 or 8 interviews, cross the street to the house opposite the key address. Starting with this house, proceed around this second block exactly as you did in the key address block.

The following special instructions apply to two irregular situations you may encounter:

If you find a block that is irregularly shaped, proceed as though it were a square or rectangle. If there are no street intersections in the key address block, simply continue along the street until you have obtained 7 or 8 interviews. If this is not possible (because the street comes to a dead end, runs into a business district, changes to an undeveloped area, etc.), go back to the key address house and attempt an interview at the house directly across the street from it. Proceed from that house in the usual manner. If you run into any unusual situation not covered above, call _____ on _____ for additional instructions.

Probing for unusual favorable experiences

Following the probing of all unfavorable experiences on Items 1 through 17, let the respondent know that you are interested also in learning of any instances in which he may have received some personalized, "out of the ordinary" treatment from telephone people with which he was especially pleased. Say something like this:

"So far I have been trying to learn about any experiences you may have had with the Company or its service that you found in some way to be displeasing or unsatisfactory. On the opposite side of the coin, I am wondering if you can think of any instance in which you were especially *pleased* by something telephone people did—any time when you felt that they really went out of their way to give good service or do something else for you that you wanted?"

If there is such an instance, and it happened locally within the past year or two, get the customer to describe it in complete detail and record what he says on an Experience Report Form.

As in the case of unfavorable experiences, use a separate Form for each unusual favorable experience the respondent describes. Enter the Field Report Card Number and Line Number at the top of the Form, but disregard the Item Number and Rating Given spaces.[7]

Now that we have seen how this duplicate survey was conducted and the sort of questions that were asked, let us look now at the results. What findings did both surveys uncover, and how did the amateurs compare with the professionals?

COMPARISON OF DATA OBTAINED BY PROFESSIONAL AND LOCAL TELEPHONE COMPANY INTERVIEWERS

Ratings

One of the first comparisons made between the professional and local interviewers concerned the ratings obtained to the 19 items in Figure 16-2. The ratings of "good" and "excellent" were combined as "favorable"; "poor" and "fair" were combined as "unfavorable." The results of this combining of the ratings were summarized in Table 16-1.

Table 16-1. Comparison of ratings obtained by professional versus local Telephone Company interviewers

	Favorable	Unfavorable	No opinion or no answer
Items 1 through 17:			
Local team interviewers	72%	9%	19%
Professional interviewers	77	7	16
Items 18 and 19:			
Local team interviewers	59	4	37
Professional interviewers	51	2	47

Source: American Telephone and Telegraph Company, "Community Relations Fact-Finding Interviews," New York, n.d., Attachment A, p. 6. (See the source note for Fig. 16-2.)

[7] American Telephone and Telegraph Company, "Community Relations Fact-Finding Interviews" (New York, n.d.), Attachment A, pp. 1–7. (See the source note for Fig. 16-2.)

It is clear from the table that the overall ratings obtained by the two sets of interviewers are essentially the same—particularly on items 1 through 17. For items 18 and 19 the professionals elicited a larger percentage of "no opinion or no answer" replies. When an item-by-item analysis was made, unfavorable ratings for both interview groups were highest on the items dealing with telephone rates (item 14), the directory (item 5), and party lines (item 10).

With respect to items 18 and 19, the local interview team obtained a larger number of opinions than did the professional interviewers. We will go into the results of the probing done on these two items separately.

Unfavorable experiences reported

In our description of the interview we pointed out that one of the procedures followed after the respondent had rated all the items in Figure 16-2 was to get him to explain why he had checked any of them either "poor" or "fair." If his reason had been some unsatisfactory personal experience encountered within the past year or so, it was summarized on an Experience Report Form. A total of 417 unfavorable Experience Report Forms were obtained—236 by the local team interviewers, and 181 by the professional interviewers. On a per-interview basis, this amounted to an average of 1.8 unfavorable experiences reported for the local team and 1.2 for the professionals.

On the 417 unfavorable Experience Report Forms were recorded a total of 452 specific problems, of which 256 were reported to the local interviewers and 196 to the professional group. The local team managed to elicit not only more unsatisfactory personal experiences from the respondents, but also a greater number of specific, identifiable problems (60 more than the professionals, to be exact). This results in an average of 1.9 specific problems or complaints per interview by each local team member, as compared with 1.3 obtained in interviews by the professional team.

Unusual favorable experiences

Relatively few respondents, roughly one in five, mentioned instances in which they were especially pleased by something that telephone people had done for them. On a per-interview basis, the outside interviewers obtained a somewhat higher number of unusual favorable experiences than did the local team. The averages here were .24 as opposed to .13. In terms of the total number of interviews conducted, this means that the professional interviewers obtained approximately 37 favorable comments, whereas the local team obtained roughly 17. It is interesting to note that when unfavorable experiences were being discussed, the local team came out ahead.

By contrast, we see that the professionals did better at eliciting favorable experiences. It is as if the respondent with a complaint was more inclined to make it directly to a telephone company representative, whereas he would be more likely to hand out compliments to a stranger.

Data obtained by special probing

The reader will recall that the last step in the interview consisted of probing for details on items 18 and 19, which concerned (1) the efforts of the telephone company to keep its customers informed, and (2) the participation of telephone company employees in civic and community affairs. The data obtained from this probing proved to be quite limited and, consequently, unsatisfactory for several reasons. First of all, the interviewers, both local and professional, were not so skillful in probing as they might have been. The quality of the interviewing varied markedly on an individual basis, although as a group the professional interviewers were the more skillful. Secondly, judging from the information obtained, respondents knew very little about the company's activities, particularly its advertising and information programs; they were no better informed about the company's community activities. Moreover, they did not seem to be able to express their opinions intelligently on either of these two items.

In summary, this last segment of the interview produced such limited data that the conclusions reached by the business research people were limited as well. Their findings were necessarily less definite than those generated by the remainder of the interview. It is a moot point whether the respondents really had no views, for example, about company participation in the community, or whether the interviewers were incapable of obtaining them. Also unanswered is whether this paucity of data is entirely a function of unskilled interviewing, or whether it is due more to inadequate dissemination of information on the part of the telephone company. If a vigorous community relations program had been in existence before this experimental survey took place, even amateurish probing might have uncovered considerable feedback simply because of information received upon which to form opinions.

HAMMOND, INDIANA, LOCAL TEAM REACTION

The local team devoted a total of 533 man-hours to this do-it-yourself community relations research project. This does not include approximately 22 hours of clerical work done in connection with the survey effort. The breakdown of time spent is as follows: 376 hours for meetings, interview training, and general instructions; 108 interview hours required to obtain

AMERICAN TELEPHONE AND TELEGRAPH COMPANY

the data; and 49 hours for analysis of the data, including a detailed report listing recommendations for action by their own telephone people in Hammond.

The final report was eleven pages in length and consisted of the following major sections:

1. A summary of ratings made by respondents in connection with the 19 items shown in Figure 16-2.
2. A compilation of the number and nature of unfavorable comments received.
3. A detailed list of recommendations for action.
4. A list of assignments for each department of the telephone company based on the action recommended.

CONCLUSIONS OF THE BUSINESS RESEARCH DIVISION

Based on the rigorous field test provided by the cooperation of the telephone people in Hammond, Indiana, the business research group came to the following conclusions:

1. In general, the package survey tool that they had developed for use by local telephone personnel worked quite well. The rating list, used as the basis for the entire interview, proved to be particularly effective and simple to administer; it enabled the interviewer to quickly determine which items the customer should be able to discuss and which ones he is uninformed about.

2. The local management team is quite capable of conducting interviews of this type. Taking into consideration both the strong and weak points, the local group did not differ significantly from the professionals in their ability to conduct the survey.

3. There is no evidence that customers are reluctant to criticize the telephone company because they are being interviewed by company representatives. On the contrary, it appears that the telephone company employees were more successful than the professionals in eliciting negative comments. Conversely, however, it is possible that they would be less successful in eliciting favorable information.

4. From all indications, the local team found the survey package quite acceptable. Even more important, they seemed to be capable of making a straightforward analysis of the sort of data the package generated, as well as carrying out a program of action based on them. Lastly, the local telephone people appeared to become quite personally involved in the study and to regard the entire experience as both worthwhile personally and useful organizationally.

5. As the data were analyzed, the single—and perhaps significant—weakness that came to light in the survey package stemmed from the probing on items 18 and 19 in the rating list. This was most likely due to the inadequate interviewing skills of the interviewers—particularly among the local teams—although the researchers admit as an additional possibility the nature and wording of the questions themselves. Since the areas covered were less relevant to the customer than the rest of the items, one might expect a higher level of "no opinion" answers and a lower yield of useful information.

On the basis of their overall experience with the Hammond, Indiana, field test, the researchers very definitely recommended that the use of the survey package by other local telephone personnel be encouraged, and suggested the following modifications to further improve it:

1. More time should be devoted to training the local interview team; one of the most notable observations about the entire study effort was that the local interviewers obtained less complete and less accurate data then they might have had they been more skilled; their lack of training was particularly noticeable with questions that required probing and on which the subject was ill-informed and the interviewee thus unable to express himself easily.

2. Procedures should be modified for classifying and recording information on the unfavorable experiences of the customer—the forms previously used were found to be awkward; as a result, the forms were revised, made up into pads, and designed to carry only one experience per page—nothing was recorded on the reverse side.

3. A separate interview checklist should be developed for questions 18 and 19, as these two items elicited practically no useful information in their original form.

THE SURVEY PACKAGE IN OPERATION

After the community relations survey package had been judged operational, so to speak, by means of the field test in Hammond, Indiana, the availability of this tool was made known to the associated operating companies of the American Telephone and Telegraph Company. The following letter[8] was one of the methods used to spread the word:

Over the years a number of companies have used various approaches in attempting to develop an effective community relations program. When the

[8] Letter dated October 30, 1963.

AMERICAN TELEPHONE AND TELEGRAPH COMPANY

local people were unable to determine specific needs of their customers of their community, they concentrated more on the informing portion of the job, i.e., providing films, central office visits and talks. These activities are worthwhile but represent only one facet of a well-rounded community relations job.

The common ingredient of the efforts in fact-finding at the local level in most companies has been interviews with customers to gain first hand knowledge of their viewpoint toward the Company. Method of sample selection, interviewing procedure and the validity of the information obtained, varied considerably among the companies.

Our Business Research Division undertook a pilot study to develop an efficient interviewing tool that would provide meaningful and accurate information from a representative cross section of customers. This new approach to help plan community relations action at the local level, which I touched upon briefly at the conference,[9] is reported in the attached. The report of the test in Hammond, Indiana, indicates in some detail the soundness of this fact-finding approach.

Copies of the report are being sent by the A.T.&T. Director of Business Research to your Comptroller. Additional copies may be obtained through your Chief Statistician.

Sincerely,

Lee C. Tait
Assistant Vice President
(A.T.&T.)

Attachment
To all Public Relations Vice Presidents

For a better idea of how this survey package was utilized by a given local telephone company, let us examine briefly what Burbank, California, did with it.

THE BURBANK, CALIFORNIA, FINDINGS

The data obtained by the Pacific Telephone and Telegraph Company in Burbank, California, are not included here in complete detail. However, a summary of the responses to the basic 19 items will give us sufficient information to be able to understand the highlights of the community relations program that was developed as a result (see Table 16-2). Five of the items that received either the largest percentage of "poor" or "fair" ratings, or the largest percentage of "no opinion" ratings, are summarized in the bar

---

[9] The conference referred to lasted for several days and was held by A.T.&T. for all the vice-presidents in the company.

Table 16-2. Summarization of 46 interviews in Burbank

Items	Poor	Fair	Good	Excellent	No opinion
1. The quality of their local service	2%	7%	50%	39%	2%
2. The quality of their long distance service	0	8	44	40	8
3. The quality of their repair service	0	4	47	42	7
4. The quality of their information service	4	4	60	30	2
5. The quality of their telephone directories	4	2	52	40	2
6. The quality of their public telephone (pay station) service	0	9	41	11	39
7. The quality of the job they do in installing or moving telephones	0	4	52	32	12
8. The condition of the telephone equipment in my home	0	2	46	46	6
9. Providing equipment that enables me to hear or be heard easily	0	4	43	38	15
10. Their treatment of party-line customers	0	2	26	8	64
11. The way they handle their customers' requests	2	7	50	36	5
12. The location of the company's business office here	0	0	60	18	22
13. The way they bill their customers	11	20	48	18	3
14. The prices they charge for their services and equipment	6	31	46	8	9
15. The way they sell their services and equipment	4	28	39	9	20
16. The type of employees they have	0	2	50	36	12
17. The benefits and working conditions they provide for their employees	0	0	24	34	42
18. Their efforts to keep customers informed about the telephone business	2	5	51	30	12
19. The participation of the company and their employees in civic and community affairs here	0	4	41	11	44

Source: Pacific Telephone and Telegraph Company, *"Community Relations (Burbank-Sun Valley),"* Burbank, December, 1964, p. 4.

AMERICAN TELEPHONE AND TELEGRAPH COMPANY

graph in Figure 16-4. Another reason for isolating these particular items is that the plans for corrective action, based on the survey data, focus upon these areas of heightened customer dissatisfaction and lack of awareness of company activities.

Billing our customers
Poor	Fair	Good	Excellent	No opinion
11%	20%	48%	18%	3%

Customer cost for service and equipment
Poor	Fair	Good	Excellent	No opinion
6%	31%	46%	8%	9%

The way we make sales
Poor	Fair	Good	Excellent	No opinion
4%	28%	39%	9%	20%

Employee benefits and working conditions
Poor	Excellent	No opinion
24%	34%	42%

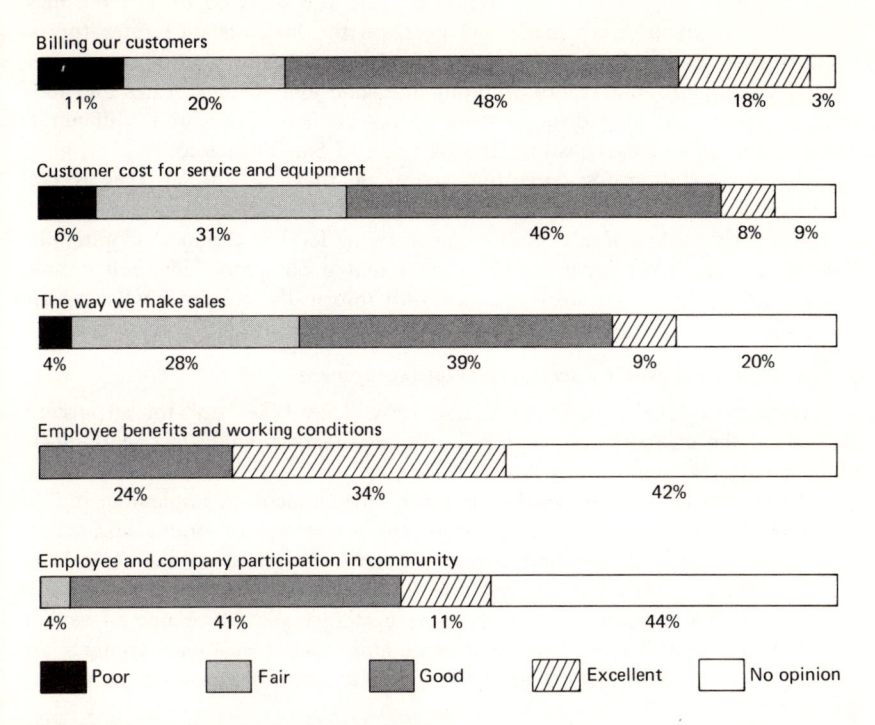

Employee and company participation in community
Poor	Fair	Excellent	No opinion
4%	41%	11%	44%

Figure 16-4. Burbank problem area

Source: American Telephone and Telegraph Company, "Community Relations Fact-Finding Interviews," p. 5.

THE PLANS FOR CORRECTIVE ACTION

The following recommendations were made for the areas of customer contact that appeared to be most in need of correction:

1. *Concerning our telephone bills*

The first step to be taken is the itemization of message unit charges. It is the team understanding that steps are being made to eliminate the message unit. If this is true, the general public should be made aware of this end of the reason behind it. It is our belief that an informed public is an understanding and better satisfied public. Message unit and lack of itemization are universal problems, not unique to the Burbank-Sun Valley area. With the media at our disposal in Los Angeles, the Company should take a more active role in attacking this problem head on.

2. *Concerning our prices charged for service and equipment*

For the most part, customer reaction again was directed toward the message unit. Comments were made, however, on the long distance rates for intrastate calls versus the new reduced rates for interstate calls.

The Company should look into our intrastate long distance rates and their relative position to long distance rates to out-of-state points. It is difficult to justify a call to Chicago costing less than one to San Francisco.

Recommendation for corrective action on message unit charges is outlined in Item 1.

Any large scale action cannot be taken at the level of the local Community Relations Team. Corrective action is such that a company-wide policy must be established. Again, we stress that we must inform the customer what we are doing. This can be done through bill inserts, advertising, etc.

3. *Concerning the way we sell services and equipment*

Here the typical comment was that we will not take "no" for an answer. To inform the customer of services and equipment available is one thing—to try to sell at every opportunity is something else.

Technique is a simple word—it is much more difficult to implement it. The problems of selling could be corrected by the proper use of timing and selling techniques. High pressure and overselling have no place in the Telephone Business. Over emphasis on selling due to indices may create an undesirable side effect.[10] The impression left with the customer should be one of service rather than that of having been sold something. Direct customer contacts are being reduced by automation—we should strive to make the most of the few we do have.

4. *Concerning the benefits and working conditions for our employees*

There was no response in general to this question, indicating that the public is unaware of our employee benefits and working conditions. Company provided benefits must be sold to our employees, for the employee is our best salesman. We have all been furnished our Benefits Plan booklets. It is suggested that all employees be provided with a supplement, comparing our overall benefits with those of other large companies. Our advertising theme should be "a good place to work."

5. *Concerning the participation of the company and our employees in civic and community affairs*

It is obvious that our efforts in this area are going unnoticed. . . . We plan to dramatize our interest in civic affairs through more effective use of the employment office windows. The first step will be to mail a notice to the various organizations informing them of the available space and how it may be secured.

---

[10] The expression, "emphasis on selling due to indices," is an in-house reference to the fact that local operating units were once measured in terms of a variety of services and equipment indices. As in any organization, these indices were used to keep track of the sales component of the overall functioning.

AMERICAN TELEPHONE AND TELEGRAPH COMPANY 257

It is suggested that if sufficient interest is displayed the company should consider purchasing a "community billboard" to be mounted on top of the Burbank Business Office building, where maximum coverage would be received through foot and auto traffic. A brief statement on the sign would relate the Company's interest in community affairs. The team feels a responsibility to stimulate more interest among employees in the affairs of their community. The employee of the month is considered as one way to publicize as well as recognize the Company's interest.[11]

[11] Pacific Telephone and Telegraph Company, *"Community Relations (Burbank-Sun Valley),"* Burbank, December, 1964, pp. 10–12. Following the completion of this case presentation, some interesting information came to the attention of the writer. A Service Attitude Measurement plan has been developed to provide additional information to telephone management people in the local community. This plan provides a practical means of measuring telephone service from the customer's viewpoint by assessing his attitude toward the quality of service on a district departmental basis. Meaningful current data are provided on specific details of service performance, pinpointed by specific customers in specific places at specific times. The method used is a mail survey directed primarily to service items in which the customer has specific interest or experience—for example, a repair service visit. A monthly series of questionnaires in this area provides a continuing flow of information. (Controls have developed to prevent repeated surveying of any one customer in too short a time—the average customer will be contacted only about once every seven years.)

17 Case 7

Promotion of seat belt acceptance and usage by the National Safety Council

CASE OUTLINE

1. Introduction
2. Background information
   a. a vignette to illustrate the obstacles faced by the NSC in Promoting safety
   b. promotion of seat belt usage as a case in point
   c. how do we cope with this communication dilemma?
3. A five-phase program developed by the NSC to cope with their communication dilemma
   a. Phase 1, literature search leading to a position paper
   b. Phase 2, critiques of the Basic Paper
   c. Phase 3, National Symposium of mass communications
   d. Phase 4, writing a technical summary
   e. Phase 5, development of a Simple Handbook for safety practitioners
4. Traffic safety workshops—first major by-product
5. "The National Drivers' Test"—second major by-product
   a. how the safety communications study guidelines helped
      —selective perception of the potential audience
      —importance of involving your audience whenever possible
      —providing for constructive tension release
      —advantage of multiple media usage plus personal communication
      —combining information with persuasive efforts
      —attention-getting dramatization
6. Handbook of safety communications—third major by-product
7. The safety communications study: a summary

THE NATIONAL SAFETY COUNCIL

INTRODUCTION

Elsewhere in this book we have stressed the point of view that the public relations practitioner must make use increasingly of research in order to guide the planning and implementation of his public relations programs. In fact, this entire book can be seen as a modest effort toward inducing the public relations practitioner to visualize his work in this light.

We have learned that research can be viewed as a process made up of nine basic steps. The first requires that the researcher be able to state explicitly the problem he is going to investigate, and the last that he note the implications of his research and carefully spell out any resulting generalizations.

One of the steps of the process—used as a point of departure, in this case—is the *literature search*. In simple terms, this involves trying to find out what others have done that may have bearing on the problem you are trying to solve. By examining the literature in a wide variety of sources, one tries to determine whether or not what he is seeking may already be known. Although in the case of public relations the researcher is unlikely to find that someone has faced *exactly* his same problem, the search may provide him with information concerning pitfalls to be avoided. In short, though he may not solve his problem, he may find out what did not work in the past.

This is what the literature search is all about. It is seldom that an individual is the first person ever to be concerned about a given problem situation. In scientific circles the literature search is old hat; an investigator would not think of trying to solve a problem without first checking the related literature.

Unfortunately, this attitude is not nearly so widespread among public relations practitioners. The action-oriented practitioner somehow regards the literature search as wasting time, and it is a rare occurrence when he takes the time to do a careful literature search. The author is aware that this attitude does not exist in a vacuum; he realizes that the available literature in public relations sources is not what it could be in terms of helpfulness—and that it is often not worthy of the time it takes to read it. However, there is much valuable material, especially in the literature of the social and behavioral sciences, that is consistently overlooked. This lack of faith in the literature is a circular process, and the only way to break the reaction is to examine every literature source that might prove to be useful in helping to solve a public relations problem.

This case, based on the activities of the public relations leadership of the National Safety Council, is one of the most exciting applications that the author has come across of the use of the literature search applied to a public relations problem area. As a result of an extensive literature search launched by the Council, a number of significant applied steps were taken by the public relations practitioners involved. Their action led to noteworthy progress in furthering one of the basic goals of the National Safety Council —the promoting of highway safety throughout the country.

BACKGROUND INFORMATION

The National Safety Council is a voluntary, noncommercial, nonprofit association dedicated to reducing the number and severity of accidents of all kinds. The group was born in 1912, when many people were still regarding the 150 year old Industrial Revolution as a "Frankenstein's monster, ravaging human life with the clicking of every cog." Many of those who were not arguing for turning back the clock were inclined to accept the loss of life and limb as one of the penalties of progress.

In that eventful year of 1912, a group of electrical engineers from the iron and steel industries got together at a hotel in Milwaukee to form what was known as the National Council for Industrial Safety. *The Chicago Tribune* prophetically announced on its front page, "One of the most important offices in the world was quietly opened this week. . . ." Although the initial impetus for the formation of the Council was to promote safety in industry, the organization soon became concerned with the prevention of *all* accidents, and in 1953 it was chartered as a public service organization by Congress.

Today, the National Safety Council has more than 9,000 members. These include industrial and transportation organizations with more than 25,000 plants and operating locations; insurance companies, associations, professional organizations that influence safety work in hundreds of branches or units; and community or state safety organizations that carry on extensive programs of safety both in this country and abroad. The financing of the Council is achieved through membership dues and sales of its publications. Also, industry, business, and private individuals contribute funds for a variety of NSC activities that are not self-supporting—such as setting up and servicing accident-prevention organizations on all levels, and public service in the areas of traffic, school, home, farm, and general safety.

With a staff of some 370 individuals headquartered in a block-long building overlooking the Chicago River, plus a volunteer army of more than 3,000 men and women, the range of activities of the NSC is enormous. First of all, the organization acts as a national and international clearinghouse, gathering and distributing information about causes of accidents and ways to prevent them. A partial list of this tremendous outpouring of information—the NSC handles more mail than any but the largest catalog houses in the city of Chicago—is as follows:

THE NATIONAL SAFETY COUNCIL

The Accident Prevention Manual for Industrial Operations (revised periodically)
Thirty monthly newsletters for different industries
One thousand different safety poster designs
An annual safety calendar
Dash cards for commercial vehicles
One hundred safety films for employees and supervisors
School lesson units
Accident Facts (an annual statistical reference book)
Public information materials for radio and television stations, newspapers, and magazines
Books, pamphlets, and leaflets directed to many audiences

A vignette to illustrate the obstacles faced by the National Safety Council in promoting safety

It has often been pointed out that the average individual in the United States is subjected to an immense volume of messages—particularly through the mass media—all of which demand his attention. They exhort him to do something, believe something, change something, or take responsibility for something. Although it is extremely difficult to estimate with any sort of accuracy, the number of commercial messages alone directed toward a single consumer has been placed at 1,500 a day.[1]

Among this welter of communications are those concerned with highway safety. In this connection, Dr. Harold Mendelsohn writes:

During 1960, the National Safety Council reports that 190,000 safety speeches were made under state auspices; 17,000,000 automobile driver manuals were distributed; 140,000 film presentations were made; 226 films and slide film presentations were produced; and incalculable amounts of space in newspapers and periodicals, plus time on the air, were devoted to promoting traffic safety in the United States. The National Safety Council estimates the dollar value of this prodigious effort to be in the neighborhood of $100,000,000 annually. Small wonder that certain experts in traffic safety have asserted that it is the "nation's most publicized cause."[2]

The topic of traffic safety is an exceedingly wide one, and all sorts of traffic safety messages can be noted at any time. However, despite massive communication efforts, the annual toll of deaths (in the neighborhood of 47,000) and of temporary and permanent injury (estimated at 1.2 million per year)[3] keeps on increasing. To be sure, on the basis of such statistics we cannot conclude that our communication efforts are either effective

---

[1] Harold Mendelsohn, in Murray Blumenthal, ed., *The Denver Symposium on Mass Communications Research for Safety* (Chicago: National Safety Council, 1964), p. 5. See also below, n. 9.
[2] *Ibid.*, p. 5.
[3] H. Gene Miller, "September Death Toll Up 2 Percent," *Traffic Safety*, LXIV, No. 12 (December, 1964), 28–33.

or ineffective, either "good" or "bad." In fact, one of the disconcerting features of traffic safety is that so many important facets of the overall problem remain imperfectly defined. For example, we still lack adequate and agreed-upon measures of what constitutes an accident; and regions of the country differ considerably in how carefully the causes of accidents are identified. In addition, we still have great difficulty agreeing on just what causes accidents and how they can be controlled. For example, what assumptions do we have concerning the *degree* to which they can be prevented? Some people generally assume that no systematic patterns of causes can be uncovered; consequently, the notion of reducing accidents is not held with any great hope. In other words, accidents are "unavoidable." Others believe that accidents *can* be prevented; indeed, one sometimes feels that these people equate accident control with disease control: with the proper vaccine the problem can be gotten rid of entirely.

To round out the picture of our inability to come to any conclusions on the effectiveness of our communication efforts in combating traffic accidents, let us look at the following quote:

Without a doubt, some of the safety programs and the individual messages have had little effect; some have had no effect and some even have had a negative effect.

The validity and effectiveness of the program and the message is, in most cases, directly related to the keenness, perceptiveness, and experience of the communications practitioner. There ae good ones and bad ones. The good ones are amazingly good in their ability to analyze and understand human motivation and human responses, having an "intuitive" wisdom, a "PR sense," a keen insight and a fine ability to empathize.

But there are many kinds of knowledge that are not available, on the basis of the sheer "intuition" (keen observation) of the best of the communications specialists. This is where research is needed: to test out different types of appeals in relation to different situations and to provide more certain guidance as to the preferred content, method and mechanism of delivery for different situations. . . .

If we move from a consideration of the safety communications themselves to the results that safety communications are designed to produce—safe driving and safe pedestrian practices—we must come to an entirely opposite conclusion that safety communications have been eminently successful.

According to statistical data presented in *Accident Facts, 1963,* published by the National Safety Council and distributed to participants in this conference, in 1962 there were 40,900 deaths in traffic accidents. But as we look over the figures for previous years, we find that there were almost as many traffic deaths in 1937 (39,643), and 1941 (39,969), despite the fact that the number of motor vehicles has more than doubled between 1937 and 1962 (30.1 million in 1937; 34.9 million in 1941; 78.6 million in 1962).

With this great increase in the number of vehicles, speed capacity, speed limits and the complexity of traffic problems, we would have expected that, between 1937 and 1962, the number of deaths would have at least doubled, and

THE NATIONAL SAFETY COUNCIL

that the death rates would have either increased, or at least remain unchanged. The fact is that the absolute number of deaths barely increased while the rates fell very sharply.

	1937	1941	1962
Total traffic deaths	39,643	39,969	40,900
Number of vehicles in millions	30.1	34.9	78.6
Vehicle miles (billions)	27%	334	767
Death rate (per 10,000 vehicles)	13.2	11.5	5.2
Death rate (per 100 million vehicle miles)	14.7	12.0	5.3

Thus, we have been presented with no proof at all that traffic safety communications are in a state of crisis or ineffectiveness. (In effect, we have been presented with no evidence at all concerning the state of traffic safety communication.)

As for the state of crisis in safety, the statistics show that none exists and that, as a matter of fact, it was a great deal safer to drive or walk in traffic areas in 1962 than it was 25 years earlier. (This is not to obscure the fact that, between 1961 and 1962, traffic deaths rose from 38,090 to 40,900. However, the death rate rose only from 5.2 to 5.3 for vehicle miles and from 5.0 to 5.2 for number of vehicles. While these inceases are cause for concern, they do not present a picture of crisis.) *[4]

It is clear from a reading of the above material that there is a great deal that has not yet been determined about the nature of the problems in the general area of traffic safety. Moreover, the role of communication in all this is quite unclear at the present time.

Promotion of seat belt usage as a case in point[5]

The seat belt is a personal protective device designed for use in motor vehicles and airplanes. The most common form of the seat belt consists of two straps, each anchored at one end to the vehicle and fitted at the other end with a buckle coupling. When fastened in place, the belt encircles the

---

* National Safety Council reports total traffic deaths for 1963 as 43,600, with a vehicle mileage death rate of 5.5.

[4] Blumenthal, op. cit., pp. 154–155.

[5] This section is quoted from a write-up of the seat belt problem area as a case (for a different purpose and to a different degree) by the author in *Communication and Public Relations* (Columbus: Charles E. Merrill Books, Inc., 1966), pp. 18–22.

passenger, holding him firmly in the seat. In case of collision or sudden stop, he is thus protected from being thrown severely against the windshield, the interior, or the fittings of the vehicle—and from being ejected from the vehicle.

The very first airplanes and automobiles made use of such devices, but only in the airplane was the seat belt developed, perfected, and made standard equipment as part of the seat itself.

As recently as World War II, seat belts were ignored by virtually everyone but a handful of safety specialists and a few visionaries who were considered crackpots. From time to time, one of the specialists or crackpots might gain the attention of a manufacturer or an organization interested in safety, but while the idea was deemed sound, at least two factors prevented a grand-scale professional acceptance in safety, health, and medical circles: (1) the absence of reliable, research-based proof of the value of seat belts; and (2) an absence of engineering standards for manufacture and installation.

The general public, however, could not have cared less. It knew nothing about the belts—or, at least, did not indicate any knowledge through purchase—in spite of the fact that as early as 1947 the devices were marketed by Nash.

From what might be considered a low point of interest in seat belts in 1947, there gradually emerged a series of events that had considerable bearing on the two factors listed above. Briefly, some of the events were as follows:

1. In 1947, Cornell University's Aeronautical Laboratory studied the action of the human body during deceleration when held in place by a seat belt. It was demonstrated that the severity of head injuries would be appreciably reduced in collision if the body were held in place with a seat belt. The report of the study was filed in 1949.

2. In 1953, under a project sponsored by the Liberty Mutual Insurance Company, the Cornell Laboratory studied the action of the human body during automobile crashes, particularly front-end collisions. It was determined that seat belts would eliminate the most severe injuries caused by the unrestrained body colliding with the windshield or dashboard.

3. In 1955, the Society of Automobile Engineers, after several years of study, issued its first seat belt standard.

4. In 1955, a National Safety Council policy statement recommended the installation and use of seat belts in motor vehicles. This statement further recommended adherence to SAE standards and called for a continuation of research and development such as that done by Cornell, Minnesota, UCLA, Purdue, and several other universities, the Society of Automotive Engineers, and various manufacturers.

5. In 1957, Cornell's Transportation Safety Research Committee an-

nounced, after studying five thousand injury cases, that automobile seat safety belts save lives and reduce the frequency and severity of injuries to car occupants "beyond all reasonable doubt."

In spite of the fact that by 1957 substantial progress had been made in overcoming the lack of research on just how valuable seat belts were in reducing death and injury and establishing engineering standards for manufacture and installation, acceptance and use of seat belts remained at a very low level. For one thing, conflicting information concerning the value of seat belts was before the public. For example, Andrew J. White of Motor Vehicle Research, Inc., of Manchester, New Hampshire, issued releases and articles to a number of publications casting strong doubt about the value of seat belts. The tenor of the attacks ranged from calling seat belts "overrated" to "lethal." The basis of the attacks included evidence that purported to demonstrate that "jackknifing" of the torso would inflict serious abdominal and head injuries, depending on how the body reacted. Such articles certainly gave anyone opposed to seat belts—informed or otherwise —support for his point of view.[6]

Further confusion resulted when *Consumer Reports,* published by the strongly pro-seat belt Consumers Union, was critical of (in its opinion) inferior products on the market and warned of the necessity for proper installation. This was further compounded by the fact that early in 1958 the General Services Administration of the United States Government established specifications for seat belt purchases which were more stringent and more limited than SAE standards. Although the GSA standards were developed as a guide to government purchases and, as such, were not strict standards of minimum acceptable quality, the effect was that there seemed to be two sets of "standards."

While the above attacks and confusion producing events did not reach as wide audience as the pro-seat belt material, it can safely be assumed that the opinion leaders and educated persons reached by it were affected somewhat, and, as a result, blocked a more immediate and widespread acceptance.

By virtue of the very nature of its organizational goals, the National Safety Council was vitally interested in the progress that had—or, more properly, had not—been made to gain widespread acceptance of seat belts by the motoring public. By the end of 1960, an estimated one million vehicles were equipped with one or more belts. The average installation was two belts in the front seat. This tiny fraction of the nation's more than seventy million vehicles was particularly disturbing to the National Safety

---

[6] At this point, one is reminded of the conflicting statements that were issued when the Salk polio vaccine was first available to the public, particularly with respect to what age groups (including adults) should be inoculated. As a result, the average individual (informed or not) was left up in the air about what to do.

Council. By this time, a considerable number of public promotions had been attempted. For example, *The Saturday Evening Post* carried a typical "personal" story of how belts saved an individual's life, then launched into the vital facts. *Woman's Day* ran a straightforward "how-to-protect-yourself" story written by a Cornell University specialist. Ford, with its 1956 models, promoted a "safety package" which included emphasis on seat belts as well as padded visors and dished steering wheels. In fact, the Ford advertisement probably constituted the first major national promotion of seat belts by a major advertiser.

In addition to these public promotions, there were many promotions of an "internal" nature—*i.e.,* attempts within certain organizations to promote the use of seat belts. For example, certain businesses, particularly motor vehicle fleet operators, encouraged seat belt usage. Police force adoption of seat belts is another example of what is meant by "internal" promotions. As a matter of fact, in 1959, the International Association of Chiefs of Police had adopted a resolution urging all law enforcement agencies to use belts, set an example for the public, and promote the use of belts wherever possible.

In spite of these various programs, a sizable task still confronted the National Safety Council to promote the use of seat belts. A distressingly small proportion of the driving public (estimated at one in seventy) made use of a device that was known to prevent injury and save lives.

How do we cope with this communication dilemma?

From our prototype traffic safety problem concerning seat belt usage, we have a better appreciation of the communication problems confronting the NSC. Not only is the scope of the task large—with the entire motoring public as its object—but it is clear that there are a multitude of other forces involved, some helpful and some detrimental to furthering the cause of seat belt usage. Also, any program that a public relations practitioner develops must be constructed with an eye to taking advantage of the work of the many organizations which share the goals of the National Safety Council, at the same time avoiding the conflicts and entanglements that the mere existence of so many organizations engenders.

Over the years the Council has done many things to encourage the use of seat belts. For example, a research study was undertaken to study the effects of a television program entitled "The Great Holiday Massacre," a documentary produced by CBS Reports, with Edward R. Murrow as narrator. During the five-day period preceding the TV program (telecast Monday, December 26, 1960), a nation-wide sample of over 700 families was interviewed. The questions elicited their views on highway safety and driving on holiday weekends, and also measured their awareness of and attitudes toward seat belts. In the five-day period following the telecast, an

THE NATIONAL SAFETY COUNCIL

effort was made to reinterview as many of the respondents in the original sample as possible. The purpose was, of course, to see what attitude changes had taken place as a result of their viewing this special program.

A FIVE-PHASE PROGRAM DEVELOPED BY THE NSC TO COPE WITH THEIR COMMUNICATION DILEMMA

Those responsible for communication programs at the National Safety Council were acutely aware of the gaps in knowledge that existed with respect to how to communicate about safety—particularly highway safety. In fact, one might say that these gaps had acquired the status of the daily weather, with everyone talking about it and no one doing anything about it.

Early in 1962 one man decided to do something about it. This was John Naisbitt, then manager of the public information department of the National Safety Council.[7] In conjunction with the Council's fiftieth anniversary celebration, an extensive mass communications study on safety was launched, thanks largely to his efforts.[8] This study evolved into five basic phases, four of which have been successfully completed, with the fifth not yet done. Let us examine each of them in turn, since collectively they constitute one of the most extensive literature searches ever promoted and encouraged by a public relations practitioner, and dramatically illustrate the value of this method of research in helping to solve applied public relations problems.

Phase 1: Literature search leading to a position paper

The first phase called for an exhaustive literature search of the topic of communication. The express purpose of the search was to pull together all of the pertinent literature and relate it to the general question of how to communicate about traffic safety. Its objectives are expressed in the preface to a final report that was the result of eight months of intensive work:[9]

[7] The present manager is Mr. Archibald McKinlay, Jr., who has more than ably filled the shoes of his predecessor. He has not only carried on what John Naisbitt started but added his own creative insights and efforts to the task.
[8] This five-phase program was known as the Safety Communications Study and was sponsored by the following organizations: American Petroleum Institute, American Seat Belt Council, Inc., American Society of Safety Engineers, Automobile Manufacturers Association Inc., Automotive Safety Foundation, Insurance Institute for Highway Safety, National Safety Council, U.S. Public Health Service, and the U.S. Bureau of Public Roads.
[9] The literature search was directed by Dr. Harold Mendelsohn, professor and Director of Research in the Radio-TV Department of the University of Denver. He was the author of the final report which summarized the literature. The report also contains a fresh viewpoint on safety communication that has provided the springboard for widespread training efforts directed toward safety communicators throughout the country.

1. To develop a comprehensive bibliography of materials pertaining to the effective communication of traffic safety messages (abstracted according to a standardized procedure using standardized criteria) and to establish a reference file of studies in this field to be used currently as well as in the future.
2. To describe critically the scope and depth of the current state of empirically derived knowledge relating to the effective communication of traffic safety messages.
3. To generate principles of effective communications for traffic safety, and to document such principles from the research that has been done in the communications of persuasion.
4. To contribute to the development of guidelines for programming in traffic safety.[10]

Using the literature search as his basis, Dr. Mendelsohn came up with a critical review of the literature, complete with a summary of conclusions that could be drawn as a result. In addition, primarily because of the inadequate treatment of traffic safety found in the literature, he developed a theory to guide the development of subsequent research and practice in this area. This took the form of a position paper entitled *"Mass Communications for Safety."*

Phase 2: Critiques of the basic paper

Eighteen leading social scientists, communication specialists, and safety experts were asked to study the position paper and write critiques of Mendelsohn's work. As might be expected, not all the experts agreed with his conclusions. These very dissensions (and agreements), however, helped to move the general literature search ahead and stimulated the development of additional ideas and new approaches to the whole question of furthering traffic safety.

Phase 3: National symposium on mass communications

After the critiques of the 18 reviewers had been assembled and compiled into one document, it was then duplicated and sent to additional experts in the safety and communications fields (there were a total of 73 recipients, including most of the critique writers). These experts were asked to study the original literature review, the position paper by Mendelsohn, and the 18 critiques, after which they were invited to attend a national symposium held in Denver in the fall of 1963. The attendees were divided into four different panels, with each panel responsible for producing a report summarizing its views of all the work that had been done prior to the symposium (the position paper and the 18 critiques). The work of the

[10] Mendelsohn, *op. cit.*, p. 2.

panels resulted in a refinement of all the thinking thus far, plus additions to the overall store of information about traffic safety.

Phase 4: Writing a technical summary

The next step was to consolidate everything that had happened in the first three phases and print it in book form. Edited by Dr. Murray Blumenthal, the work was published by the NSC in 1964 under the title *The Denver Symposium on Mass Communications Research for Safety*. Part I of the volume consists of the original review of the literature and the position paper produced by Mendelsohn. Part II contains selected portions of the critiques and questions that were raised by the original 18 writers. The final part is devoted to how the information obtained can best be applied to the general problem of traffic safety. Of particular interest are several pages of questions that Dr. Blumenthal felt a practitioner—that is, one directly concerned with and working in the field of traffic safety—should ask himself about his work.

Phase 5: Development of a simple handbook for safety practitioners

The final phase of the Safety Communications Study is the only one that is incomplete at this time. It consists of producing a handbook for the safety practitioner, one that is simple and concise, yet explicit as possible with regard to what guides can be provided to the applied communicator trying to reduce traffic accidents. This handbook, in one sense, represents the most difficult portion of the whole study effort. Among the perplexing problems involved are: translating communication theory and psychological and sociological concepts into a form that can help a safety practitioner construct his messages; deciding the format to put them in and what media combinations to use; and figuring out how mass communication techniques should supplement face-to-face techniques. We will return to these tasks in more detail a little later.

Now that we have considered the sequence of events embodied in the Safety Communications Study, let us turn to an examination of the highlights of the practical or applied by-products of this elaborate literature search. In short, what good has the literature search accomplished for the safety practitioner?

TRAFFIC SAFETY WORKSHOPS—FIRST MAJOR BY-PRODUCT

One direct by-product of the elaborate communication study has been a series of workshops at which the findings of the study are translated into explicit guidelines for the safety practitioner. To date, workshops have been held in Lansing, Chapel Hill, Boston, Denver, and Waco. Let us look at some of the details of how they are conducted—details that are essentially common to them all.

The workshops last a day and a half, running from 8:30 a.m. to 11 p.m. the first day and ending at 1:00 p.m. on the next. Between 40 and 50 safety practitioners are in attendance. They are divided into eight panels of approximately six persons each, the whole emphasis of the workshop being on participation.

The safety practitioners are continually working on developing actual materials to bear on some particular applied problem; the format of their work is essentially one of theory first, then practice. The participants are exposed to theory-based material that presumably has relevance for the practitioner, and the practitioner is then required to demonstrate how he would apply this theory to practice, with the emphasis on *now;* let us consider some examples.

After the comparatively neutral introductory lectures (devoted to such things as an examination of the communication process with all its complexities), the first of a series of action-oriented exercises is introduced. Projected on a screen is a series of rectangles arranged at various angles to one another. One participant in the audience is called upon to communicate to another participant (who is not permitted to look) what is on the screen. The "receiver" is asked to reproduce the pattern solely on the basis of what the "sender" tells him. In order to simulate most safety communication situations, the receiver is not permitted to ask any questions. The result of this exercise: few sender-receiver teams are able to accomplish this communication objective successfully; the objective: dramatic reinforcement of the earlier lecture material that stressed the complexity of the communication process.

Following an exercise such as this, the participants are required to describe in detail which factors of the various media (and of the community in which they are utilized) help and which hinder getting safety messages across to any particular publics or subpublics. This is then followed by a request for a list of predominant attitudes and values of the various groups to be reached and for the participants' ideas on how these attitudes and values can either help or hinder his safety communication objectives. This reveals what the participant knows about his target audiences and shows how his knowledge can help him in practical communication situations—not yet covered in the workshop.

While the participants are still recovering from this exercise, they are thrown yet another series of questions for which they must provide detailed answers with specifics. For example, they might be asked: "What media mix would you use to reach the following subpopulations in your community to promote fire safety in the home?" Difficult subpopulations are provided, such as school-age children, the elderly, housewives, adult men, voters, persons of low socioeconomic status, and lawmakers. Each panel is required to come up with its recommendation on what media mix it would use and *why*.

A different type of problem is introduced in the following statement:

> A body of people in the community does a lot of driving and quite a bit of drinking. It has been exposed to the alcohol and gasoline don't mix preachments, but the lesson doesn't soak in. In fact, since most members have never had a serious accident, and since they *feel* more relaxed when driving with alcoholic fortification, these messages nudge the group toward a more stubborn fixation that alcohol and gasoline do mix.[11]

Here the participants are required to come up with recommendations on how they would cope with this sort of problem—also in explicit terms, not in generalities.

Next, a change of pace occurs; once again there is a return to more theory, perhaps with a presentation such as "Attitude Formation and Opinion Change in the Persuasion Process." Following this, it is back to practice again. Maybe the participants are required to rewrite a safety message, or to answer another practical question involving a specific program of action.

By now we have considered enough of the details of a typical workshop to have a feeling for what goes on. The points to emphasize in conclusion are as follows:

1. The literature search provided the means by which the lectures on theory can be developed authoritatively. With this tremendous store of information, workshop directors can become true experts.
2. The literature search provided those running the workshops with up-to-date information on what the facts are with respect to safety communications and their impact; they could be certain about what we know and what we don't know, at least at the present time.
3. The literature search provided the experts with the best possible basis for judging what infomation from the social and behavioral sciences is most likely to be helpful to the safety practitioner.

"THE NATIONAL DRIVER'S TEST"—SECOND MAJOR BY-PRODUCT

One of the major by-products of the Safety Communications Study has been the development of specific and general guidelines for safety practitioners. These guidelines have been used in a variety of ways; for example, they were injected into the workshops described above, into a series of articles written by Arch McKinlay, Jr., for *Traffic Safety,* and into brief, concise brochures distributed by the Insurance Institute for Highway Safety. Perhaps most importantly, these guidelines proved to be of sig-

---

[11] Archibald McKinlay, Jr., "The Safety Communications Workshop: A View from the Podium," *Traffic Safety,* LXV, no. 10 (October, 1965), 26.

nificant value in one of the most elaborate, and unquestionably successful, television programs yet to be telecast dealing with the topic of driving safety knowledge.

We really can't reconstruct precisely how and why "The National Driver's Test," an hour-long CBS News special, came into existence. CBS had not produced a program directly concerned with driving safety since "The Great Holiday Massacre" in December, 1960. Hence, CBS thought it about time that a program dealing with traffic safety be provided. The question remained, however, what sort of program? Fred W. Friendly, former president of CBS News (then Executive Producer of "CBS Reports"), had found himself in the position of having his driver's license suspended unless he took and passed the refresher test given by the New York State Department of Motor Vehicles. In the process of fulfilling this requirement, Friendly became acutely aware of how much he had forgotten about what is required to be a safe driver. This experience intrigued Friendly greatly, and the beginnings of a program idea began to take shape: why not develop a refresher driver's test for all drivers in the country and make television the medium by which the test is administered. Such an approach could be useful in furthering the cause of traffic safety and be a very dynamic program besides. Consequently, the second ingredient was a request by Friendly that such an idea be explored. During the process of this feasibility research, the people at CBS became acquainted with the work of the Safety Communication Study. As a result, all the necessary parts of the jigsaw puzzle were now in place. It was clear that the program was feasible, and its success appeared to be a foregone conclusion.

The results of these ingredients' coming together are now history. The program was produced and shown on May 24, 1965, on the eve of the annual Memorial Day highway slaughter that has become so commonplace in the United States.

Briefly, the program worked as follows: a driver's test was developed and broadcast over the CBS television network; the viewers were encouraged to actively participate by taking the test as given during the program; and additional opportunities for involvement were provided for by giving them almost immediate feedback on how their answers compared with other viewers. The producer-writer, Warren Bush, brings this and other points out when he writes:

> Nearly 50 million official test answer forms were printed and circulated to provide the homeviewer with a psychological incentive to see the broadcast and to take an *active* part in it. The test was also designed to induce the participation of viewers who did not have an official test answer form. Low scorers and others concerned with their test results were immediately provided with an anxiety-freeing recourse prior to the termination of the broadcast, *i.e.,* an opportunity to enroll in, or start, a National Safety Council Driver Improvement Program within their own communities.

THE NATIONAL SAFETY COUNCIL

A sense of group participation was created by providing viewers with an opportunity to compare their test results throughout the course of the program with those of a four-city probability sample of 2000 drivers who began the test a few minutes immediately prior to the broadcast. (The test results of the sample group combined with additional survey questionnaires provided a bonus feedback for post-program research purposes.) Finally, the project was designed to support an established testing theory that the function of a test should be to advance as much, or more information than it seeks to elicit from the respondent.[12]

What were the results of the program? By any standards it was an overwhelming success and is likely to become a classic. It has already been compared to such other communication phenomena as Kate Smith's World War II bond-selling program and to Orson Welles's 1938 broadcast simulating the invasion of the earth by Martians. On the basis of survey data this program was "on" in more than 16 million homes and was viewed by some 30 million persons. Nielsen ratings for the period following the broadcast revealed that the program was far and away more popular (it received the amazing rating of 30.5) than such favorites at that time as "Bonanza," "Peyton Place," and "Beverly Hillbillies;" it even outdid the rating received by the Gemini IV space shot.

More than one million completed test answer forms were mailed to CBS following the program. In addition, some 52% of these returns (more than 500,000) contained additional information about the person taking the test. The spirit of these additional remarks, which were completely voluntary, is summarized in the following statement on one of the answer forms: ". . . thought you might like to have this for your research."

How the safety communications study guidelines helped

Our focus in this case is not on the details of the program itself, but on how the information obtained through the elaborate literature search directly helped to shape this immensely successful venture. We will consider a half-dozen instances of this.

Selective perception of the potential audience. One guideline used in the programming was the principle that people filter out or otherwise ignore messages that do not interest them or that they are tired of hearing about. The literature suggests that this often happens when the word *safety* is used. People have come to expect that they will be preached at, and they don't want any of it. For this reason the word *safety* was used not at all in the program title and only sparingly elsewhere. Instead, the program was given the more intriguing or challenging ("I am a good driver; I'll easily get 100%") title, "The National Driver's Test."

[12] Warren V. Bush, "The Test," *Television Quarterly,* IV, no. 3 (Summer, 1965), 25.

Importance of involving your audience whenever possible. A second generalization of considerable importance is that a communicator should avoid, whenever possible, letting his audience merely sit there and listen or be talked at. The results of passivity are usually loss of interest, low impact, minimum behavior and attitude change, and so forth —all undesirable results from the standpoint of a communicator. Consequently, a considerable effort was expended toward involving the audience, by providing an opportunity for them to actively "take" the test with a real test answer form. Immediate feedback was provided (the viewer learned how well he did right away), and what's more, he could compare himself with a cross section of fellow drivers the country over and see how well he "stacked up"—another device for producing involvement. Lastly, the notion that he could contribute to scientific research (a highly esteemed phrase these days) was also an additional incentive to the viewer. In short, a number of powerful inducements to be active, not passive, were deliberately built into the program.

Providing for constructive tension release. The communication and persuasion literature also revealed that it is not enough to arouse in the audience feelings of anxiety or tenseness about their shortcomings or their flirtations with danger. The communication must also indicate to the recipient how he can constructively cope with these problems. This was accomplished by having Walter Cronkite suggest to the audience that they write to Howard Pyle, the President of the National Safety Council, for information on how to enroll in the Council's new driver-improvement course.

Advantage of multiple media usage plus personal communication. We know that audience penetration is best if we do not depend upon a single medium, but, rather, if we utilize a multiple-media approach. Also, we know that reliance solely on the mass media is not so effective as coupling them with a personal communication, or face-to-face effort. In preparation for the program itself, an incredibly varied communication attack was launched through the newspapers, through strategic mention on nationally viewed TV programs such as "To Tell the Truth" and "I've Got a Secret" and via articles in tremendous number of company house organs. The face-to-face supplementary approach was achieved through the approximately 300 local safety councils working in cooperation with the National Safety Council.

Combining information with persuasive efforts. There is reason to believe that successful persuasion takes place when the recipient is not aware that he is being persuaded. The same can be said for incidental learning, or learning that takes place without the subject's realizing that he

THE NATIONAL SAFETY COUNCIL

is being taught something. A child watching TV ads doesn't realize that he is taking in information even though he is not in school. The principle is this: without the negative associations that many adults associate with "teaching," information can sometimes be quite effectively imparted.

This idea was very emphatically used in the CBS driving safety program. Although it was billed as a test, the show was essentially a short course in defensive driving, a theme currently being pushed by the National Safety Council. By skillful combinations of test questions, visual aids, actual filmed shots of driving accidents and preventive measures, and correct answers to all of the questions asked (supplemented by information on how the "other fellow" did), considerable teaching was built into the program without the respondents even being aware that this was, in fact, the objective.

Attention-getting dramatization. In safety communication we have to walk a virtual tightrope between making our persuasive efforts dramatic enough and yet sufficiently realistic to accomplish the general objective: namely, to make the recipient realize the seriousness of traffic accidents today. We know from the research literature that if the warnings are too stark or too frightening, the recipient can literally reject them in a variety of ways, the most common being forgetting them. Psychological blockage works most effectively.

Careful study was given to the scenes depicting various accidents; they could neither be too gory nor too tame to attract attention. Also, preprogram publicity had been directed to pointing out that the cars shown had been driven by humans and were not radio controlled. This had two desirable effects: the scenes were made more believable—"it could happen to me"; and they afforded the viewer a degree of reassurance in that the occupants were not smashed up beyond recognition.

Many other principles that had been derived from the literature search and follow-up work were carefully and calculatingly built into the television program—in fact, some 20 or more specific guidelines were utilized. Clearly, "The National Driver's Test" program is a classic example of the blend of theory with practice, and the results of this blend more than justified the whole effort.

HANDBOOK OF SAFETY COMMUNICATIONS— THIRD MAJOR BY-PRODUCT

The last phase of the Safety Communications Study, the development of a simple handbook for safety practitioners, has already been briefly described. We noted then that this phase is still under way. Although it deserves a little more attention as the third major by-product of the total study effort, we can only indicate in tentative terms what its contents will be.

The handbook of safety communications is being written by Arch McKinlay, Jr., the present manager of the public information department of the National Safety Council. He is a logical person to write the handbook for several reasons: (1) He was personally involved in much of the overall safety communications study, even though the project had been initiated by his predecessor prior to his arrival; (2) He and Dr. Harold Mendelsohn together conducted the various workshops described earlier as one of the major by-products of the study. His experiences with the workshops have added to his insights of the problems that a safety practitioner faces; (3) As a public relations practitioner himself, he is fully aware of the difficulties inherent in being an applied communicator, regardless of the particular goals; (4) His present position as manager of public information for the NSC gives him access to considerable pertinent information and data that someone who was not in his position would not be privy to.

Because of the unfolding nature of this third major by-product, the best thing we can provide for the reader is a general working outline of the projected handbook, an outline which, of course, is subject to change. As one reads the proposed chapter headings and subheadings and considers the direction of the emphasis, it appears that the safety practitioner is uppermost in McKinlay's mind.

Guidelines for Safety Communicators (*Tentative title*)

Chapter 1: Mass Communication: An Absolute Requirement for Accident Reduction

    Increase in people to be reached
    Limitation of traditional means
    People's dependence on mass communication
    The reach of mass communication

Chapter 2: Potential of Mass Communication

    Conveying information
    Persuading
    Preselling
    Reinforcing
    Triggering innovators
    Modifying attitudes

Chapter 3: Pitfalls of Effective Safety Mass Communication

    Boomerang (negative reinforcement)
    Nervousness
    Blockage
    Scapegoating
    Derailment
    Annoyance
    Boredom
    Confusion
    Distortion

THE NATIONAL SAFETY COUNCIL

Chapter 4: The Process and Complexity of Mass Communication
    Two orientations
    On-going process
    Variables
    Hooking into the process
    Feedback

Chapter 5: Attitude Change
    When attitudes can be changed
    Kinds of attitudes
    Attacking all three dimensions
    Centrality of attitudes

Chapter 6: How To Get Through
    Selective exposure
    Selective perception
    Selective retention

Chapter 7: Choice of Media
    Print vs. electronic
    Mass plus personal
    Combination of media

Chapter 8: Content
    Rational plus emotional
    Threat with release
    Varied repetition
    Source build-up
    Slogans
    Humor

Chapter 9: Predispositions
    (not yet outlined)

Chapter 10: Relayers
    (not yet outlined)

Chapter 11: Idea Spreading
    (not yet outlined)

Chapter 12: Planning
    (not yet outlined)

Chapter 13: Evaluation
    (not yet outlined)

SAFETY COMMUNICATIONS STUDY: A SUMMARY

In this case we have given our attention to the concept of the literature search—to the notion that one element of problem solving, regardless of the problem, is to find out what others have done and learned about their difficulties in the area in which we are interested.

We suggested that this process is essentially foreign to most present-day practitioners. Most public relations practitioners tend to move directly into problem-solving steps primarily on the basis of their own experiences (one might call this a "personal" search) and of those of their associates in their own organization. A smaller group of practitioners do a partial literature search, in that they may do some reading, some talking with outsiders, and some utilizing of their own company's research department, if one exists. This group may even take some of the time set aside for a literature search to hire consultants or private research organizations to help them obtain reliable information.

The last segment of public relations practitioners, and by far the smallest of the three described here, engage in a true literature search, in the sense that it is traditionally practiced by research scientists.

This case has been devoted to examining the work of a few public relations practitioners (and a multitude of other individuals harnessed for the task) who belong in this third category. We have examined briefly the sequence of events surrounding the Safety Communications Study spearheaded by the National Safety Council. We have seen how the literature search literally revitalized the ability of the NSC to cope with the ever-increasing job of promoting (and achieving) safety in the United States. We have examined three major by-products[13] of this literature search (workshops, "The National Driver's Test," and a handbook of safety communications), all of which have directly aided the safety practitioner and influenced enormous numbers of Americans with regard to the importance of learning to drive safely. Lastly, what we were not able to examine, but must leave to the imagination of the reader, is the tremendous storehouse of knowledge generated by this literature search that will have practical implications for safety practitioners for years to come.

In summary, this case is a testimony to the enormous potential force that the literature search represents for the public relations practitioner. It is hoped that one day this potential will be fully realized.

[13] Another major by-product of this literature search has been the establishment of a Mass Communication Center at the University of Denver. This development is too recent to be included in any detail in this case, however. Among other things, the Center will conduct research in the area of safety communication, coordinate teaching of safety practitioners from all walks of life, serve as a repository of information about safety communication, initiate publications of all sorts (particularly books) dealing with safety communication, and spur development of specialized communication materials to further the goal of safety for us all.

Index

Adams, Phelps H., vii
Air Transport Association, 138
Airport Operators Council, 138
Alfred Politz Research, Inc., 186, 192
American Association for the Advancement of Science, 224
American Dairy Association, 184, 196, 199, 200, 201, 202, 203
American Telephone and Telegraph Company, 240, 244, 245, 248, 255
Applied research, 207
　See also Scientific research
Attitude, innoculation of, 150

Basic-question approach in interviewing, 79–92
Basic research versus applied, 207
Best-obtainable-evidence. *See* Problem-solving continuum.
Birch, Stephen, 157
Blough, Roger, 138, 145, 154
Blumenthal, Murray, 24, 261, 263, 269
Braden, William, 157
Bush, Warren V., 273

Cabot, Hugh, 107, 108
Canfield, Bertrand R., 239
Carter, Roy, 110
Case method, 36, 37, 105–110
　See also Exploratory studies
Chapin, F. Stuart, 40
Clark, Bardsley and Haslacher, 170, 171, 174, 178, 180, 181
Cloze procedure, 110
Communication process, 24–27

decoding and encoding, 27–28
primary and secondary reference groups, 27
Communication theory model, 19–24
　media stage, 21–24
　message stage, 24
　overlapping fields of experience, 21
　recipient stage, 24
　sender stage, 19–21
　"seduction" quality concept, 22–24
Content analysis, 97
　See also Scientific research
Content response code, 110
Cooper, R. Conrad, 145
Culture shock, 125
Cunningham, Robert B., vii

Danish, Roy, 175–177
Data, analyzing and interpreting, 98–99
　collection, 77–95
　obtaining, 52
　preparing, 97
　reporting on, 98, 99
　See also Research process
Decoding and encoding, 27–28
　See also Communication process
Deming, W. Edward, 68
Descriptive studies, 39, 40
　and explanatory studies, 44–49
Dowell, Edwin E., vii
Doyal, Frank, vii
Druck, Kalman B., 183

Eisenhower, Dwight D., 112, 113
Encoding and decoding, 27–28
　See also Communication process

INDEX

Explanatory studies, 41
  and descriptive studies, 44–49
Exploratory studies, 36–39
  case method in, 36, 37
  planned naïveté in, 37

Fairless, Benjamin F., 139–141, 145
Feedback, 28, 29
  and public relations, 29
Festinger, Leon, 199
Flesch formula, 110
Flesch, Rudolph, 110
Framingham National Bank, 86, 87
Frutchy, Fred, 17

Gagarin, Yuri, 226

Hargood, Margaret J., 40
Hypothesis, 38
  developing, in research process, 51, 52
  See also Scientific Research

Individualistic state, 12
Interviewing, 78–80
  basic-question approaches, 79–92
  direct, 80–82
  direct and indirect, 89
  face-to-face, 78, 79
  indirect, 82–92
  mail survey, 78
  modified projective device, 86
  modifiers of accuracy, 92–95
  motivation research, 83
  projective techniques, 83
  and public relations, 8–17
  and quantifying, 98, 99
  remote, 78
  Rorschach Ink Blot Test, 84
  sentence completion, 88–91
  structured disguised test, 85, 86
  structured versus unstructured questions, 80, 81, 83, 84

Thematic Apperception Test, 84

Jackling, Daniel C., 156
Jeppson, Lawrence S., 138

Kahl, Joseph A., 107, 108
Kennecott Neighborhood Theater, 158, 159
Kennedy, John F., 145
Kerlinger, Fred N., 42
Kish, Leslie, 40

Larry, R. H., 154
Literature search in research, 51

Mail survey, 78
Mass Communication Center, 278
McGinnis, Robert, 40
McKinlay, Arch, Jr., viii, 267, 271, 276
Media stage, 21–24
  "seduction" quality concept, 22–24
  See also Communication theory model
Mendelsohn, Harold, 261, 267, 268, 276
Message stage, 21
  See also Communication theory model
Miller, H. Gene, 261
Motivation research and interviewing, 83
Murrow, Edward R., 266

Naisbitt, John, 267
National Association of Science Writers, 224
National Driver's Test, 271–273
National Safety Council, 263
Neu, Frank R., vii
New England Consultants, 86
Nonscientist and scientist, 11–13

INDEX

Opinion Research Corporation, 143
Oppenheim, A. N., 91, 92
Osgood, Charles E., 110

Pacific Telephone and Telegraph Company, 257
Parten, Mildred, 70, 72, 73
People-to-People Program, 112
Perception, 84–92
   structural, versus function, 84, 85
Population, 58
Price, Daniel O., 40
Problem-solving continuum, 12
   scientist and nonscientist, 11–13
   and applied disciplines, 13–16
   and survey research, 16, 17
Projective techniques, 83
   modified projective device, 86
Public relations, definition of, 5
   and feedback, 29

Ray, William S., 42
Recipient stage, 24
   See also Communication theory model
Reference groups, 27
Reliability of interview, 92, 93
Research process, 50–53
Response code, content of, 110
Robinson, Edward J., 5, 11, 12, 17, 19, 20, 25, 42, 47, 54, 61, 69, 100, 263
Roper, Elmo, 202
Rorschach Ink Blot Test, 84

Samples, 58, 61–69
   cluster, 243
   function, 60, 61
   size, 69–72
Scientific research
   basic versus applied, 207
   content analysis, 97
   definition of, 9

dependent variable, 41
descriptive and explanatory studies, 44–49
descriptive studies, 39, 40
explanatory studies and hypothesis, 41
exploratory studies, 36–39
hypothesis, 38
interviewing, 78–80
nonprobability sampling, 62–67
   accidental samples, 63, 64
   purpose samples, 65, 66
   quota samples, 64, 65
population, 58
probability sampling, 67–69
   errors in, 68, 69
   and nonsampling errors, 67, 68
   random, 67
and public relations, 8–17
and quantifying, 98, 99
reliability, 92, 93
research process, 50–53
S–R model, 44, 45
samples, 58, 61–69
types of studies, 36–43
universe, definition of, 58
validity, concept of, 93–95
Sender stage, 19–21
   See also Communication theory model
Sentence completion technique, 88–91
Selltiz, Claire, 36, 63
Selvin, Hanan C., 40
Semantic differential, 110
Structural perception, 84, 85
Structured disguised test, 85, 86
Structured questions in interviewing, 80, 81, 83, 84
Study design in research process, 52
S–R model, 44, 45
Suci, George J., 110

Tannenbaum, Percy H., 110
Taylor, Wilson L., 110
Thematic Apperception Test, 84

Tipton, Stuart G., 138
Tyson, Robert C., 145, 154

Universe, 58
Unstructured questions in interviewing,
    80, 81, 83, 84

Validity, 93–95

Worthington, L. B., 154

Kirtley Library
Columbia College
8th and Rogers
Columbia, MO. 65201